COLLEGIATE CULTURE AND LEADERSHIP STRATEGIES

Ellen Earle Chaffee
William G. Tierney

with
Peter T. Ewell
Jack Y. Krakower

American Council on Education **M** Macmillan Publishing Company
NEW YORK

Collier Macmillan Publishers
LONDON

Macmillan Publishing Company
866 Third Avenue, New York, N. Y. 10022

Collier Macmillan Canada, Inc.

Library of Congress Catalog Card Number: 88-1517

Printed in the United States of America

printing number
1 2 3 4 5 6 7 8 9 10

Library of Congress Cataloging in Publication Data

Chaffee, Ellen Earle.
  Collegiate culture and leadership strategies / by Ellen Earle
Chaffee, William G. Tierney with Peter T. Ewell, Jack Y. Krakower.
      p. cm.
  Bibliography: p.
  ISBN 0-02-905291-2
  1. Universities and colleges—United States—Administration—Case
studies. 2. Organizational behavior—Case studies. 3. Educational
anthropology—United States—Case studies. I. Tierney, William G.
II. Title.
LB2341.C467 1988
378.73—dc19   88-1517
                                                                    CIP

Contents

Preface

Our purpose in exploring seven different collegiate cultures is not unlike that which Margaret Mead expressed regarding her own work: "As the traveler who has once been from home is wiser than he who has never left his own doorstep, so a knowledge of one other culture should sharpen our ability to scrutinize more steadily, to appreciate more lovingly, our own." Similarly, our aim is to foster a more acute self-assessment of organizational culture and a greater awareness of the leadership strategies that can influence daily institutional life. Meant as a diagnostic aid, not a prescriptive primer, this book will have met this goal if it enables readers to both scrutinize and appreciate more fully the colleges and universities so central to America's future.

Case-study research requires two fundamental ingredients: exceptionally kind interviewees and good road maps. About four hundred people provided us with the material that comprises this book, and we benefited greatly from listening to their thoughts and concerns about higher education. As we traveled throughout the nation, down country lanes and up city streets, we were impressed by the countless individuals who work long hours for relatively low pay because they believe in a vision of American higher education.

Conducting case-study research that combines both qualitative and quantitative approaches also requires considerable support from other team members. Dr. Peter T. Ewell and Dr. Jack Krakower contributed to the research design, interviews, and theoretical framework for this book. They spent many hours reviewing earlier versions of the book and providing helpful criticism. Dr. Ray Zammuto, Dr. Rolf Norgaard, Shelley Niwa, and Dee Lowrance also aided us at critical stages along the way.

We conducted the case studies and began this manuscript when we were at the National Center for Higher Education Management Systems (NCHEMS) in Boulder, Colorado. Subsequently, we have returned to administrative and faculty life. Ellen Chaffee is

Associate Commissioner for the State Board of Higher Education in North Dakota, and Bill Tierney is a faculty member at the Center for the Study of Higher Education at The Pennsylvania State University. Although time has passed since we visited the campuses for this study, the individuals and their collegiate cultures remain distinct in our minds. It is to these individuals and their institutions that we dedicate this book.

Ellen Earle Chaffee   William G. Tierney
Bismarck, North Dakota   University Park, Pennsylvania

September 1987

PART ONE

Introduction

"Doubt is not a pleasant condition, but certainty is an absurd one."

—*Voltaire*

―――――――――――― ONE ――――――――――――

The Cultural Drama
of Organizational Life

Asked for his advice on acting, Spencer Tracy once remarked, "Just know your lines and don't bump into the furniture." On the stage of organizational culture, such advice becomes wholly inadequate. Actors within collegiate cultures have few if any scripts to go by. And as for the furniture, the most visible props—roles and governance arrangements—are not the ones we tend to bump into. Rather, we most often trip over perceptions and attitudes, the intangibles that escape our attention even as they make up the fabric of daily organizational life. As a result, effective leadership has to do not only with planning and adaptation but also with interpreting and communicating institutional values and understanding organizational processes. *Collegiate Culture and Leadership Strategies* is a hands-on study for executives, researchers, and students who want to better understand how organizational culture can support or impede decision-making strategies in a complex and changing environment.

As we enter the organizational life of a college or university, we enter a theater-in-the-round in which a multitude of actions and perceptions determine institutional performance on a variety of fronts. For this study we have walked on seven such campuses.

On each campus we observe a cultural drama in process, one that is unique to that institution. We also encounter, however, a common desire to understand the dynamics of culture and its influence on institutional performance. Our observations emphasize the diagnostic over the prescriptive. Growing interest in organizational culture has encouraged practitioners and researchers alike to view it as a new management approach promising to cure all organizational ills. This is a mistake. We eschew quick-fix meth-

3

ods and simplistic principles in favor of a nuanced, in-depth study of the role of culture, strategy, and leadership in promoting organizational effectiveness.

Those who work in organizations may read these cases and our conclusions in search of a list of dos and don'ts. Most management-oriented books provide such lists, and it may be disconcerting, even irritating, not to find them here. Someday it may be possible to approach organizational culture in this way, but we doubt it. If we have learned anything significant from this work, it is the need to respect the integrity and uniqueness of each institution, to learn its identity in the same way that one learns to know a valued friend. Through practice, we have learned what to look for and how. We have learned, as outsiders, to immerse ourselves deeply enough to develop some understanding of an institution's culture. As insiders, those who work in organizations need to learn to gain perspective, to transcend their own immersion. The stories of other organizations help provide perspective by giving frames of reference within which the reader can seek similarities and differences. Our task will be to tell the stories as faithfully as possible and to help the reader become immersed in the stories and use them to gain perspective on any organization, including one's own.

Although colleges and universities are among the clearest examples of organizational cultures, we have directed attention to underlying issues in management and organizational life that transcend the college campus in both application and importance. Many key questions we address are asked as frequently in corporate board rooms as they are in the halls of Old Main:

- Why and in what respect is culture important in organizational life?

- How can leaders match decision-making strategies with organizational culture to meet long-range missions and goals?

- What happens when top executives fail to properly interpret or communicate their organization's culture to its members or its external constituents?

- How can executives develop decision-making strategies that will address environmental change, institutional values, and cultural tensions?

- How can leaders strengthen the link between organizational culture and institutional mission to achieve their vision of the future?

By addressing these and similar questions through an exploration of seven institutional cultures, we attempt to provide a rich context within which executives and researchers can examine both daily decision-making and long-range policies. Each case study provides the reader with a real grasp of organizational culture and decision-making styles not possible through anecdotal snapshots typically found in management guides and research literature on strategy. The cases deal with both public and private institutions with small to medium enrollments. Each points out in poignant and instrumental ways how an organization is a web of meaning collectively spun by all participants. Embracing complexity, the case studies attempt a dense, multifaceted interpretation of organizational life that moves beyond tidy "how-to" guidelines to broach the "why" of culture and strategy.

A distinctive feature of these case studies is their close integration of qualitative and quantitative approaches. We have endeavored to portray these institutions as living cultures. Yet behind these seven engrossing stories lie detailed interviews and a variety of ethnographic methods. These in turn are supplemented by statistical and quantitative studies and a recently developed, highly regarded instrument for assessing institutional performance. Although each case is examined in its own terms, the multiple studies, conducted simultaneously, resonate with each other and prompt useful comparisons and distinctions.

Practical insights into key dimensions of organizational culture emerge from these seven cases. These dimensions include the values held by members of the organization, the structure by which the organization accomplishes its activities, and the understanding members develop about the nature of the organization's context or environment. These dimensions provide, in turn, a useful framework within which to explore many of the elements of culture, such as:

- The role of symbols and the symbolic dimension of instrumental decisions and actions

- Organizational saga or the role of history and the varied modes of its interpretation

- The role of time and space as cultural parameters and their use in leadership and decision-making styles

- The use of information as a token in a cultural system of exchange and its relation to power and position.

These and other elements become strands in the web of meaning that is an organization's culture. By making leaders more aware of this web and of the need to spin it more consciously, this book will help enable them to effect positive change rather than merely react to circumstances. When leaders understand the important link between culture and strategy, they are better able to act in the abstruse environment in which higher education currently finds itself.

In the context of these cases we delineate strategic options along three general dimensions: linear or goal-oriented strategy, adaptive strategy, and interpretive strategy. Interpretive strategy sees the organization as playing a role in creating its environment, in part by the manner in which leaders communicate and interpret institutional goals and values. While all three dimensions contribute to organizational effectiveness, interpretive strategy provides an important and often necessary context for effective decision-making. As executives assess what strategy means to their organization, they are discovering the strategy of meaning. Simply put, the value of strategy lies foremost in its capacity to manifest and motivate the very best of an organization's cultural values.

Before we enter these seven institutions to explore the important link between culture and strategy, it is useful to take a step back and consider the role of culture in management and institutional performance. Additional questions are also in order. How does a cultural view of organizations differ from other research perspectives? How did we set about studying the seven cases under consideration? By addressing these questions, we will develop key concepts and issues common to all of the cases and suggest how a study of this kind can be a significant diagnostic tool for those in leadership positions.

The Role of Culture in Management and Performance

Even the most seasoned executives often ask themselves, "What holds this place together? Is it mission, values, bureaucratic procedures, or strong personalities? How does this place run and what does it expect from its leaders?" These questions often arise in moments of frustration, when seemingly rational, well-laid plans have failed or have met with unexpected resistance. They are also frequently asked by members new to the organization, who are at a loss to know "how things are done around here." Questions like these seem difficult to answer because no one-to-one correspondence exists between actions and results. The same leadership style can easily produce widely divergent results in two ostensibly similar institutions. Likewise, institutions with very similar missions and curricula can perform quite differently because of the way their identities are communicated to internal and external constituents and because of the varying perceptions these groups may hold.

Institutions are certainly influenced by powerful external factors, such as demographic, economic, and political conditions, yet they are also shaped by strong forces that emanate from within. This internal dynamic has its roots in the history of the organization and derives its force from the values, traditions, processes, and goals held by those most intimately involved in the organization's workings. The most fundamental construct of an organization, as of a society, is its culture. An organization's culture is reflected in what is done, how it is done, and who is involved in doing it. It concerns decisions, actions, and communication both on an instrumental and a symbolic level.

The anthropologist Clifford Geertz writes that traditional culture "denotes an historically transmitted pattern of meanings embodied in symbols, a system of inherited conceptions expressed in symbolic forms by means of which men communicate, perpetuate, and develop their knowledge about and attitudes toward life" (1973, p. 89). Organizational culture exists, then, in part through the actors' interpretation of historical and symbolic forms. The culture of an organization is grounded in the shared assumptions of individuals participating in the organization. Often taken for granted by the actors themselves, these assumptions can be identified through stories, special language, norms, institutional ideology, and artifacts that emerge from individual and organizational behavior. The socialization processes used to introduce new members to the culture and maintain continued loyalty and morale are also significant cultural mechanisms in organizational life. That is, the way faculty and administrators become and remain socialized to an institution is a critical element of culture. Such mechanisms

include both formal and informal activities, styles of communication, temporal and spatial cues, and a variety of institutional
bonding mechanisms, such as hiring practices, award and incentive structures, tenure review, and position advancement.

Institutional leaders, however, often have only an intuitive
grasp of the cultural conditions and influences that enter into their
daily decision-making. In this respect they are not unlike most of us
who have but a dim, passive awareness of cultural codes, symbols,
and conventions that are at work in society at large. Only when
we break these codes and conventions are we forcibly reminded
of their presence and considerable power. Likewise, administrators tend to recognize their organization's culture only when they
have transgressed its bounds and severe conflicts or adverse relationships ensue. As a result, we frequently find ourselves dealing
with organizational culture in an atmosphere of crisis management, not reasoned reflection and consensual change.

Our lack of understanding about the role of organizational culture in improving management and institutional performance
inhibits our ability to address the challenges that face higher education. As these challenges mount, our need to understand organizational culture only intensifies. Like many American institutions
in the latter part of the twentieth century, colleges and universities
face increasing complexity and fragmentation. As decision-making
contexts grow more obscure, costs increase, and resources become more difficult to allocate, leaders in higher education need to
understand institutions as cultural entities. As before, these leaders
must continue to make difficult decisions. These decisions, however, need not engender the degree of conflict that they usually
have prompted. Indeed, properly informed by an awareness of culture, these decisions may contribute to an institution's or system's
sense of purpose and identity. Moreover, to implement decisions,
leaders must have a full, nuanced understanding of the organization's culture. Only then can they articulate decisions in a way
that will speak to the needs of various constituencies and marshall
their support.

Equally important, an awareness of culture enables us to recognize those actions and shared goals most likely to succeed and
how they can best be implemented. Effective administrators intuitively understand that they can take a given action in some institutions but not in others. They are less aware of why this is true.
Bringing the dimensions and dynamics of culture to consciousness
will help leaders assess the reasons for such differences in insti-

tutional responsiveness and performance. This will allow them to assess likely consequences before they act, not after. Indeed, the most persuasive case for studying organizational culture is quite simply that we no longer need to tolerate the consequences of our ignorance—nor, for that matter, will a rapidly changing environment permit us to do so.

Although organizational culture influences all aspects of institutional effectiveness, daily management concerns can inhibit practitioners from recognizing its impact. By encouraging a broad perspective, the concept of organizational culture encourages practitioners to

- Consider real or potential conflicts not in isolation but on the broad canvas of organizational life
- Recognize structural or operational contradictions that suggest tensions in the organization
- Implement and evaluate everyday decisions with a keen awareness of their role in and influence upon organizational culture
- Understand the symbolic dimensions of ostensibly instrumental decisions and actions
- Consider why different groups in the organization hold varying perceptions about institutional performance
- Orchestrate innovation and change in the organization, mindful of how such change will impact on and be constrained by the culture.

Many managers intuitively understand the importance of organizational culture and their actions sometimes reflect the points mentioned above. The case studies that form the heart of this book are meant to bring this awareness to a more conscious level and thereby render leadership strategies more effective.

A Cultural View of Organizations

"The difficulty in studying culture," notes Andrew Masland, "arises because culture is implicit, and we are all embedded in our own cultures" (1985, p. 160). If administrators are to implement effec-

tive strategies within their own cultures, then an appropriate perspective is needed, one that will help make explicit the essential
elements of organizational culture. Traditional perspectives, oriented toward quantitative measurement of objective structures
and patterns, do not adequately capture the dynamics of culture.
Similarly, conventional variables such as size, control, and location
are little help in understanding what holds an institution together.

In considering appropriate perspectives on culture, it is helpful
to consider, as Marvin Peterson (1985) has done, the broad continuum of research perspectives. Peterson notes that two competing
theories about organizations have developed. The first theory is
oriented toward the traditional paradigm that considers organizational reality as objective facts. The other theory exists within
a cultural paradigm that emphasizes an organization's ability to
socially construct its reality.

Peterson notes that the traditional paradigm

> views organizational elements as objective, accepts them as positive
> facts, and is concerned with predicting events. The major focus is
> on structures, observable behaviors and organizational elements, and
> respondents' attitudes and self reports. Theories are posed in terms of
> how one set of variables varies with others and the concern is to test
> them. The methodologies are primarily reductionist and quantitative
> in nature. (1985, p. 9)

The cultural paradigm views an organization as a social construction where participants constantly interpret and create organizational reality. This view sees the organizational world as more
than a conscious set of demographic data and figures; the organization's understanding of itself is not merely the sum of its parts.
Rather than view the organizational universe as a finite set of
knowable elements, the researcher studies how the participants interpret and make sense of their organization to themselves and to
others. The history of the organization, individual perceptions, and
present-day circumstances combine to produce organizational reality. The imperative for the researcher is to gain a dynamic view
of the organization that successfully interprets the participants'
understanding of their culture.

Although it is helpful to understand research and practice in
terms of these two paradigms, our assumption is that successful
researchers or administrators must understand that most endeavors in organizations occur along a broad continuum. For example,
higher education administrators have the difficult task of trying
to predict enrollments when budgets are restricted and competi-

tion for students is high. Administrators often try to capture new markets in their quest for financial security. At the same time, however, administrators must be mindful of what new markets mean for the organization's culture. Instrumental decisions affect cultural realities. Cultural interpretations affect instrumental decisions. The struggle for the researcher and administrator is to understand and operate within both paradigms.

Administrators and a good number of researchers are accustomed to that portion of the continuum informed by the traditional paradigm. That is where much of the research has occurred in higher education, and its assumptions are still broadly held. In recent years, however, considerable activity has shifted attention toward the other end of this continuum. The best of this recent work moves beyond tidy, constricted social-science approaches and attempts a dense, multifaceted interpretation of larger issues and emerging trends.

Although still not widely prevalent in higher-education research, the cultural paradigm parallels a widespread shift in perspective that is occurring in the social sciences and humanities. The shift, often referred to as a "turn to interpretation" (Rabinow and Sullivan, 1979), finds researchers and practitioners struggling to develop a more appropriate way to study social behavior and events. Interest in this multidisciplinary mode of inquiry has been sparked not by wild-eyed radicals but by some of the most respected minds of this century: Georg Gadamer (1979), Michel Foucault (1973), and Clifford Geertz (1973, 1983), to name but a few.

Interest in this new line of inquiry has already made an important impact within the business community. In the last ten years, management strategies such as linear and adaptive planning have been seriously questioned, with organizational culture now emerging as a topic of central concern. Books such as Peters and Waterman's *In Search of Excellence* (1982), Ouchi's *Theory Z* (1981), Deal and Kennedy's (1982) *Corporate Cultures*, and Schein's *Organizational Culture and Leadership* (1985) have become landmark studies of managerial and organizational performance.

Important research is now being conducted on institutions, organizations, and subunits of organizations as distinct and separate cultures with unique sets of ceremonies, rites, and traditions. Initial attempts have been made to analyze leadership from a cultural perspective (Burns, 1978; Bennis, 1984). The role of symbolic and cultural communication has been examined by March (1984), Feldman and March (1981), Putnam and Pacanowsky (1983), Trujillo

(1983), Tierney (forthcoming-b), and Pondy (1978). Similarly, organizational stories and symbols have also been investigated (Hirsch and Andrews, 1984). It is significant to note that a number of theorists suggest that there is an identifiable deep structure and set of core assumptions that may be used to examine and understand organizational culture.

Although interest in organizational culture is now widespread, the lack of research on this topic in higher education has been noted by numerous writers (Chait, 1982; Dill, 1982; Masland, 1985; Tierney, 1988). Noting the growing interest in imported management techniques, David Dill has commented, "Ironically the organizations in Western society which most approximate the essential characteristics of Japanese firms are academic institutions. They are also characterized by life-time employment, collective decisionmaking, individual responsibility, infrequent promotion, and implicit, informal evaluation" (1982, p. 307). Instead, research in higher education has moved toward defining managerial techniques based on strategic planning, marketing, and management control.

Nevertheless, higher-education researchers have made some progress in studying campus cultures. Research in the early 1960s concerned primarily student cultures (Becker, 1963; Bushnell, 1960; Pace, 1962). Since the early 1970s, Burton Clark has pioneered work on distinctive colleges as cultures (1970), the role of belief and loyalty in college organizations (1971), and organizational sagas as tools for institutional identity (1980). Recent work has included the study of academic cultures (Becher, 1981; Freedman, 1979; Gaff and Wilson, 1971), leadership (Chaffee, 1985a; Tierney, forthcoming-a), and the system of higher education as a culture (Clark, 1984). Although it may be unfamiliar reading for some, this study of collegiate cultures and leadership strategies finds itself in good company. It parallels the work of many respected higher-education researchers, and it echoes a concern in the social sciences and humanities generally that we embrace the complexities of social life.

Culture and the Case-Study Method

The rationale for case studies is straightforward: If we are to improve higher-education management, we must understand colleges and universities as socially constructed organizations and discern what can make them more effective. This cannot be done through armchair research but only through intimate contact with daily institutional life at a number of campuses. By departing from traditional lines of inquiry, our exploration of these seven institutions allows us to attempt a multifaceted interpretation of organizational life. Case studies are an appropriate vehicle because they allow for what anthropologist Clifford Geertz calls "thick description." The richness and complexity of organizational life on these seven campuses prevent us from embracing simplistic answers while encouraging us to broach larger issues.

Although case studies of the kind presented in this book operate within the cultural paradigm rather than the traditional paradigm, our intention from the outset has been to wed both quantitative and qualitative approaches. This is apparent in the origins of this study. Our current research was prompted by an earlier, inductive study of turnaround management at fourteen private colleges (Chaffee, 1984a, 1984b). The question posed in this earlier study was simple: Faced with real, objectively apparent decline, how did these colleges attempt to turn themselves around? Although the problem concerned social fact, the strategy most effective at these institutions was cultural, a matter of interpretation rather than social fact. The central importance of organizational culture and its interpretation and communication prompted, in turn, the present study into collegiate culture and leadership strategies.

Appendix A to this volume presents a discussion of the research methods that underlie this book. For the purposes of this introduction, a general description of our approach will help place the story of each institution in proper context. The guiding principle of the research was to construct a multifaceted approach to the study of organizations. We did not set out to prove hypotheses. Although we did not assume that perception is always reality, we gave credence to the idea that organizations are social constructs. We assumed that participants' perceptions of problems, solutions, and culture go a long way toward determining organizational health. Aside from general issues foreshadowed by this approach, we permitted specific questions to arise in the field.

The research team conducted the study during the academic year 1984–85. To the extent that a small sample permits, we selected institutions in order to examine the applicability of our findings to diverse kinds of institutions. The key structural dimensions on which the selection rested were size, control, and the possibility of using time-series data. Because the Institutional Performance Survey (IPS) developed at the National Center for Higher Education Management Systems (NCHEMS) offered valuable data and was thus an important component of our research design, we limited the possible institutions to the 334 four-year colleges and universities that participated in a 1983 IPS survey. The research sites ultimately selected, whose stories are told in this volume, include four public and three private institutions, of which three are colleges and four are universities. Located throughout the United States, none of these institutions is smaller than 900 students or larger than 7,500.

The research design for this study follows from our belief in the importance of multiple methods. Not only did we seek to integrate qualitative and quantitative approaches, we also found that multiple case studies, conducted simultaneously, added further richness to the project. Moreover, we placed considerable importance on the longitudinal dimension of our inquiry.

Case studies involve essentially qualitative research, yet we have found it important to employ quantitative techniques as one way to confirm, modify, and extend our observations. The IPS offered a useful means of correlating perceptual and empirical evidence and raising important questions for our return site visits. Although augmented by quantitative research, qualitative methods lie at the heart of this study.

Detailed interviews following multiple formats were supplemented by a variety of ethnographic methods. Four forms of interviews conducted by four different team members provided for cross-checking of research findings. These formats included structured interviews, open-ended interviews, sessions in which specific questions were raised that related to initial findings, and interviews that sought to confirm perceptual evidence developed earlier in the study. For additional information about how we gathered data and conducted the case studies, please see Appendix A.

In an effort to avoid a onetime snapshot of an institution, we placed particular emphasis on longitudinal analysis. We made every effort to place events and people into an historical context. Our assumption is that for a portrait of an organization to have any meaning, it must be fleshed out, thick in description and rich in nuance. Cultural research is best conducted when researchers can observe a full cycle of time, in this case a full academic year at an institution. Repeat visits to each campus were thus an essential element in the research design. Were we to have made only one visit, we would have missed a number of important and, at times, crucial insights into the dynamics of organizational culture and processes of organizational change.

Because colleges and universities are not two-dimensional entities, such as one would find on an organizational chart, but a complex, highly interrelated collection of people, we have presented our observations in the form of a vivid portrait, not a wearisome report. Data presentation of this kind is consistent with recognized anthropological methods but is in many respects new to higher-education research. Instead of merely reporting incidents to the reader, we have sought to involve the reader more fully in the interpretation of the data. One goal of our work is to enable the reader to step into our place and know the institution so well that the reader can interpret the data and reflect on the nature of our observations and the validity of our conclusions.

Rather than tell the reader about information, we present quotes and institutional portraits that show the organization's culture at work. Throughout this book, we use quotations only if they exemplify what we heard from a variety of individuals; they are never exceptions to the rule. Resisting the temptation to portray institutions as their promotional literature would have them appear, we have treated each case as if we were putting together a giant puzzle without having the picture on the box. Our observations represent a highly candid portrait collectively drawn by institutional members. Although at times unflattering, it is also genuine.

Due to the method and style of our research, we wish to acknowledge and extend our appreciation to the many individuals we interviewed and observed. Although all individuals, institutions, and locales are camouflaged to ensure anonymity, the people who are portrayed here remain fresh in our minds. Virtually everyone provided us with helpful advice, encouragement, and oftentimes friendship. These are perilous times for higher education. Hence, honest portraits of institutional life must necessarily encompass the full range of human activity—from the courageous to the mundane.

One assumption of our research is that studies of organizations need to move away from inaccurate pictures of individuals as heroes or of static roles inhabited by powerless functionaries. We owe a special debt to the college presidents who allowed us to enter their institutions. Their courage is especially appreciated because we portray in this study not the exceptional college, with all of its success, but the mainstream of higher education, with all of its problems. We sought to offer a true cross-section of faculty and administrators, with both their genuine commitment to education and their human foibles. Throughout this book, our desire has been to emulate the candor of the individuals with whom we have spoken by portraying situations and people in as lifelike and fair a light as possible.

The Ingredients of This Book

Upon reading these introductory comments and certainly upon studying the seven cases, the reader is most likely to come away thinking of culture not unlike E. B. White thought of the future: "It seems to me no unified dream but a mince pie, long in the baking, never quite done." Such a realization should not tempt us to leave the kitchen. Organizational culture remains a critical ingredient in institutional life and performance. The seven institutions represented in this study each have their own recipes for organizational culture—be they conscious or unconscious, planned or haphazard. By exploring these cultures we wish to assume no special authority in judging them; instead, we are grateful for the opportunity to gain insight into their dynamics and processes.

The next chapter suggests ways to read the case studies in order to take lessons from them to understand one's own institution. Then, the seven cases in this study have been divided into three sections. The groupings and their respective headings suggest connections among the cases that have emerged in the course of our inquiry. The first section includes two institutions where culture is viewed in terms of continuity. The next section is an appropriate home for three institutions now struggling to accommodate change within organizational culture. The final section chronicles the search of two institutions for organizational and cultural identity. By no means a given, the organization of the chapters is offered as a provocation for further discussion and as a first step in launching the reader into his or her own interpretation of organizational reality. The concluding chapter in this volume addresses the challenge to leadership that these cases and, more generally, studies of organizational culture present. Appended to this volume is background information that enables researchers and administrators alike to reflect on the nature of our conclusions and the methods by which we arrived at them.

Meant as a diagnostic tool, not a prescriptive manual, this book will find its ultimate usefulness if it encourages administrators to reflect on and operate within their own culture with greater awareness. These seven cases provide a rich source of information and there are many lessons to be learned through close reading and reflection. The overly zealous should bear in mind Mark Twain's admonition:

> We should be careful to get out of an experience only the wisdom that is in it—and stop there; lest we be like the cat that sits down on a hot stove lid. She will never sit down on a hot stove lid again—and that is well; but also she will never sit down on a cold one anymore.

The cultures described in this study are each baking at a temperature unique to that institution. What each of us can gain through a study of this sort are better means and greater confidence in taking—and influencing—the temperature of our own organization.

TWO

The Search
for Dynamic
Equilibrium in
Organizational
Culture

This chapter provides the reader with a brief tour guide. Just as reading about foreign cultures before going abroad prepares tourists for their trip, developing a general understanding of the dimensions and dynamics of organizational culture will give the reader an understanding of what to look for and a way of seeing what otherwise may be invisible. We provide three road maps. First, we consider dimensions of culture that will be found in any organization. Second, we discuss dimensions of strategy that parallel the dimensions of culture. Third, we suggest ways for the reader to embark on a reading of the seven cases so that comparisons can be made among the seven colleges and universities and with the reader's own institution.

The three general dimensions of culture are *structure, environment,* and *values.* They are highly interdependent and interpenetrating. Speaking of them separately is convenient, but the reader should bear in mind their interactive tendencies, as depicted in Figure 2.1.

The *structural* dimension refers to various ways in which the organization accomplishes its activities, including programmatic, fiscal, and governance mechanisms. Structure is more than the roles and relationships one can see in a formalized organizational

ORGANIZATIONAL CULTURE

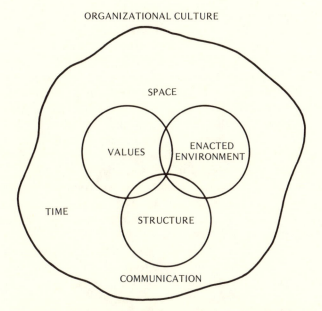

Figure 2.1. Dynamic Equilibrium in Organizational Culture

chart, encompassing also the processes by which activities are accomplished. In this light, structure involves both the formal and informal aspects of decision-making, as well as both the day-to-day operations of an organization and its long-term planning. We investigate not only who reports to whom vis-à-vis the organizational chart, but also who interacts with whom on informal levels. We study not only the formalized roles and tasks of each worker, but also how the participants interact with one another and how work activities are passed from one part of the organization to another. Pertinent to the structural sphere are the roles of specific individuals and the lines of communication and information that the array of these roles creates.

Decision-making and the role of the leader assume special significance within this dimension. The mechanisms for shared governance and the roles of the president come under scrutiny when one investigates the structure of higher education institutions. We will discover campuses where the structural role of the president is particularly constrained and other institutions where the president has assumed a powerful position. Similarly, we will visit a university where collective bargaining has stymied communication, inhibiting shared governance, and another institution where collective bargaining has helped clarify roles and responsibilities, making communication more effective.

The *environmental* dimension of organizational culture includes, but is by no means limited to, the objective context of people, events, demands, and constraints in which an institution finds itself. Yet this dimension is more than a set of facts. In the context of our study, this dimension might be more aptly referred to as the *enacted* environment (Smircich and Stubbart, 1985), or the understanding organization members develop about the nature of the organization's context. For example, it includes their definition of the organization's potential clientele (locale, ethnicity, ability, social class, age) and their understanding about the prospects for recruiting that clientele (demographics, competition, key factors that attract them). Other discussions of organizational environment often assume that it is a comprehensive, objective, intractable set of facts. Our reference to the enacted environment includes any such facts that come to the attention of the organization, but excludes those that do not. We also highlight the capacity of organizations to create their environment through selective attention and interpretation.

An organization's perception of its environment provides useful information about the way the institution perceives itself. Do participants, for example, view the organization's relationship to its environment as one of dominance, weakness, or selectivity? How participants respond to such a question helps explain why similar organizations utilize different decision-making strategies. By noting that organizations not only respond to, but help define their environment through selective attention and interpretation, we observe once again that organizations are less a matter of objective fact and more an ongoing process of cultural definition.

The third dimension in this framework of organizational culture is *values*. Pertinent to this dimension are the beliefs, norms, and priorities held by members of the institution. We are especially interested in values that pertain to the organization itself and in the extent to which values are congruent among individuals and subgroups.

These values are most apparent in the institution's mission and the quality and direction of its leadership. The mission expresses the college or university's core set of values and its underlying ideology. Institutional mission can provide a collective understanding of the institution and play a key role in defining for members what the institution can and cannot do. It not only provides the rationale and criteria for developing curricular programs but also provides standards for performance and self-criticism. Useful questions about organizational mission pertain to how the institution defines and articulates it. Is it used as a basis for decisions? How much agreement exists among the community about the institution's mission? And how has the mission changed over time?

The nature of an organization's leadership is, in many respects, the most tangible expression of its values. The nature of leadership in an organization extends beyond a transactional exchange between a leader and his or her subordinates. Of particular interest in this context is the extent of transformational leadership within an institution, or leadership that seeks to satisfy higher needs of followers, engaging the full person in the life of the organization (Burns, 1978). It is by this kind of leadership that institutional values and constituent support are cultivated.

Three themes move through the model of culture shown in Figure 2.1: time, space, and communication. Time is relevant as history, tradition, and habit influence behavior; as members conjure up a desired future; and as individuals pace their current activities. Space issues provide symbolic as well as instrumental contexts for action. Spatial relationships among individuals in the institution and between the institution and its constituents provide valuable information about organizational structure, environment, and values. Communication is the primary vehicle through which members perceive and interpret their world, so it is the sine qua non of organizational culture. Oral and written discourse and a host of nonverbal acts provide clues through which we can better understand the cultural dimensions.

Each cultural dimension (structure, environment, and values) and each theme (time, space, and communication) changes according to its own internal logic but not independently of the others. They may change in tempo with one another, or each may turn at its own speed. A central task of leadership is to comprehend the parts and their relationships. Structure influences leadership by way of historical context; the power of a leader is determined in part by institutional history. Leaders articulate values and interpret the environment. Leaders help the organization seek a dynamic equilibrium, but they do not do so divorced from the organizational dimensions of culture. Leaders influence culture, and culture defines leadership.

Complex organizations cannot reach an optimum state. They cannot even reach equilibrium, except perhaps for fleeting moments. The constant challenge is to seek equilibrium. However well some of these seven institutions are doing, improvement is possible. Institutional life has no end point at which someone declares winners and losers. An organization may be perceptibly better or worse at the end of a president's term in office than it was when that president began, but in either case the new president faces important challenges. The nature of those challenges becomes clearer when the case studies are read with the cultural perspective in mind.

The framework provides a means of diagnosing the points at which an institution's progress toward dynamic equilibrium may be hampered by elements that are out of balance. We propose that institutions need structures, enacted environments, and values that are congruent. Institutions also need to use time, space, and communication to reinforce and develop those congruencies. When the dimensions are incongruent, one undermines the other instead of reinforcing it. The institution cannot develop momentum toward equilibrium when it is headed in diverging directions. The cases contain areas of both congruence and divergence, and it is to eliminating the latter areas that we recommend leaders direct their attention. Strategy is a primary tool for leaders to use in seeking congruence.

Strategy, Culture, and Leadership

The title of this book, *Collegiate Culture and Leadership Strategies*, is meant to suggest that leaders can nurture and influence organizational culture through the strategies that they implement. Although the specific terms were developed in another context (Chaffee, 1985b), our study calls upon three dimensions of strategy that roughly parallel the three dimensions of culture outlined above. These three types of strategy are linear, adaptive, and interpretive. We hasten to note that strategy is often incorrectly perceived as a product rather than a process, as an answer rather than a means to ask appropriate questions. As phrases containing the modifier "strategic" continue to multiply, some administrators tend to forget that strategy is, and always has been, a way of looking, listening, and thinking. It is less a solution than a means of arriving at one.

An analogy to the individual person places the three models in a familiar context. Individuals have machinelike linear systems, adaptive systems, and cultural systems. The skeleton is an example of a linear system, in which characteristics and relationships are highly predictable. Skilled observers can easily identify the location and nature of a break in the skeletal system, and they can predict the behavioral consequences of a given skeletal type or abnormality. These properties make the skeletal system similar to a predictable, rational, goal-oriented approach to strategy.

Of the three cultural dimensions outlined in Figure 2.1, the one that tends to predominate within a linear strategic approach is the formalized component of the structural dimension. Perceiving the organization's internal and external environment as a complex set of forces, administrators assess goals and plan actions so that the organization's ends are achieved. They chart a course to keep internal disputes at a minimum and external competition as distant and ineffectual as possible. This perspective does not consider the informal aspects of the structural dimension, the assumption that the participants enact their environment, nor organizational values.

Strategy can also be adaptive in nature, just as people adapt to circumstances and changes, both physically and psychologically. If they hunger for attention and get it by screaming, they learn to scream more. If they lose one sense, they become able to learn more from their remaining senses. These capacities parallel the adaptive approach. In such an approach, the predominant cultural dimension is environmental. By perceiving the organization's environment as a complex, ever-changing set of consumer or constituency preferences, administrators can utilize adaptive strategy to align the institution with its environment through a process of organizational change. One might think of the adaptive approach to strategy in biological terms. Evolutionary and ecological in nature, adaptive strategy seeks to adapt an organization to its environment, to help it find its niche. Organizational values are ignored or subordinated to the demands of the environment, and organizational structure exists to meet environmental exigencies.

In the third part of our analogy, people are cultural and symbolic systems. They receive, process, and send messages; they develop beliefs about the organization and specific situations; they express emotions and affiliations in complex relationships with other people. These are the least predictable, the least susceptible to analysis, and the most complex human capacities. They are also the most fundamental in terms of their capacity to distinguish humans from other animals and one human from another.

Similarly, a third approach to strategy is interpretive and tends to emphasize the values dimension of organizational culture. Such strategies proceed from an understanding that the organization can play a role in creating its structure and its environment. Leaders accomplish this by communicating and interpreting institutional goals and values. Interpretive strategies enable constituencies to understand the organization and its environment and motivate them to support its mission.

Each of these three approaches to strategy can contribute to a college or university's effectiveness. On the basis of our research to date, we offer three assertions. First, effective organizations need effective functioning in all three models of strategy. They cannot afford to tolerate inattention to any of them. However, because of its emphasis on communicating and interpreting institutional mission, interpretive strategy has special significance to higher education and particular relevance to the seven institutions portrayed in this volume. Its importance derives from its articulation of institutional values, which in turn provide a framework within which to incorporate and orient linear and adaptive approaches. In this respect, interpretive strategy is less a strategy in its own right than a way of implementing and integrating a wide variety of strategic options.

The second assertion follows from this view of the importance of all three strategic models: The models are interactive. Just as a person who learns she has multiple sclerosis must come to understand what that means for her life, people in organizations that experience disaster must come to understand the meaning of the disaster for them. In both cases, people have choices among meanings. Disaster can mean the end of hope, the beginning of struggle, or the opportunity to see the future in radically new ways.

The third assertion is that the three models are hierarchical. At the top of the hierarchy is the interpretive model, followed by the adaptive, and then the linear. When we say hierarchical, we do not mean sequential. Events can enter or leave the system at any level, and it is not necessary to go through the adaptive level in order to move between the linear and interpretive. By hierarchical, we mean that the interpretive model, complex enough in itself, embraces also the complexities of the adaptive and linear models. The adaptive model incorporates the linear elements of the person or organization, but it does not include interpretive elements. The linear model excludes both adaptation and interpretation.

The hierarchy of the models explains why the interpretive

model is critical to organizational welfare. When considered as an interpretive situation, every event, every decision, becomes an opportunity to remind college constituents of their common allegiance. Moreover, the combination of strategies most likely to succeed will be a natural extension of an institution's unique identity. Colleges and universities will certainly continue to plan and adapt, but they must do so in a context of shared values and beliefs. To improve institutional performance, leaders must simultaneously employ all three strategy models and seek a dynamic equilibrium with the dimensions of organizational culture.

Culture expresses organizational identity, strategy consists of organizational action, and leadership is based on individual action. When leaders engage in planning, they are conducting linear strategy and dealing with the formalized structural dimension of the organization's culture. Using the curriculum as an example, the list of majors offered and their course requirements, course sequences, and course schedules are structural aspects of the culture that respond well to planning and linear strategy. Such components of the curriculum can be expressed in charts, lists, or tables. Changes tend to reflect rational thoughts about what structure will best meet specified goals. We will see at Present State College that student attrition was related to a structure that permitted students to take most of their major courses without prerequisites or a general education background. The college reduced attrition by implementing rules about course requirements and sequencing.

The environment changes and so does the organization's interpretation of its environment. Dealing with these shifts calls for change-oriented leadership through adaptive strategy. At this level, we are dealing with relatively large changes such as program creation, termination, or modifications that reshape the orientation of the program. Such changes occur even on relatively stable campuses. We will find exceptional stability at Rural State College, but not stagnation. The college is working toward a new M.A.T. program in mathematics that will strengthen its in-service outreach for practicing teachers and constitute its first graduate program outside elementary and special education.

Leaders use verbal and nonverbal communication as their primary tool for interpretive strategy, through which they express and modify the values of the organization's culture. In the case of the curriculum, such leadership often comes from the faculty. They express collective values and shape the identity of the institution as they determine the substance and extent of the institution's general education requirements and decide whether such options as individualized instruction or cooperative education will play a central role in the curriculum. Notice that their decisions on such issues mean little without corresponding adaptive and linear changes to implement the interpretive decisions. For example, at Mission University we will discover that the president expresses a commitment to a values-oriented education. Despite a major annual conference on ethical issues, however, students do not perceive this commitment in much of their on-campus experience.

One of the most important challenges leaders face is to achieve cultural integration. Lack of integration, persisting over time in areas that are central to organizational functioning, tends to culminate in crisis. So, for example, we will see Covenant University struggle under a long-term crisis arising from its leaders' inability to translate the university's historic emphasis on community, faith, and human dignity into a governance structure that expresses those values. The crisis was precipitated by environmental forces—declining resources—but it was exacerbated by a former president who did not deal with those forces in a manner consistent with the values. A consistent approach has not yet been worked out, nor has a satisfying revision of the historic values emerged.

On Reading the Cases

The picture we are trying to paint of culture, strategy, and leadership may be difficult to grasp. Virtually all management and leadership literature culminates in a series of recommended steps. When managers read professional literature, they look for what they should do in their daily lives. Managerial cookbooks are popular because they offer formulas for success. We offer no recipes for managers. What these cases have to offer the reflective reader is a fresh perspective that generates insights. Beyond the basics of management, formulas do not apply. Every important organizational situation has unique properties that call for creative moves. The more a manager develops his or her sensitivity to such properties, the more creative and successful the response.

That is why we did not organize this book differently. Rather than taking each case in its entirety, we might have taken several themes, one per chapter, and used vignettes from the cases to illustrate the themes. That is the organization for a typical management book. However, managers do not experience organizations in such a fashion. We believe it is necessary to present the case studies as the participants experience them, and equally necessary to approach the reader as she or he experiences life in an organization.

In observing and analyzing the seven institutions that form the basis of the study, we have found it essential to understand each case as fully as we can in isolation from others before we look across cases for generalizations. We recommend that readers immerse themselves in each case. Read interactively, stopping on occasion to imagine the setting and think about one's own actions in a similar setting. Speculate about how a given problem could have been prevented, or whether it would be enjoyable to work for a particular president or institution. Only after the reader becomes involved personally with each institution is it possible to join us in looking across institutions for common denominators.

We have provided brief introductions to each of the three sections of the book. The sections deal with culture and continuity, change, and identity. Figure 2.2 shows how we envision the relationships of culture, strategy, and leadership in the three sections. Leadership and strategy influence the cultural dimensions of structure, environment, and values. Conversely, organizational culture influences leadership and strategy. No organizational element is free to operate unaffected by culture's power. At the same time, however, leaders can exert pressure so that cultural change may occur.

An organization with a coherent identity, such as those depicted in the next part of the book, has a strong sense of what it stands for—so strong that it is apparent to observers, newcomers, and old-timers alike. The identity is structurally consistent. Some elements of the culture may be latent or slightly divergent, and some elements of strategy or leadership may be trying to take the organization in new directions. These "imperfections" are represented at the top of Figure 2.2 by the fact that the three solid circles do not overlap perfectly. But overall, the organization's identity is clear enough to indicate the kinds of behaviors that are in or out of bounds. Such institutions are close to dynamic equilibrium. The cultural dimensions of structure, environment, and values are aligned with one another, and the institution's leadership and strategies accentuate a coherent identity of the organization. We find this to be true of the first two cases, Rural State and Family State. The fact that both colleges exist in relatively stable envi-

Part 2. Culture and Continuity

Part 3. Culture and Change

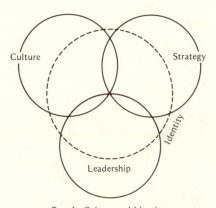

Part 4. Culture and Identity

Figure 2.2. Continuity, Change, and Identity

ronments probably is not coincidental, so we have labeled their condition as continuity.

Change, often instigated by forces beyond the organization's control, can shake or prevent dynamic equilibrium. As shown in the middle of Figure 2.2, culture, strategy, and leadership pull apart from one another. As they do so, they begin to move beyond the boundaries of a coherent identity. When many liberal arts colleges began to offer programs in business, health, and other professions, they strained their formerly well-defined cultures. Responses to what administrators perceived to be environmental demands caused structural and normative contradictions within the culture. Some leaders in such situations drew a larger circle of identity by a strategy that attempted to reinterpret the mission, others did not. The result for each institution was movement away from equilibrium. In two of the cases contained in Part 3, the force for change was declining resources; in the third, it was growth. Change need not be hostile to be disruptive.

The two cases in Part 4 show so little overlap among culture, strategy, and leadership that one must question whether a coherent identity exists at these universities. Organizational structure, values, and environment have little to do with one another, but operate instead as if they are independent spheres. Triad University would have belonged in Part 2 of this book during the first half of its existence. Now, however, it has a tripartite governance structure, a predominantly linear strategy, and very little unified leadership. Much of the public continues to equate the university with its original college or secondarily with its newest college. The university as a whole and its third college are relatively invisible.

R&D University, on the other hand, has not had a coherent identity since its former incarnation as a research center. Within the cultural sphere, its stated values are only loosely expressed in its structure. The university's formal leaders, especially the academic vice president, have a strong sense of the desired culture and identity, but their vision is not widely understood by the faculty, nor is it adequately supported by available resources.

It is ill-advised to question whether the institutions in Part 2 are better than those later in the book. A central tenet of the cultural view of organizations is that we need to be concerned about organizational health over time. The cause for an institution's financial well-being today may precipitate its downfall tomorrow. An inert definition of institutional mission today may provide a highly regarded student body, but it may also cause a crisis when environmental contexts change. The search for dynamic equilibrium belies static judgments at any given time concerning whether one institution is better than another.

Our overall assessment, then, is that the first cases are neither better nor worse than the last. Regardless of our groupings, we find institutions and programs within them that are strong in academic reputation, service to their region, financial welfare, or morale. In all cases, leaders face major challenges as well as opportunities to improve. Some would find the colleges in Part 2 parochial, those in Part 3 high in potential, and those in Part 4 stimulating for their dynamic tensions. On the other hand, most participants in the first group are very comfortable, those in the second group are often confused, and some of those in the third group are deeply concerned and frustrated.

This kind of ambiguity is the rule, not the exception, in organizations. Our aim is to help the reader diagnose the cases and, ultimately, his or her own organization through the conceptual models. Once a diagnosis becomes clear, the range of alternative prescriptions and their potential costs and benefits are easier to identify.

To guide the reader further, we have provided section overviews, case introductions, and a final chapter. The section introductions point out some of the key themes and dilemmas of each case and compare the cases with one another. Each case begins with an introduction that foreshadows major elements and dynamics of the institution. In the concluding chapter, we revisit the model of culture as illustrated by the cases.

During our visits, we came to regard these colleges and universities as friends. Like individual friends, they have many plusses and a few quirks. For the reader who has not visited these campuses, getting acquainted with them will be more like reading a play than making friends. The critical, thoughtful reader can learn much from the characters and situations. The applications to one's own life may not be immediate and obvious, but they can be profound.

PART TWO

Culture and Continuity

Erik Erikson once commented that a personal sense of identity "provides the ability to experience one's self as something that has continuity and sameness, and to act accordingly." On the broad stage of institutional life, the same might be said of organizational culture. Shared values and an active, consensual understanding of one's mission provide a cultural coherence that, over time, results in continuity.

The two state colleges discussed in this first section both display considerable continuity in their values, structure, and environment. In this respect they offer a helpful introduction to the concept of organizational culture. At the same time, change is upon them.

Rural State College and Family State College are both relatively small public institutions in relatively rural locations. Although separated by thousands of miles and although the environment of one is agricultural and the other blue-collar, the colleges are similar in many ways. Both show signs of cultural strength and congruence. Interpretive strategy is implicit, built into their cultures. Their environments are relatively stable and homogeneous, and the colleges' adaptive movement is correspondingly slow. In both cases, the president is a strong presence in the institution, and he is "one of us" in geographic and academic background. Yet the colleges also share at least two elements that could lead to conflict—both have begun to hire new faculty members from different kinds of backgrounds than the old-timers, and both aspire to change their names from "college" to "university." Like many public institutions, they are struggling with self-definition, which in turn

31

reflects upon how they see themselves and portray themselves to others. What is the mission of a public institution in the late twentieth century? What kind of faculty member should be recruited? Should research play an increased role in the life of the institution? Whether these questions will develop into important new themes for the colleges remains to be seen. They could constitute signs of impending divergence in the values and structure of the institutions.

Because of the similarities in the two institutions, they offer valuable opportunities to compare and contrast what is different. For example, one president is low-key and leaves many cultural elements implicit, taking them for granted. The other president has high energy and makes use of numerous social, physical, and communicative reinforcers of the culture. How are the colleges' curricular adaptations similar to or different from each other? The drive for university status seems to be real at Rural State but primarily symbolic at Family State. If so, why might that be the case, and what can one predict for the future?

Despite the comfortable clarity and congruence of culture, strategy, and leadership in these colleges, one may well wonder whether something is missing here. Have they missed some opportunities, such as new clientele or programs that would enliven the place? Do they have feasible, unexplored options for a fresh interpretation of their mission?

In many ways, Rural State and Family State represent situations that many would call ideal. They are doing well as institutions, most people at each college like being there, and they do what public institutions are supposed to do—serve the educational needs of the people who support them. They have a strong sense of identity and pride. Yet, as in the children's game, it is fair to ask whether there is anything wrong in this picture.

THREE

Rural State College

An organizational culture extends far beyond merely a group of individuals who inhabit roles. Rather, in the words of Clifford Geertz, it concerns an organization "suspended in webs of significance the actors themselves have spun" (1973, p. 5). Webs of significance take shape not only through individual action and change but also through historical processes and institutional forms. At Rural State, as at many organizations that have not been inundated by systemic change from the outside, the culture of the college is not readily apparent. Relative continuity has allowed the institution to internalize rather than articulate its cultural norms. As a result, the socialization of individuals into roles occurs implicitly, not explicitly. Likewise, strategic decisions are conceived and executed in an environment whose parameters and values are understood and shared by a large majority of the participants. The information for such decisions is available not as a compiled set of data but as local knowledge present throughout the culture's web of significance.

This chapter investigates how socialization occurs and how decisions and strategies become implemented in an organizational culture that has not experienced rapid transformation. Among the seven cases we present, Rural State College is perhaps the best example of a stable culture. However, it would be wrong to attribute to the institution a prelapsarian innocence or perceive its situation through a Rousseau-like vision of an untouched culture. Quite to the contrary, evolutionary change and its impact on the organization are pressing issues precisely because the institution is now recognizing the need to interpret and articulate its own cultural identity in an increasingly complex environment.

As the institution evolves from a state college to a university, administrators are asking themselves how to maintain the degree of confidence that Rural State currently enjoys. Indeed, environmental change can come about much more quickly than expected, and administrators need to be able to respond with equal rapidity. For example, both our visit in the fall and the IPS found the institution to have high morale and an extremely collegial environment. By our spring visit, however, morale and collegiality had plummeted. As we will describe, a presidential hiring decision and a hostile state legislature that viewed colleges as "ivory towers" caused much consternation among faculty and administrators. The metamorphosis of Rural State poses particular problems for an increasingly new administrative team who must recognize both the strains and the opportunities presented by its changing culture.

Regional Service and Efficiency

In seventy-two years Rural State College has had five college presidents, all of them locally born and raised. Throughout its history the college has relied on local actors as it transformed from a normal school to a teachers college, then to a comprehensive liberal arts institution, and is now making plans to become a university. These transformations have occurred as much for political reasons as for educational ones. One state historian of higher education comments:

> The principal consideration in the locations of most of these institutions was not how best to serve the people of a great state in its development for hundreds of years to come, but how many votes can you bring to the combination. . . . The institutions were distributed for votes and the counties able to deliver the most votes got the institution.

Rural State College is located in the northwest quadrant of a largely agricultural state. The city of Rural garnered enough votes to create one of three state colleges. It is the principal four-year institution of higher learning in the western half of the state. Two universities reside on the eastern border of the state, along with two state colleges. The final state institution resides in a less-populated portion of the western half of the state.

The institution's student body can be characterized as primarily working class and rural. People sometimes refer to Rural State as a "suitcase" college, since many students return home on weekends. The tuition cost reflects the working class character of the student body; it is $837 per year for residents and $1,472 for nonresidents. Rural's enrollment has fluctuated from 2,700 in the late 1960s to

2,200 in the early 1970s and currently stands at 3,100. Applications have increased 10 percent for the next academic year. With a continuing-education program that enrolls 4,000 and a special-education program enrollment of 1,000, Rural's service to the community and state is considerable. The college exists in a city of 35,000, which makes it the major metropolitan center in the northwest quadrant of the state. The institution presently has a full-time faculty of 138. Forty-four percent of the faculty hold Ph.D.s; 24 percent hold either graduate or undergraduate degrees from Rural.

Change is taking place both in academic structure and administrative posts. Within the last year, in a move to cut costs and enhance the possibility of university status, the nine divisions of the college were reorganized into five schools: nursing, business, education, arts and sciences, and graduate. A new administrator from outside the Rural State College community has been appointed as the new dean of the school of arts and sciences. The former dean of the education school has assumed the post of acting academic vice president en route to his own retirement.

Rural is the most efficient provider of higher education in the state in terms of cost per student in comparison to the other five state postsecondary institutions. However, financial belt-tightening by both the federal and state governments may cause problems in the future. The current downturn in the agricultural market combined with the bottoming out of the state's oil revenue suggests growing fiscal stringency.

Local Knowledge in a Stable Culture

Organizational culture at Rural State is tied closely to the daily lives of its constituents. The institution's evolution reflects the fortunes and misfortunes of the agricultural state. The region has a homogeneous population and ethnic heritage. The state's minority population is 4 percent and the largest minority—Native Americans—remain outside the mainstream of state or college authority. The state, like the college, has remained culturally stable. Actors who work at the college become intertwined and caught up in the life of the state through the institution. One individual mentioned, "I'm from Rural. I was born and raised in Texas, but I've been here fifteen years. I'm a product of this state now. My thinking, my way of life reflects that."

The economic realities of the college remain linked to those of the state, which traditionally has relied on small farms for its revenues. During the 1970s, when oil was discovered in the region, it appeared that the economic fortunes of the state and, therefore, the college were on the rise. By 1984, however, oil revenue had virtually dried up and once again small-farm revenue took on greater importance. Indeed, in 1984 projected state revenues from oil dropped by $75 million within a three-month period due to the oil glut. Additionally, farm supports, and particularly small-farm support, came under attack from the Reagan administration so that subsidies once relied upon no longer existed. To make matters worse, as the college president noted, "The drought this year has driven hay up to $90/ton when it should be around $25/ton. Money is real tight right now." Thus, the economic boom times have been replaced by the threat of a recession or possibly a depression.

The state has always been a strong supporter of agriculture; other interests, such as education, have been of secondary importance to the legislature. The year under study provides one example. In the legislature's attempt to balance the budget, everyone acknowledged that the two hardest-hit areas were higher education and human services. As one individual noted, "We were the whipping boys for the legislature. Obviously things are really tough out there, but higher education and human services took the brunt." Indifference to higher education, however, turned toward antipathy. One individual familiar with the legislative process commented:

> The faculty sit in an ivory tower and just want more money. They don't exist in the real world. They have a country club mentality and that doesn't go over very well in this state. They want salaries of $35,000 and $40,000, just like at an Ivy League school. Well, we're not that.

Such statements reflect an ethic that values farm work. The liberal arts and "ivory-tower" professors seem far removed from the practical, everyday problems of the farmer.

The state has a long tradition of minimal government interference in the life of its people. Deficit spending or increasing the taxes of individuals or businesses would be beyond the ken of state officials. Given these political, economic, and cultural realities, Rural State College forges ahead, intent on transforming itself into a university and led by one of its own—President Carl Johnson. To the college community, the attainment of university status signified natural growth and evolution. As we shall see, however, the college's future was not similarly perceived by a majority of the citizens of the state, nor by the state legislature.

A week before the legislature scheduled its preliminary session on the budget, the president called an impromptu staff and faculty meeting. People arrived at a meeting that had no written agenda, with less than a day's notice. They packed the hall to await the president's word. Prior to the meeting, the president explained:

> I'm a believer in people knowing where they've been and where they're going. I have a meeting today and I want to explain to them what is going to happen down there in the legislature. It's the first pitch of the first inning of the ball game. I want them to know they might get raises, but they shouldn't raise or drown their hopes with what they hear on the news Thursday night. If they hear on the evening news that there'll be no raises, that will have a demoralizing effect and I don't want that to happen. People have a right to know what's what. Whoever shows up at the meeting, shows up.

His meeting with the different constituencies went well; he spoke straightforwardly and succinctly, and answered whatever questions the audience had. After the meeting one individual noted characteristics of the president.

> The man is just honest. He doesn't pull any punches. If he has something to say to you, he just tells you, and if you have an idea or something, you feel free to go to him and talk to him about it. He really trusts us. He's fond of saying, "When you buy a bull you buy him to do the job." He hired all of us, and he respects the people who work for him.

When asked how change takes place and where he gets his ideas, the president referred neither to strategic-planning models nor to managerial objectives. Rather, he said:

> I carry a lot of ideas, plans, in my head that I never put down on paper—like grandma baking a cake. She didn't have a recipe, she couldn't tell you the specifics, but she sure could bake a cake. . . . I try to listen to all constituencies—and new ideas often come from young faculty. You'll get more new ideas from two new faculty than from ten older ones. They will reinvent the wheel and, in so doing, they'll find something different and new, and sometimes they're persistent enough to actually make it succeed.

CULTURAL NORMS

Mottos and slogans often play an important role in the life of an institution. Moreover, they can point to underlying cultural norms that frame daily life at the college. At Family State we will hear the

president use the term "excellence" to help his constituencies interpret the kind of institution he leads. One did not hear words such
as "excellence" or "quality education" at Rural State. Rather, a re-
sounding theme echoed by all constituencies was that Rural State
provides "service to the community." The phrase fits the ideology
of a state that places high value on serving rural constituents. The
point is not that one institution concerns itself with excellence and
another does not. Rather, we point out the slogans used by institutions to highlight how a particular institution sees itself and how
others see it. The way one sees and portrays the institution's role
affects both the decision-making process and the decisions themselves.

As we shall see, problems can arise when one violates norms
and expectations. Many faculty and administrators stay at Rural
because of the culture. They feel they can effect change, come
up with new ideas of their own, and work on different tasks. For
example, a broadcasting professor developed films on the history
of the state and college; a geologist/statistician developed models
for tracking and developing alumni; several professors set to work
on overhauling the general-education curriculum; and another
group worked on redesigning the institution from nine divisions
into five schools.

The impetus for creating five schools came from the administration. They felt that the change would cut costs and enhance
prospects for gaining university status. Cost efficiency was a familiar theme both at the college and in the state house. Moreover,
universities tend to have particular governance structures; the reorganization was an additional sign to the legislature and state that
Rural State was indeed a university. Throughout all of this change,
the actors received presidential input and initiative. One individual, when asked if the president ever said "No" to an idea, stated,
"Sure he does. Most often, however, I've heard him say 'Wait' or
'Have you thought about this?' He rarely just says 'No.'"

The atmosphere of initiative and the ability to effect change ran
throughout the institution. For example, the move to change from
state college to university status reportedly came about through
the impetus of the student body and the alumni. The state board
and legislature approved the change, but certain citizens protested.
Although the college made a positive effort to lay out the need for
such a move and show that it would not cost the state or taxpayer
any additional money, the ballot lost in a statewide referendum.
The college won every county except eight. Opposition came from

the most populous counties in the eastern part of the state, where two universities and two state colleges are located.

One local legislator commented:

> It's a travesty that the universities are located on the eastern border of this state. They brag that they are getting students from the next state over. We are subsidizing those out-of-state kids! This is an affront to the citizens of this state, and those are the very scalawags that said Rural shouldn't become a university because we want to serve the western citizens of this state. East versus West. It's like this with every issue.

Undaunted, Rural continues to try to effect the name change. The next step will be an appeal to the state board of higher education. Most individuals interviewed expressed resolve and confidence that the change to university status will occur within five years.

Social functions at Rural State are not common; the president, for example, does not have people over to his house regularly for suppers or luncheons. Written letters of congratulation rarely are forthcoming from any administrative office. The president has an "open door" policy, but the awareness of the open door does not come about by written notification or specified schedules. "If faculty members have a problem, they usually go right in and talk with him," said the president's secretary. "He's very flexible. His schedule is pretty open."

Socialization of new members into the organization occurs by informal means, such as talking with the deans or colleagues, rather than through formalized meetings and written agendas. A new faculty member commented on these informal means and compared them to a larger university where the individual previously taught:

> The dean was helpful in telling me what to do, everybody was. People just came by and told me how this gets done, and how to get something if I needed it for a class. At the university there were piles of documents that I could read. Requisition requests, committees, new faculty meetings. Here it's different. When I first arrived everybody told me I could take coffee at 9:30. Take coffee? I'd never heard of such a thing, but here everybody goes over and chats over coffee at 9:30. On Fridays at 3:00 some of us also go out for donuts as a way to unwind.

Thus, the way one learned about the institution was through oral, informal means.

The differences between the community and the college—"town and gown"—also were minimal. Rural State and the city's actions and desires were almost synonymous. As the college's admissions officer, the registrar hires one graduate to drop off Rural State College's latest brochures at area high schools and local businesses. One civic leader said:

> People in the community feel it's our college—and that means the people in the northwest quadrant of the state. The credit goes to the staff and faculty because they're active in service clubs and the college has always had an open door for us. If you go over to the Dome [the gym], you'll see senior citizens there all the time. The college is ours because the president made it ours.

The president reiterated the point by talking about who he considered key constituencies.

> You have to listen to a lot of people who won't even show up for meetings. We think people are important and we want people's ideas. The senior citizens, for example. Our housing is tight, so we have some girls living with the senior citizens in the retirement home. The elderly have always been here. We helped them sandbag the town when the flood came. We fed them in our student union. Our students know where they come from—they know who grandma and grandpa are, and those are vines of solidarity.

A CHANGING CULTURE

Vines of solidarity, however, can both grow and wither, or develop in new directions. In the 1960s the college either recruited its faculty and other professionals from within the state or attracted individuals who came to the college with the intent of settling down. Now individuals come because of a tight job market, or they conceive of the position as a stepping-stone to a job elsewhere. The ability of the organization's culture to persist in the face of rapid change and turnover will be sorely tested in the next few years. Further, while university status can be viewed as a positive step, a continued march on the road to improvement, university life may well alter the forms and processes currently at work in the organization's culture.

Recent and forthcoming changes in administrative personnel heighten the prospect of considerable cultural transformation. In 1984 the academic vice president and dean of education resigned. In addition, the president, vice president for business, and the director of continuing education and public relations will retire within the next five years. Thus, an entire new cadre of top personnel will take over from an administration whose ways of doing things reflected the state's culture. Change is bound to occur.

One top official in the state suggested the kind of person he would like to see become president. "The college needs a contrast to Carl Johnson. I'd want someone forty-five years old, moderately ambitious, who does not want to spend the rest of his career here. It will be difficult to follow Johnson's act." Another individual commented, "We need an academician with university experience. Someone outside of the state who can present different ways of doing things. Sometimes I think we are a little too inbred." Other individuals said they wanted someone born and raised in the state.

Change already has occurred. The new dean of arts and sciences wants his faculty to undertake small-scale research projects and publish articles. Although he has no desire to create a "publish or perish" mentality, his requests have created dissent on the part of some faculty members. "We came here to get away from that kind of demand," complained one individual. One can expect that changing cultural norms will gradually alter the future composition of the faculty.

Another transformation concerns the reconfiguration of academic divisions into schools. Although most faculty members saw very few changes in their daily life because of the reorganization, different forms of socialization are likely to emerge. Reflected one science professor:

> There's been little change. Science and math used to have a backyard get-together in the spring, and I noticed that just the math department had one this spring. But they wouldn't have been upset if someone from science showed up. We both share a secretary—although we want our own secretaries. But overall, I'd say there's been little change.

However, when new individuals arrive, they will identify not with the "science and math" division, but the individual department in which they reside. Bureaucratic differences such as secretarial assignments mean that different communication patterns will occur.

One change underway concerns the selection of a new dean for the school of education. The president formed a search committee that selected one internal candidate—the acting dean—and two outsiders to be interviewed. The overwhelming faculty favorite was the acting dean. After interviewing all three candidates the president decided: (1) to downgrade the graduate dean's position to a director, (2) to move the incumbent from graduate dean to dean of education, and (3) to name a faculty member returning from leave with a new doctorate as director of graduate studies. On an instrument level, the president's reasoning appeared sound. None of the candidates for dean fit what he wanted; he did not want a "maintainer," he wanted a "mover and shaker." The graduate dean's position was not really a full-time position because there were not many graduate programs. The president checked with the accreditation agency and it approved what he wanted to do. His candidate for director of graduate studies is a woman, which will put a female in a top administrative post. He knows the director of continuing education will retire in two years, and he has considered combining graduate studies with continuing education because he has confidence in the new graduate director. The move also will save thousands of dollars, which is critical in an institution where cost-effectiveness is essential. However, his decision met with widespread criticism.

"The search committee spent a lot of time for nothing," said one observer. "I don't like it, because it's not very trusting. He's closed that open kind of communication. He just did it." Another individual echoed the criticism: "I don't care what the decision was, he didn't do it right. If you make a decision, then we need to talk about it. A president should never have people afraid to go and talk with him, and that's what he's done. I've never seen him do anything like this before." Finally, one person noted, "I've never seen morale so low. The legislature hit us, and now this. It was a surprise to everyone. I feel sure it wasn't premeditated, but it sure has caused bad feelings."

The president's decision points the way toward a new social order at Rural State. He recognized a need for change in education similar to what was occurring then in arts and sciences; to hire the popular candidate would not have produced new ideas and programs. Consequently, the individual who has been instrumental in maintaining the ideology and status quo of the institution—President Johnson—is also the one who has begun to point the college toward its new path. As he begins to wind down his career he is setting in motion the college's future orientation.

Clearly, one fundamental change that most constituents would like to see is the college's change to a university. Indeed, the president wants new ideas, and that was one of his rationales for hiring the individuals he did. However, downgrading a dean of graduate studies to director because the college did not have enough for a dean to do may have unintended yet important symbolic implications. That is, one critical structural component that separates a university from a college is its graduate offerings. What will external constituents think when they see that Rural State has cut costs by eliminating a position central to the function of any university? Rural State exists through implicit cultural norms and codes. Cost-effectiveness and service are the underlying institutional philosophy. As the college prepares for university status, it must develop a greater awareness of its cultural fabric and the capability to interpret and articulate cultural transformations both to internal and external constituencies. Interpretive strategy of this kind is currently lacking at Rural State, and its development would ease the cultural transformations that are now beginning to occur.

Rural State has long existed in a homogeneous environment largely protected from outside change. Nevertheless, it is possible that environmental factors could radically restructure the institutional climate. At present an air force base in town accounts for a substantial portion of Rural State's clientele. Closing the air force base would not only adversely affect the college student population, it would cripple the local economy. A more likely prospect, however, is that the base will stay open and the agricultural economy will suffer. Within a decade, it is forecast that the adult population will have leveled off and thereby decrease Rural State's student clientele. In a depressed economy, however, many expect the college's market to be maintained. If farming and oil production continue to decrease, many workers will return to higher education for retraining in different vocational careers.

Curiously, while the actors and culture may come under pressure due to rapid transition, the mission of the institution most likely will not change dramatically. Individuals speak of mission in one of two forms: geographic or substantive. First, one hears a familiar refrain, "We serve the needs of the people of the northwest quadrant of the state. I don't just mean students, I mean everybody who has higher educational needs in the northwest quadrant." Second, one hears how the former teachers college is changing: "The mission is changing. We were into teacher education, but now we're shifting into liberal arts." The first refrain accentuates how the actors—and the state—see the college. The universities serve the needs of the eastern portion of the state and, with or without university status, Rural State serves the needs of the northwest quadrant. Presumably, if the institution became a university they might say they serve "the needs of the western half of the state," thereby encroaching on the territory of the weaker area state college. Nevertheless, the clientele will remain the same, and the emphasis remains on geography.

The IPS results pointed out that, more than any other institution surveyed, Rural State sees its academic programs and student body increasing in diversity. Interpreting this information points out how the institution sees itself. When asked what diversity means to them, individuals continually commented that the institution is changing from a teachers college to a comprehensive liberal-arts college. These comments reflect a process that has extended over fifteen years. For over ten years the college has offered the bachelor of arts, bachelor of science, the master of science, the associate of arts, and the associate of science degrees. The BS degree offers 31 majors, and the BA degree offers 24 majors. The college moved away from teacher education in 1970, yet fifteen years later constituents still see themselves becoming more diverse. A new administrator noted: "The myth persists that everything is a support service to teacher education, and it's just not that way anymore." Resources, power, and curricular design have clearly shifted from the school of education to other centers of power. Consequently, image needs to catch up with reality; an awareness of current changes must supplant the memory of those that have long since transpired. Even though the institution's mission is unlikely to undergo radical restructuring or change, its culture is likely to experience rapid transformation as new individuals fill top-level positions in what is otherwise a small, close-knit community.

Information in Decision-making

The committee structure at Rural State establishes a formal process for informal communication and decision-making. The institutional culture implicitly supports specific practices and procedures. One example of this structure is the most recent long-range plan conducted by the college. The institution involved faculty, administrators, staff, and community people in a process that took the better part of a year. They set institutional goals and helped create a camaraderie and impetus for making the college into a university. When asked about long-range planning, virtually all individuals spoke of their participation in the process and were familiar with its finer details.

At one point, the planning process involved over five hundred people meeting in small groups in a hotel ballroom to discuss strategies and plans for the future. The president commented on the process as one example of how he feels all people should be involved. "They know they had a lot of influence," he said. "We pay attention to the classifieds [staff] as well. Everyone counts here.

Our long-range plan shows how people learned what we're about." Throughout the process, however, the administration continually informed the actors that their thoughts were neither decisions nor plans that would be used as a blueprint; rather, the actors offered information and suggestions to different committees and groups. Eventually their input filtered its way up a hierarchical system and the president decided what was to happen.

By all accounts, the president has the respect and ear of the legislature and board. "If I had to choose any president in this state," said one knowledgeable professor, "I'd choose Carl. He's for us. He knows the legislature. He's been a rancher in this state. We've done very well by Carl." A member of the state board echoed the professor's comments: "We like dealing with Carl. The board perceives him as competent, honest, hard-working. There's a confidence with Carl that you don't get with other people. When he comes to you, you know he's not going to pull any punches. He's a straight talker."

One individual described the decision-making structure in this way: "If you ask people for their input, then you had better listen to it and use it. If you don't ask people, then you had better keep people informed about what's going on." The president at Rural State normally acted in both ways. He constantly sought people's ideas and input, and he kept people informed of what he deemed they needed to know. Thus, one can understand the shocked feelings of faculty when they heard that the president had chosen a new dean without consultation or information-sharing.

The system expects—and receives—decision-making by an individual, yet he requests and receives input from multiple constituencies. Indeed, throughout the research process, more than at any other institution, the president used "we" rather than "I." That is, men in leadership roles often use the first person singular in reference to decisionmaking and planning (Henley, 1977). This president, however, quite often used the first person plural.

This language and other symbols provided the sense that the administration based decision-making and governance on a shared authority wherein one individual had final say, yet the process itself was informal and input came constantly from all sides and angles. As a young administrator noted:

> Carl really sees himself as first among equals. He's not authoritarian. He's created a symbolic niche by talking with people, relating things to people in a fair way. When I arrived here I almost felt I didn't have enough guidance. The president's attitude, though, was "I hired you because you know what to do and if you don't, you'll ask me."

IPS data confirm these observations about the college's decision-making process. Among the seven institutions studied, respondents at Rural State rated their college highest on the credibility of top administrators, highest on collegial decision-making regarding resource allocation, and lowest on autocratic decision-making regarding resource allocation. Nevertheless, when compared to the 1983 survey, the 1985 IPS results indicate a growing perception of centralization in major decisions.

The role of information and communication in the decision-making process remains informal yet is supported by various formal structures. These structures include committees such as curriculum, a newly created dean's council, and the faculty senate. The faculty senate receives information from committees prior to passing on issues to the president and perhaps the state board. Actors on these committees and throughout the college community share an implicit awareness of the organization's culture. A high degree of informality governs their work. Committees worked from written agendas handed out prior to the meetings and specified times and votes existed. Nevertheless, formal rules did not inhibit informal processes.

Another manifestation of the president's emphasis on a team approach to decision-making is his reliance on top administrators, particularly the academic vice president. One individual related, "He works things out through his academic vice president. He's there if you need him, but the person we go to for day-to-day advice and suggestions is the academic vice president. That's why the replacement is so important to us." Again, instead of an iron-fisted ruler at the top who arbitrarily made decisions, one finds an individual who makes decisions, but to interpret those decisions as arbitrary or dictatorial belies the institutional culture in which they are made.

For an institution in 1985, Rural State is woefully inadequate in its accumulation of statistical data and information systems that would inform decision-making. There is no director of institutional research other than a quarter-time professor of earth science who enjoys the manipulation of data as a hobby. Little information exists on where students come from, why they choose to attend Rural State rather than another institution, why they drop out, and where they go to work after they have completed Rural State College. Retention and attrition studies contain no conclusive data or sophisticated statistical methods that inform the administration about what measures to take if a problem arises.

The lack of institutional data is in part due to the actors' personal awareness of the college's constituency—to an extent that is impossible nearly anywhere else. Another factor is the institution's wariness of outside consultants providing them with data that is either unreliable or misperceived. Finally, institutional data are unnecessary at times, insofar as Rural State College works from assumptions that further its goals, mission, and decisions. Rural State College attracts about 80 percent of its students from eight nearby counties—the northwest quadrant of the state. The rural nature of the state demands in large part that students attend college during the week and either go home to help out on the farm or go home to return to the womb, so to speak, on the weekend. Consequently, a study telling administrators where students come from is perceived as unnecessary. The same can be said about a study of retention. If students leave Rural State College and go to one of the universities, it is because the institution does not offer specific degrees and the university does. Administrators are intuitively aware of students who want to major in programs Rural does not offer and why a student leaves to complete such a program elsewhere. In the early 1970s outside consultants provided Rural State with seriously misguided information about institutional enrollment. When administrators are innately suspicious of outsiders and statistical data, then inaccurate projections only confirm to the institution that it should rely on its homespun judgment.

Given the importance of local knowledge to the organization's culture it is not startling when the registrar, who is also director of admissions, talks about the causes of healthy enrollment trends and says, "That's a wonder. I don't know where the kids come from in that sense. I just know we keep getting them." When an institution identifies as closely with its market as does Rural State, administrators have intuitive knowledge within their purview. When an institution wants to go after university status to attract public monies it feels it should be getting, then statistical summaries that may prove their case wrong are not only unnecessary, they can be harmful. Finally, when someone tells the institution that they will face declining enrollments in the 1980s, and instead the college has shown steady enrollment increases over five years, then administrators wonder about the significance of long-term projections that do not take into account their awareness of local conditions.

Local knowledge is an important key to Rural State's success. A refrain that one hears quite often is that the college has the lowest cost-per-student ratio in the state. This seemingly well-managed organization has been developed not through the sophisticated manipulation of data bases but through the use of an intuitive approach to problem solving. However, transforming this approach from the institution to the state level remains difficult. Even though the institution is fiscally sound and managed more than competently in financial terms, the state would not consider increasing revenues for a well-run organization. "My severest criticism of this state is that it does not reward efficiency. It rewards inefficiency," said one observer. In a curious twist on Callahan's *Education and the Culture of Efficiency*, the state not only fails to reward efficiency, but it also forgoes the bureaucratic checks and balances used by other state systems to measure efficiency.

CULTURAL DYNAMICS AND CURRICULAR CHANGE

The inception and development of a master's degree in math education reflects some of the dynamics of the organization's culture and the ways that the institution uses its surrounding environment to adapt to changing or perceived needs on the part of its clientele. A faculty member recalls, "A few years back, [the math department] got a request from the field for graduate level courses in math education, with the emphasis on math." The continuing education director and the president gave their input concerning the worth of the program. On a casual basis, the math chair and other math faculty talked with high school and elementary school teachers and discovered a need. The department found that teachers wanted solid training, but they did not have the time or resources to go East to one of the universities for that kind of training. In 1983 the math department surveyed the field by sending out questionnaires; the respondents wanted to have graduate courses in math education. Rural State discovered that there are substantially fewer math teachers with a master's degree in the western part of the state than in the eastern half. The college attributes this difference to the lack of graduate course offerings by a university in the western half of the state and the students' inability to pay to go elsewhere.

After the department drew up the master's degree proposal, it went to the curriculum committee and presented the idea. The curriculum committee, after little debate, passed the resolution and it then went to the faculty senate, which voted for it. The president supported the measure all along, and there are plans to submit the proposal to the state board.

As the program currently stands, selected centers—local high schools—will offer courses each quarter. Courses will emphasize math education rather than, for example, foundations of education, or classroom principles. An instructor from Rural State or an adjunct faculty member will offer the classes, generally one night a week per quarter. In the summer, students will take courses at Rural State and will either commute from their homes or live in college dorms. The program has been set up so that students will supplement their two summers on campus with courses provided in their local area. The faculty plan to rotate their centers until the demand has lessened; they will begin the course offerings in areas that have been designated as high in demand. When they have exhausted the "northwest quadrant," they hope to move into the western area where the other state college draws its clientele but does not offer graduate programs. Rural State College tentatively has arranged for the other state college to have its faculty teach one or two of the courses, but control and the summer program will remain with Rural State.

Recruitment of students is a relatively simple affair since the continuing education director has a firm grasp of the local market, many professors at Rural State College are from the local area, and the public-school teachers themselves have either attended Rural State or are aware of its presence. Prospective students will find out about courses through a mailing to individual teachers and departments of math and science. Admission and registration have been streamlined so that students will know when they apply whether they will be accepted, and they will be able to go to class the first night to register. The program illustrates an adaptive strategy that is natural for Rural State College. The college acknowledges a previously untapped market, and the overall reputation of the institution will be enhanced by additional graduate course offerings.

By incorporating math education into its curriculum, Rural State strengthens its mission and institutional identity. Although the topic never came up within informal circles or formalized decision-making structures, the mission of the institution and the incorporation of this new program are a perfect fit for one another. As has been mentioned, people speak of the mission as "serving the needs of the northwest quadrant of the state," and math education serves that population. Math education is an example of how Rural State initiates changes that are consistent with its ideology.

Moreover, the program has ramifications beyond the scope of math education in the northwest quadrant of the state. Individuals recognize that an additional program at the graduate level will further enhance Rural State's assertion that it is in fact a university and that the state should allow it to be recognized as one. The second way people speak of the college's mission is in terms of the changing nature of serving teachers. While the emphases may change, the inclusion of a graduate-level, teacher-education program is a natural progression that will create a climate for university status. Nevertheless, the college is keenly aware of encroaching on another institution's turf—hence the hesitation on the part of Rural State to offer graduate level courses in the southwest quadrant. The college has designed the program primarily for its local constituency; if it develops a larger regional offering it plans to use faculty from another local college to offer its courses.

Culture as Identity, Culture as Limit

The development of a graduate program in math education reflects both cultural norms and processes within the institution and the college's service to local constituents. The relative success of the institution has much to do with the homogeneity of its organizational culture and the extent to which it mirrors that of its environment. As with any culture, however, minorities do exist. How these individuals and groups gain access to and interpret the daily institutional life and activities may differ radically from the norm.

One local group that has been left out is the Native American population that lives on two reservations within the state's northwest quadrant. Because Native Americans have different communication structures and cultural attitudes, the processes deemed natural for the overwhelming portion of the local constituency often leave minorities such as Native Americans by the wayside. But people with differing racial or ethnic origins are not the only ones with different cultural norms. The homogeneity of the culture can also work against people who are new to the organization. Likewise, the entrance of key individuals into the organization can also threaten long-standing cultural norms and expectations. As we have noted, a number of high-level administrative positions will be filled in the next five years. It remains to be seen how this change will affect the culture and the key actors who help shape it.

Trice and Beyer have noted that:

> rites and ceremonials most often will be used in modern organizations to express the ideologies of dominant elites, who are likely to have the biggest stake in maintaining the status quo. The question thus arises as to whether rites and ceremonials tend to impede organizational adaptability by making change more difficult. (1984, p. 666)

Another way of looking at "rites and ceremonials," however, is that they can help maintain institutional identity during periods of upheaval and change. Interestingly enough, a prominent feature of Rural State's culture is the virtual absence of these forms of socialization. Individuals who might expect some form of congratulation or recognition for their work do not receive a letter from the president extolling the worth of their efforts. An artist who exhibits in a local show receives little notice or recognition from a culture that does not place art at a premium. In the past, Rural State has had little need for elaborate rites and ceremonials because its homogeneous culture is widely internalized among its constituents. However, impending changes may make the college community more aware of its culture and of the need to interpret and communicate its values and goals in order to elicit support from an increasingly heterogeneous body of faculty, administrators, and students. This kind of interpretive strategy may well provide a welcome sense of continuity during a period of considerable transformation.

Change is already occurring at Rural State and more is anticipated as personnel shifts take place. The new dean of arts and sciences encourages faculty to enter a previously neglected area—research and the publication of articles—to the consternation of long-time faculty members who have grown accustomed to other expectations. Eventually he wants to see tenure decisions based in part on scholarly publication. He is also seeking released time for faculty research, yet an increased emphasis on research can only increase the average cost per student for the institution. This would undermine a source of great pride for current leaders of the college.

When people speak of the kind of individual they would like to see in the presidency, they quite often speak of many of the qualities President Carl Johnson has—honesty, knowledge of the state system, and a frankness with those he contacts. At the same time, people ask for someone different. They recognize the needs of the 1980s and the changes that have taken place since Johnson inherited Rural State Teachers College back in the mid-1960s. "I'd like to see someone with a broader scope than just Rural State," opined one individual, "someone who has a broad array of experience, and someone who thinks organizationally, in a formal sense. Of course, the interpersonal atmosphere must remain."

Therein lies the paradox. The point of this comment is not that one style of management is right and another wrong, nor that different points in organizational time necessarily demand different leadership and managerial styles. The speaker's remark reflects a sense that the institution must prepare for the future. The interpersonal atmosphere is due in large part to the consistent cultural paradigm from which Rural State always has worked. Even the progression of change from normal school to teachers college to comprehensive institution was predicated upon stability and a singular world view of how to accomplish tasks and set goals.

Rural State in the 1980s, however, will have faculty and administrators who do not necessarily come from the area. The professoriate is likely to be more geared toward individuals who will begin at Rural State and then move elsewhere on the academic ladder, instead of an academy that sees its professorial life begin and end at Rural State. The state board is likely to choose an individual as president who will not have a tenure similar to the two decades of service rendered by his or her predecessor. Substantively, then, what was once implicit in the organization as "the interpersonal atmosphere" will either be made explicit or dropped.

Decision-making processes and the kinds of information assimilated by and shared within the organization will undoubtedly change, as will the intuitive approach to strategy and leadership. It could not be otherwise. Although the institution's mission and its dedication to serve a specified clientele will likely remain intact, the impending transformation in organizational culture may prove to be more considerable than any of the actors suspect. Many point to the shift from college to university status as a watershed event in the institution's history, yet to recognize its full implications requires understanding that it is an underlying cultural transformation. Rural State's prospects for the future depend in large measure on whether it can recognize and successfully interpret these changes, not merely experience them.

FOUR

Family State College

The intensity of an academic culture is determined not only by the richness and relevance of its symbolism for the maintenance of the professional craft, but by the bonds of social organization. For this mechanism to operate the institution needs to take specific steps to socialize the individual to the belief system of the organization. . . . The management of academic culture therefore involves both the management of meaning and the management of social integration. (Dill, 1982, p. 317)

Family State College offers insight into the role of symbolism and social integration in an organizational culture and shows how administrators can utilize the management of meaning to foster understanding of the institution and motivate support for its mission.

This chapter provides our clearest example of an institution's use of interpretive strategy. As discussed in Chapter 2, interpretive strategy orients metaphors or frames of reference that allow the organization and its environment to be understood by its constituents. Unlike strategic models that enable the organization to achieve goals or adapt to the environment, interpretive strategy proceeds from the understanding that the organization can play a role in creating its environment. In dealing with its environment through symbolic actions and communication, Family State College has imbued in its constituents a strong feeling that the institution has a distinctive purpose and that the programs reflect its mission. By invigorating old roots and values with new meaning and purpose, the president of Family State has largely succeeded in reconstructing tradition and encouraging a more effective organizational culture.

As with all strategies, however, the utilization, strengths, and weaknesses of a particular approach are circumscribed by institutional context. This chapter explores questions that arise with the use of interpretive strategy. These questions include how the institution responds to its environment, how it articulates its mission, how new individuals become socialized into the system, and how the system changes. Decision-making processes, patterns of communication and socialization, and still unresolved issues of curricular renovation and faculty development provide perspectives on these questions.

A Family-style Atmosphere

Founded in 1894, Family State College exists in a fading mill town. Throughout its history the institution has fulfilled its mission as a career-oriented college for the working class in nearby towns and throughout the state. "I came here," related one student, "because I couldn't afford going to another school, and it was real close by." Fifty percent of the students remain in the local area after graduation, and 30 percent more reside in the state. In many respects the city of Family and the surrounding area have remained a relatively stable environment for the state college due to the unchanging nature of the working-class neighborhoods. An industrial-arts professor explained the town-gown relationship: "The college has always been for the people here. This is the type of place that was the last stop for a lot of kids. They are generally the first generation to go to college and college for them has always meant getting a job."

Like many of its counterparts, Family State began as a teachers college. With the drop in demand for teachers, combined with the rapid increase of college-age students in the 1960s, the college successfully altered its programs and changed to a comprehensive college that currently offers twenty-one degrees. The institution has 3,400 full-time students and 3,000 continuing-education and graduate students. The largest number of students enroll in business, nursing, communications/media, special education, computer science, education, and industrial technology.

The college has adapted to a variety of environmental circumstances in proactive and reactive ways that fostered growth. The call for courses in high technology in the region prompted, in turn, more courses in business. Substantially reduced demand for high school industrial-arts teachers forced similar institutions to drop their programs. Family State, however, added a segment in industrial technology for businesses and kept teacher education, thereby being one of the few remaining institutions in the region to offer coursework in industrial-arts technology and teacher education. At present, because no other institutions continue to offer the industrial-arts teaching credential, Family State has a steady stream of majors. When the demand for industrial education returns, the institution will be ready to expand its program. Before any other of the state institutions, the college implemented a computer-science major that captured a new market. These new programs have been successfully grafted onto the college without altering the central mission: to serve working-class students in the surrounding area.

When Family State's president arrived in 1976, he inherited an institution in equilibrium yet with a clear potential to become stagnant. The institution had low visibility in the area and next to no political clout in the state capital. Family State was not a turbulent campus in the late 1970s; rather, it was a complacent institution without a clear direction. In the past decade the institutional climate has changed from complacency to excitement and constituents share a desire to improve the college. "It's because of him [the president]," said an administrator. "Danny works so hard that you feel like you're really doing it for the good of the community, the students. It's not for your own gain or something, it's like a family." Throughout the interviews individuals consistently mentioned the "family atmosphere" that had developed at the college.

A faculty union for all state colleges coexists amicably with the administration at Family State; both faculty and administration note the low grievance rate by the faculty. Explained one faculty member:

> There's not much to complain about because we're involved in the decision-making and the president listens to our different concerns. I'm in the liberal arts, and it worries me that business courses are growing so rapidly, but I've spoken with the president. It concerns him too, and he will be an advocate for us. He believes in academic excellence.

Results from the Institutional Performance Survey confirm these observations. In both 1983 and 1985, Family State respondents reported the lowest level of conflict among the case-study institutions.

The president's visibility pertains not only to faculty input but to virtually every level of the institution. As one individual noted:

Everything used to be fragmented here. Now there's a closeness. The reason is, he's everywhere. He'll walk in your office and you never feel he's trying to catch you. He'll talk decisions out with you, you know where he stands. If he agrees with your ideas he'll say, "Ok, go with it. Whatever decision you make I'll back you." The bottom line, though, is Danny must have academic excellence.

One potential problem with a president being "everywhere" is an inability to let subordinates make decisions. One individual associated with the president at Family commented on presidential overinvolvement:

He realizes he gets into too much. It's the penalty he pays for accessibility. His enthusiasm can get in the way; fortunately, he realizes it, and will most often let go. He'll pawn off jobs on people who should actually be making the decisions, so his overmanagement isn't really a problem.

Nevertheless, the IPS responses pointed out a curious contradiction. Respondents believed that Family State had formal policies and procedures and a very centralized decisionmaking structure. On the other hand, Family State appeared to be a personal place with a family environment. How can an institution governed by centralized processes be family-oriented at the same time? Consensus exists that when cutbacks occur, they are done on a prioritized basis, and they are based on what objectively seems best for the institution. One critic of the administration provided an explanation:

Power is so diffuse here, I don't know where it is. Everyone does get involved, but no one decides, really. It's centralized because the decisions that are made are made by the president. It's family oriented because everyone talks about the decisions. There's lots of information.

The individual in charge of public relations noted:

Nothing gets published without people knowing Danny's read it. Everybody on this campus feels important because he pays attention to people as individuals and makes them take care in what they do. He'll say to some guy, "Ok, now how can we make this better." Nothing is ever just good enough, it can always be improved.

On the whole, faculty members share the president's enthusiasm and confidence. When asked about the direction of the college, its mission, and the method used to sustain and carry on its primary function, one faculty member said, "Our mission is pretty secure. I don't see too much change in the next couple of years, because we identify with a particular market."

However, problems have begun to appear with the curriculum.

Prior to the president's arrival, the college created programs that were unique to the state college system, such as computer science. Since the mid-1970s, however, other state colleges have created similar courses and majors. "Ten years ago," noted a professor, "we had programs that were unique to us. Now most of the other state colleges have our programs, so there's nothing to keep us unique. Academic leadership is extremely weak. No one has taken charge of the curriculum."

Individuals spoke of the mission of the college from two similar angles; either the mission referred to the balance between career-oriented and liberal-arts programs, or the audience for whom the college had been founded—the working class. That is, in 1965 the college created a nursing program that easily fit into the mission of the college as a course of study for working-class students. The industrial-technology major is another example of a program that responded to the needs of the surrounding environment and catered to the specified mission and clientele of the institution. Although people spoke about the mission of the college in terms of both program and clientele, the college's adaptations concerned programmatic change, not a shift in audience. Rather than alter or broaden the traditional constituency of the institution, the college tried to create new curricular models that would continue to attract the working-class student to Family State.

How Things Get Done: Decision-making Processes

Family State's decision-making process used a formal structure that nevertheless accommodated informal activity. Initiatives often began at the individual or departmental level, as with proposals to create a new program. Eventually the new program or concept ended up in the college senate—composed of faculty, students, and administration. A subcommittee of the senate decided what action should be taken and recommended that the idea be accepted or defeated. The senate then voted on the issue. Once it had taken action, the next step was presidential—accept the proposal, veto it, or send it back to the senate for more analysis. The final step was approval by the board. All action worked within the confines and time constraints of budgetary approval by the state legislature.

The president consults with the treasurer (the chief fiscal officer) and the academic vice president to determine which new programs to implement. Every year the state outlines programs that will be given priority consideration. In part, Family State's administrative team determines which programs to include in its budget by considering how those new programs mesh with state funding priorities. Ultimately, the president decides what direction the college will take on policy matters, as he did when the college applied for a medical-technology major.

"The good thing about Dan, though," said one administrator, "is that you can come back to your idea if you present him with new data. He'll always listen. It's participative decision-making." However, another individual commented, "Danny doesn't really have a charismatic vision of this place or its future. Just 'We're number one' and 'Students come first.' There's no cohesion to the programs we offer." Formalized processes allowed for individual initiative and creativity, but some individuals felt that a cohesive plan for Family State's future did not materialize through these formalized decisions.

Formal structures notwithstanding, a strictly linear map of decision-making would be misleading. Most often the actors made decisions by widespread discussion and dialogue. Widely circulated information prepared different college audiences to actively discuss topics and agendas pertinent to the college's operation. As they debated issues and exchanged ideas, proposals eventually became decisions. The president's decisions existed in concrete, but individuals saw those decisions as building blocks upon which further, more participative decisions were made. In an interview, a former board member and onetime student noted, "The president provides us with a great deal more written information than we have ever received before." Vehicles for information included an alumni newspaper, bulletins in the local press, and meetings in which the president provided the audience with ideas and plans for the future. Thus, informal conversations and informative written material acquainted people with ideas that eventually became formal decisions.

The environment of the college provided rationales for change and prompted many of these decisions. Dwindling demand for teachers required that the college restructure its teacher-education program. A statewide tax that eliminated "nonessential" programs in high schools reduced the demand for industrial arts at Family State. New requirements by state hospitals brought about a restructured medical technology program. However, the college did not use primarily an adaptive strategy. The president noted, "I don't believe that an institution serves its culture well if it simply adapts. The marketplace is narrow and changes quickly."

As a consequence, the college continues to orient itself to its traditional clientele—the working people of the area. The city and the surrounding area have remained a working-class region throughout the college's history; the town has neither prospered and become middle class nor has it faded into oblivion. Continuing-education programs and the courtship of adult learners have broadened the clientele of the college while maintaining its traditional, working-class constituency.

In addition to the immediate community, an equally important component of the decision-making process is the state government. Even without powerful representation in the statehouse, the institution has prospered in recent years, primarily through the activities of the college president. The president is a vocal advocate for the institution and uses information effectively to lobby key legislators on funding and program issues. One source of political clout, for example, is the number of students in a senator's district who attend Family State. Unlike its counterparts, the college attracts students from throughout the state. This capability allows the president to actively interpret institutional excellence to a variety of audiences in a manner to which they can immediately relate. Nevertheless, Family State maintains close identity with its local constituency and has not recruited international or out-of-state students.

Use of Symbols: Socialization and Interpretation

Although the college has adapted to its environment, the administration—particularly the president—has brought about these changes through an interpretive strategy based on the conscious use of symbols in the college and surrounding environment. The president accentuates process, concern for the individual as a person, and the central orientation of serving the students of Family State. He does so through several vehicles, foremost among them being communication with constituencies and the strategic use of space and time.

COMMUNICATION

The president believes in the power of the written word, especially with respect to external constituencies. It is not uncommon to read about Family State or the president in the local press. A survey by the college revealed that the local citizenry had a positive, working knowledge of the president and the college. The president attends a multitude of local functions, such as the chamber of commerce, United Way meetings, and civic activities. He also invites the community to the college campus. The president has seen to it that the library and other facilities are open to the public.

The college has established a private foundation to attract gifts, primarily from corporate donors in the local community. The courtship of local business leaders has reinforced ties with the community, but with a new group of people who previously took little interest in Family State. Local business leaders most often do not live in town, and their children do not attend a public state college. Consequently, potential wealthy donors had never considered giving money to the institution. The president imitated the private college model so that the institution could raise money in ways other than through alumni donations. As one individual said, "Danny is the perfect fund-raiser."

The college also has reemphasized alumni relations to garner popular and financial support for the changes it made. In addition to continuing alumni meetings, the president hired a full-time alumni director to orchestrate the activities of the office. Symbolic gestures, such as including the alumni onstage at commencement, provide yet another vehicle for recognizing the alumni as an important component of the institution. Mailings go out three times a year to keep alumni informed of the institution's activities. Through these increased efforts the college has raised over $2 million for an endowment.

Although mailings and written information are important vehicles for sharing information with external constituencies, oral discourse predominates among members of the institution. Internal constituencies appear well informed of decisions and ideas through an almost constant verbal exchange of information using both formal and informal means.

Formal means of oral communication include task forces, executive council meetings, and all-college activities. At these gatherings individuals not only share information but also discuss possible solutions to problems or alternatives to a particular dilemma. The timely use of information is encouraged by the president, who will himself present problems to his executives and demand a solution or response to the dilemma within a matter of days. "When Danny asks to have something," observed one individual, "you don't avoid what he wants. He wants something quickly and you better communicate an answer—or at least a response to him—quickly."

The president's communicative style percolates throughout the institution. Information from top administrators is communicated to particular audiences through weekly meetings of individual departments. One vice president described the process:

> The president's executive staff meets once a week and we, in turn, meet with our own people. There's lots of give-and-take. I can also go to Tim [another vice president] and tell him casually that I think we're doing something wrong, and he'll listen. The key around here is that we're involved in a process to better serve students. Open communication facilitates the process. God help the administrator or faculty member who doesn't work for students.

Informal channels of communication at Family State are an equally important, if not more important, means for sharing and discussing ideas as well as developing an esprit de corps. The president hosts several functions each year at his house near campus. He brings together disparate segments of the college community, such as different faculty departments, for a casual get-together over supper, brunch, or cocktails. "This is like a family," explained the president. "Too often people don't have the time to get together and share with one another food and drink in a pleasant setting."

It is not uncommon to see many different segments of the institution gathered together in public meeting places such as the cafeteria or a lounge. In discussions with faculty, staff, and administrators, many people showed a working knowledge of one another's tasks and duties and, most strikingly, the student body. Consistent themes that ran throughout the institution were working long hours, attendance at extracurricular events, and relating to one another on an interpersonal level that often involved humor.

One individual who had recently begun working at the college noted, "People smiled and said hello here. It was a friendly introduction. People said to me, 'Oh, you'll really love it here.' It was that wonderful personal touch. When they hire someone here they don't want only someone who can do the job, but someone who will also fit in with the personality of the place." Another individual noted that, soon after he arrived, the president commented on how well he did his work but was worried that he wasn't "fitting in" with the rest of the staff. What makes these comments interesting is that they are about a public college. Such institutions often have the reputation of being impersonal and bureaucratic, as opposed to having the "personal touch" of private colleges.

While the institution can gain identity through the management of meaning, faculty must also gain identity through becoming socially integrated within their discipline. At present, faculty in particular do not feel that their professional development is especially high. Indeed, the IPS reported a fairly strong consensus that faculty quality was low. The academic vice president noted how few applications he received for small faculty grants. The president likewise observed that he had seen little real leadership on the part of faculty members regarding curricular overhaul. The situation is compounded by the inability of the academic vice president to exert curricular leadership. His historic role as leader of the curriculum has shifted to a mandated evaluator for collective bargaining. Currently the academic vice president conducts, for example, over two hundred faculty evaluations each year. Because collective bargaining takes up so much of his time and the faculty are reluctant to take charge of the curriculum, little curricular change has occurred.

A professor in a service area that did not offer a major commented: "If you don't have a major here you're treated as a second-class citizen. My program area has good people, but we have no power or respect." Another faculty member noted:

> We've got to hire to a design—get people who really want to be here, instead of just running after a Ph.D. Too many faculty members compare themselves to the elite institutions in this state instead of ourselves. The administration needs to think about what kind of people they want here—and I don't just mean nice people.

Further, he noted that the tight job market for academics provided an abundance of applications for a teaching position. Many individuals preferred to teach elsewhere, but they were simply glad to get a job at a nice institution with an inspired administrative team. Due to the tight job market, few faculty could leave, but it appeared that many would leave if a suitable position became available.

People mentioned that all segments of the institution were available to one another to help solve problems. Every Monday afternoon the president held an open house at which any member of the college community could enter his office and talk to him. All segments of the community used the vehicle. As one administrator reported, "That's sacred time. The president wants to know the problems of the different constituencies. People seem to use it. He reflects through the open house that he really cares."

The president's concern for all segments of the institution and his demand for excellence were best symbolized by his hard work and diligence. One longtime administrator said:

> When you see the president working as hard as he does, going to all the student activities, attending meetings, and walking through the campus, you know that he's not really asking anything more from you than he is from himself. He really cares not just about you as a teacher or administrator, but as a person.

The president frequently articulates his vision of institutional excellence in his speeches and writing. One individual commented: "When I first came here and the president said that 'We're number one,' I just thought it was something he said, like every college president says. But after awhile you watch the guy and you see he really believes it. So I believe it too."

The president confirmed his conviction:

> We are number one in a lot of programs. We'll go head to head with a lot of other institutions. Our programs in nursing, communication, industrial technology can stack up against any other state college here. I'd say we're the best institution of this kind in the state.

We see again how terms such as "excellence" and "quality" are comparative in nature. The president believed the institution "excellent" in comparison to other state institutions. The faculty, however, relate not only to the institution but also to their discipline. They compare themselves not only to colleagues at regional state colleges but also to colleagues at research universities. Interviews confirmed IPS results that Family State's faculty perceived their professional development to be low.

When addressing both internal and external audiences, the president frequently mentioned that in the near future the institution will move toward university status:

> I did it for two reasons. First I figured that the best defense is a good offense. I wanted to tell the politicians out there that we are the best in the state. That we could become a university. That will make them think twice before they try to close any programs down. Second, I want people here to believe as I do in our excellence. We have nothing to apologize for.

The president's plan for university status was one avenue whereby the actors could feel that they were comparable to their counterparts in nearby universities. Although few people really believe that the institution will become a university, the claim has been an effective tool in impressing upon audiences that the college is a quality institution.

The desire to change from a state college to a university is fairly common. We saw the same aspiration achieved, thwarted, and rekindled in the previous chapter at Rural State College. When state colleges want to set dramatic improvements in motion, they will frequently compare themselves to universities. In the case of Rural State, the desired shift in status generated real structural and programmatic change. Although the state has yet to permit the name change, few doubt that Rural State will become a university in the next several years. With Family State, on the other hand, the expressed desire to be a university proceeds largely from symbolic concerns. Although a welcome and effective expression of excellence, it has yet to take root in actual change, nor is it likely to in the foreseeable future.

SPACE AND TIME

The president's use of space is an important element in his leadership style and implementation of strategy. He frequently extends his spatial domain beyond the confines of the college campus and into the city and surrounding towns. Conversely, invitations to the community to attend events at the college and utilize the library and other facilities have reduced spatial barriers with a city that otherwise might feel excluded. Informal gatherings, such as suppers at the president's house or luncheons at the college, have brought together diverse constituencies that otherwise have little reason to interact with one another. Moreover, the president has attended to the physical appearance of the institution, making it an effective symbol to his constituencies that even the grounds demand excellence and care.

A student commented:

> If a student hasn't gotten to know the president in a year then it's the student's damn fault. Everybody sees him walking around here. He's got those Monday meetings. He comes to all the events. I mean, he's really easy to see if you've got something you want to talk to him about. That's what's special about Family. How many places can a student get to know the president? We call him "Danny"—not to his face—because he's so familiar to us.

The president's symbolic use of space sets an example emu-lated by others. His open door policy, for example, permeates the institution. Administrators either work in open space areas in full view of one another or the doors to their offices are physically open, inviting visits with colleagues, guests or, more importantly, students. The openness of the president's and other administrators' doors creates an informality throughout the college that fosters a widespread sharing of information and an awareness of decisions and current activities.

The president is also a visible presence on the campus. He spends part of every day walking throughout the institution for a casual inspection of the grounds and facilities. These walks pro-vide a way for people to talk with him about matters of general concern and enable him to note something that he may not have seen otherwise. Administrators, too, interact with one another and students not only in their offices but on the other's "turf." One administrator stated, "The atmosphere here is to get to know stu-dents, see them where they are, and not have a host of blockades so students feel as if they are not listened to."

It was also significant to many of the participants interviewed that the president had bought a home close to campus and consid-ered himself a local citizen. In addition, his children attended Fam-ily State College, which furthered the perception that the president truly believed in the quality education provided by the institution.

Our discussion of communication and space already has made reference to time. The president continually integrates formal and informal interactions with his constituencies. According to his sec-retary and a study of the presidential calendar, about one and one-half hours per day are scheduled as "free time" that he uses as he sees fit—for reading, writing, or perhaps walking around the campus. The president regularly schedules meetings with his executive circle or individuals such as the treasurer. The meet-ings revolve around both a mixture of formal agendalike items and ideas or problems that either the president or his lieutenants feel they have. Although his schedule is generally very busy, it is not difficult to see the president. His secretary makes his appoint-ments. She notes that if a faculty member or administrator asked to see the president, she would schedule an appointment when he is available in the very near future. Students, too, can see the president, but his secretary generally tries to act as a gatekeeper to ensure that the students really need to see the president and not someone else. The president's secretary has worked for him for over sixteen years. She makes all of his appointments and is the sole person between him and the public.

Finally, the president spends much of his time in the evenings and during the weekend attending college functions. As one individual noted:

> It's tough to keep up with him. I went with him one night and he had me going to a soccer game after work, an open house in a department, and then to one or two other activities. By nine o'clock I was pooped and ready for bed, but he insisted we attend the rathskeller [a student pub] "just for ten minutes." Well, of course, ten minutes for him is really a good half hour of working the crowd, getting to know the students, their concerns, how things are going for them and what he can do for them. You'd think after all that he'd want to go to bed himself. But no, he had me drive him home and we had a nightcap and he listened to my concerns.

The president's awareness of patterns and styles of communication and his conscious use of time and place are perhaps best illustrated by a meeting we had during one of our site visits to Family State. We waited in the president's outer office with the director of institutional research. The president was late for our appointment. Five minutes later he entered, dressed in an impeccable blue suit with a red handkerchief filling his lapel pocket. As he munched on an apple the secretary took a phone call and said, "It's the regents, sir." He looked at us and and said, "I'm not being a very good host, but I promise I will be back in five minutes." He walked into his office and shut the door. The institutional research director said. "The regents always come first, always. That's the way it is."

The door swung open and the president walked out to greet us. "Would you like a Coke or a drink or something?" he asked. "I'm going to have one." When he returned with the drinks he said:

> I'm sorry for being late. I knew about your appointment and had planned to be back here on time, but I was walking around the campus for forty-five minutes, and just at the last minute I made a detour to check out the cafeteria, to see how things were going. I met a guy down there who works in the kitchen and he and I have always said that we should play cribbage some time—he's a cribbage player—and wouldn't you know he had a board with him today and he asked me to play. So I did. He beat me too. So I wasn't doing anything very presidential in being late for you. I was just walking around the campus on this beautiful day, and playing cribbage in the kitchen with a friend.

The president's disclaimer notwithstanding, his actions are presidential in that they develop and reinforce an institutional culture. His effective use of symbols and frames of reference, both formally and informally, articulates the college's values and goals and helps garner support from faculty, students, staff, and the community. This does not imply, however, that presidents should necessarily spend their time walking around campus or playing cribbage with the kitchen help. What is effective at one institution is unlikely to work at another. Nevertheless, the role of symbolic communication that we witness on this campus, buttressed by tangible, constructive change, provides valuable clues about a dimension of strategy often neglected at other institutions.

Culture and the Need for Change

Family State works from an explicit mission to provide educational opportunity to the working-class population of the state and, specifically, its local area. In recent years it has strengthened its mission statement to include community service and outreach. The college serves a relatively underdeveloped area that has not participated in the state's general economic recovery. The ethnic population has remained relatively stable—Irish, Italian, French, and Finnish. In addition to reaching out to all of these groups, the college also has sought out new constituencies in different ways. For example, the town fathers—the wealthy business owners of the region—traditionally had not been affected by the college. Through the president's courtship they now donate funds to the college.

In many ways the individuals who work at the college reflect the background of the clientele they teach. Many of the administrators come from working class backgrounds and a sizeable number either attended the college or have lived in the community for over twenty years. The homogeneity of atmosphere, then, comes not only from a like-minded administrative team, but also from a community that has remained stable during the last hundred years. The president stated:

> Look, I'm a product of this kind of place. I didn't go to a private college. People would never call me an ivory-tower intellectual, and that's fine by me. I believe in publicly supported education for children who otherwise would not be able to attend school. We still offer an

education to first-generation college students. And it's an excellent education, too.

People come to believe in the institution by the ways they interact and communicate with one another. The ongoing cultural norms of Family State foster an implicit belief in the mission of the college as providing a public good. In this sense staff, faculty members, and administrators all feel they contribute to a common good—the education of working-class students. When individuals apply for work at Family State, they are considered not only on the basis of skill and qualifications but also on how they will fit in to the cultural milieu. Socialization occurs rapidly through symbols such as open doors, the constant informal flow of communication punctuated by good-natured kidding, access throughout the organization, dedication to hard work, and above all, commitment to excellence for students. When people speak of their mission, they speak of helping people. Members of the college community work from the assumption that an individual's actions do matter, can turn around a college, and can help alter society.

Belief in the institution emerges as all the more important given its unstable economic and political environment. The district in which the college resides has little political clout, and consequently the institution is not politically secure. Rapidly shifting jobs in a tight market necessarily demand that the institution have flexibility in its programs. Although the college has created programs such as medical technology and communication/media, it has not made widespread use of adaptive strategy. Growing competition from its peer institutions has prompted administrators to think about ways for the college to sharpen its competitive edge in the market.

Interpretive strategy is the principal means through which ideas become implemented here. Interpretive signals in the use of communication, space, and time, presidential pronouncements of excellence, attention to immediate and short-range plans, the upkeep of facilities, and the belief that the mission has historical accuracy and social significance all foster a sense of concern for and dedication to the institution. The active presence of the president binds institutional actors together in a shared cause that demands much work and dedication, and the acceptance and friendship of one's colleagues. We have, then, a college with a leader who interprets current actions in terms of the intrinsic public worth of the institution's mission and actors who believe in its ideology. Family

State accurately reflects an institution that "has an explicit system of general beliefs that give large bodies of people a common identity and purpose, a common program of action, and a standard for self-criticism" (Higham, 1974, p. 10).

At the same time, the institution can—and must—act with its environment by developing new programs. Although the realities of state fiscal policies will determine in part which programs the college adopts, curricular options remain open to the actors at Family State. The use of interpretive strategy by the president and his administration has created an atmosphere of trust and dedication in which change can take place. Adaptive programming in the mid-1970s set the climate for creating academic excellence. What remains to be done in the 1980s is to maintain quality while creating new structural and curricular conceptions of the institution. Both faculty and administrators are coming to realize that they have not offered strong, innovative leadership in curricular affairs.

Faculty identification with their discipline also demands more attention. Over 20 percent of faculty and administrators received their degrees from the institution. Slightly over half of the faculty holds a doctorate. With an eye to satisfying accreditation agencies, the institution seeks individuals who hold terminal degrees. At the same time, it appears that the institution needs to consider what kind of faculty it wants. Instead of hiring individuals who would rather be at a research institution, Family State might consider what kinds of individuals best fit the institutional atmosphere.

Family State's success notwithstanding, the future will demand change. One individual noted, "The reputation of an institution rests primarily on what it does with regard to its curricular offerings. We haven't done anything new for too long a time." In the institution's quest for excellence, it must attend to the management of social integration in disciplinary fields and to curricular renovation. Thus far, interpretive strategy has been successful at Family State because the effective use of symbols and communication has been linked with instrumental actions that have produced tangible, constructive change. However, if these pending issues are not addressed in the next several years the administration runs the risk of prompting a cynical response to the dedication, beliefs, and ideals it has thus far successfully cultivated.

PART THREE
Culture and Change

The manner in which institutions deal with change says much about their organizational culture. As values and norms come under pressure due to changing circumstances both internally and in the environment, leaders and constituents must reevaluate the purpose and direction of the institution, and this, in turn, influences the organization's structure— "how we do things around here."

Mission and Covenant universities are religiously affiliated, while Present State College is public. Change at Covenant and Present State was stimulated by decline, at Mission by growth. All three institutions are relatively high in their use of linear strategies to deal with change. They have developed goals and plans to position themselves. At Present State, for example, important changes took place in the physical plant and grounds, while Covenant relied heavily on more efficient financial management. Adaptive approaches to change are also fairly high at Mission and Present State, where academic programs have been added and dropped in rather large numbers. The institutions have dramatically redefined their traditional clientele in order to adapt to the changing demands of their markets. Covenant has used adaptive change less dramatically, primarily in a compartmentalized outreach unit that takes academic programs to new geographic locations. None of the three has dealt actively with mission development or other interpretive strategies.

Endowed with well-established values and goals, Mission University has responded to its high-tech environment. Whether this adaptation is an appropriate extension of its mis-

sion or whether it signals a growing tension in the institution's culture is a matter of campus debate. The curriculum is more diverse at Mission, both in content and in delivery modes, than was true of either Rural State or Family State. Curriculum change has occurred at something approximating evolutionary rates, but change is real and dramatic. The lack of an explicit interpretive strategy to guide such change may account for the differences of opinion on campus about its appropriateness.

The organizational culture of Mission University presumably grew out of its religious values and history. Is that evident in the Mission of today? To what extent is any erosion or change in culture attributable to the declining proportion of members of the founding order on the faculty and administration? Mission's president is like that of Family State in his attention to physical detail, but his communication style is radically different. The president at Mission is physically close—in fact, he lives in a dormitory among students—but he is personally remote. Although he takes great interest in values as the foundation of the university, and although one typically expects the president's major concerns to permeate a campus, the university's commitment to values-oriented education is not widely and uniformly perceived. Why?

For Present State College, change has been radical and swift. Abrupt changes occurred in the physical setting, the curriculum, and the atmosphere of the campus when the new president arrived. He has created a new order, the theme of which seems to be the creation of a "tight ship." With efficiency and market considerations as the dominant factors in change, the identity of the college has lost any clarity it may have had. In some ways, this president is similar to the one at Mission in his interest in details and his personal remoteness. However, the president at Present State is less academic, more oriented toward management. At Mission University, a sense of community within the campus receives at least lip service, perhaps more, but at Present State its primary expression is the president's displeasure when faculty fail to attend campus events. This is true despite—or perhaps because of—the fact that Mission has many more distinct factions among its faculty members (the wide variety of academic disciplines and religious versus lay faculty) than Present State has. Without cul-

tural roots, the college may find little long-term benefit from operational improvements.

At Covenant University, change occurred through a combination of declining resources and internal strife that eventually led to a faculty union. Like Mission, Covenant has religious roots. Unlike Mission, those at Covenant long ago confronted factionalism, especially faculty (largely lay people) versus administration (largely members of the religious order at the time of the confrontation). The confrontation not only drew lines between factions, but it also created new factions, including pro- and anti-union faculty and union/nonunion faculty. One may well speculate whether Mission might eventually change in similar ways and why it has not done so already.

The union arrangement has solved some problems, yet has exacerbated others. Important elements of Covenant University are frozen by antagonism and hostility. Although change is slow, perhaps too slow, at Rural State and Family State, the actors have an easy informality and collegiality that keeps the potential for change alive. Those conditions stand in sharp contrast to the hierarchical, procedural orientation at Covenant. The president here is remote physically, personally, and bureaucratically. He is far less visible within the institution than any we have seen so far.

Institutional survival has depended upon the university's highly attractive location, its profitable extension programs, its fiscal restraint, and its ability to attract large numbers of foreign students. Those factors may prove to be sufficient to maintain the university for a long time, but low faculty morale and high faculty turnover could take a serious toll. Healing the wounds of the university will probably require leadership that can transcend the factions and elicit a common bond of humanity among the faculty and administration, as well as an interpretation of the university's mission that does more than reiterate its history.

Confronted with new situations, each of these institutions has in one respect embraced change, yet in another has guarded itself from the cultural self-reflection that change requires. As a result, their ability to cope with change successfully becomes directly proportional to their willingness to recognize and interpret cultural transformation.

FIVE

Mission University

"American higher education," write Gerald Grant and David Riesman, "is much too protean to be summed up in any neat formula. Any number of contradictory trends are going on at the same time" (1978, p. 8). The case study discussed here highlights some of the "contradictory trends" that are at work within an institution as it transforms itself from a small, single-sex, liberal-arts college into a comprehensive university.

Insofar as collegiate institutions are dynamic systems, ruptures in institutional history and culture are bound to occur. Collegiate administrators face a balancing act as they attempt to respond to current conditions and demands and also retain the institution's essential focus. Simply stated, the demands of the 1980s differ from those of an earlier period. Consequently, management strategies and curricular offerings must change if the institution is to remain viable.

Yet strategies based on current circumstances not only pertain to the institution's past, but also provide indications about where the institution intends to go in the future. What cultural ruptures can occur for an institution that dramatically changes the way it sees itself? What strategies can managers take to adapt an institution to present-day demands, thereby providing fiscal security without sacrificing cultural cohesion and continuity?

The particular assumption at work in this case study is that institutional identity is communicated to different constituencies in a variety of ways—through curriculum, institutional structure, symbolic processes, and long-range plans, to name but a few. Central to an institution's identity is its mission, through which it articulates its distinctiveness and ideology. In the 1980s colleges and universities are struggling to maintain a historical identity while adapting to changing conditions. Resisting adaptation and change can lead to institutional stagnation; conversely, the wholehearted embrace of adaptation at the expense of institutional identity and culture may have equally serious consequences. Mission University provides one example of an institution that struggles with the correlation between its mission, how it sees itself, and adaptive strategies implemented by a reform-minded administration.

Growth and Change

Established in the nineteenth century, Mission University is a religiously based institution located in a major city that has experienced rapid growth in high technology. The institution was initially a small men's college; at the turn of the century it became a university when the board of trustees added the College of Engineering and the College of Law. The College of Business Administration began in 1926. It was not until the last twenty years, however, that the three professional schools gained prominence at the institution. Throughout its history the university has emphasized its dedication to the liberal arts.

In the 1960s the university admitted women. In the past two decades the institution has grown from 800 men to over 6,000 men and women. As significant as the switch from a single sex to coed university is the institution's growth in the professional areas. In 1985 university enrollment divided equally between the undergraduate and graduate schools. The business school was renovated twenty years ago and continues to undergo improvement; the engineering school will soon inhabit a new $9 million structure. The student body primarily reflects the institution's religious orientation, although all faiths and denominations are welcome. Average SAT scores range in the middle 500s. Thirty-five percent of the student body have direct ties with the alumni. Ten percent of the students are minority. Seventy percent of the student body come from the state in which the institution resides, and another 20 percent of the students come from surrounding states.

The institution has a full-time faculty of over two hundred, less than 10 percent of whom are from the religious order. Most of the religious faculty teach in the liberal arts. The administrative structure has undergone both personnel and structural changes. In 1984 the vice president for student affairs resigned and a member of the religious order replaced him. A new vice president for business and finance also took over in 1984. In the last five years the schools of engineering and business have had new deans; the

law school's dean resigned in 1985. The College of Humanities and
the College of Sciences recently were consolidated into the College
of Arts and Sciences. The president and academic vice president
both come from the religious order. They assumed their positions
at the institution in the late 1970s. The institutional charter man-
dates that the president be a member of the order. The board
of trustees is an active group of executives, lawyers, educators,
alumni, religious men from the order, and faculty members.

Most observers of collegiate America in the 1980s would envy
Mission University's current status, location, and fiscal condition.
The institution has consistently raised SAT scores and admissions
requirements. Faculty research and scholarship have increased.
Its location in a rapid-growth area has enabled the institution to
increase enrollment rather than concern itself with decline. The
beautiful campus enhances the institution's desirability on the part
of middle- and upper-class parents who want to send their children
to a good school in a safe area.

Rapid growth and a wealthy clientele have generated an endowment with a market value of over $50 million; the net worth
of the institution currently stands at over $120 million. Funding
for fully endowed chairs has increased during the past five years
from less than $3 million to over $10 million. The university annually receives over $10 million in gifts. In short, the university's
health is indeed high in many respects; the IPS results bear out
constituent awareness and belief in the institution's vitality. There
is very high consensus that the institution's finances and enrollment are stable, and that investors receive an ample return on
their investments.

The University's Mission

In becoming a university with multiple programs, the institution
has also sought to maintain its mission statement and basic goals.
The university has emphasized three guiding points in its mission:
academic excellence, service, and "an education of the whole person, an education seeking to answer not only 'what is,' but 'what
should be.'" The quest for academic excellence occurs through
rigorous training that prepares students for graduate schools or
well-paying jobs in industry. A student mentioned, "I really don't
think students should come here if they don't know what they
want to do. They should know as freshmen if they want to be a

doctor, or lawyer, or whatever." The director of career planning and placement agreed that students generally had little difficulty in finding jobs, in part because of high motivation. They knew what kind of employment they wanted and, oftentimes, their families were well connected.

The adult graduate clientele from industry provided a highly motivated, academically superior student who easily fit the institutional mission of academic excellence. The adult population furthered the second aspect of the institution's mission, that of service. According to the goals and guidelines of the university, service is one of the core values of the institution: "[Our] school exists, then, for service: service to the community; service to the people of God; and service to the world in which it labors to uphold faith, to preserve cultural traditions, and to spread the gospel of charity."

The university considers the community to include the large businesses in the area that the professional schools serve. The School of Business, for example, offers six programs and attracts many full-paying students from local firms. The strategy allows them to attend classes before work or to take evening courses toward a master's degree.

Finally, the holism of the curriculum reflects the institution's desire to base curricular decisions on how students could become more broadly educated within a values-centered framework. As one professor stated, "We are here to educate students for academic excellence. But beyond that—and this is the uniqueness—is to have students excel in a vocation as well as develop their ethical and moral values, to become leaders with the mission of serving humanity."

Annually, the university offers a quarter-long symposium on a morally relevant topic such as poverty or nuclear war. Three religiously oriented courses and one ethics course fit into the general education requirements. Many professors mentioned that they focused class discussions and assignments on ethical issues. Nevertheless, more than one student noted:

> Values really don't affect me all that much. We've pretty well decided on things from our families anyway, by the time we get to college. A few professors talk about ethics, but it's really just minor. What education is really about here is getting a good job when you've finished.

The faculty's concern for ethical issues notwithstanding, the institution's values orientation no longer seems clear to many constituencies. A discussion of the environment will help explain why people perceive that the institutional mission has become blurred.

Environmental Impact on Mission

The environmental changes have affected the constituencies from which the university chooses its clientele. One administrator noted, "We live in a community that still has chickens on the front porch and yet it is the center for high technology in the state." Likewise, the university began with the explicit mission of educating undergraduate students, and it has evolved into an institution whose population is now equally divided between graduates and undergraduates. These two factors—growth in the area and its increasingly professional orientation—shape the environment in which the institution operates.

The university's traditional constituency, Christian undergraduates, has remained stable over time. The institution has maintained ties with its religiously affiliated high schools in the area, and enrollments have remained high from these feeder schools. As the university has broadened the geographic area from which it attracts students and as similar religiously affiliated institutions have experienced decline, parents find it increasingly desirable to send their children to Mission. Although the university remains in the hands of the religious, there is no sense of religious discrimination; the institution recruits and freely admits students from other religious faiths and denominations. Indeed, one student had a comment similar to many we interviewed: "Oh no, there's no problem at all about religion here. You wouldn't even know this place is [a religious college] except for the church over there." Although increasingly nominal, the institution's religious orientation persists as the university maintains its traditional clientele while enlarging its niche.

The institution is located in an area whose local population is over 30 percent minority. The university has found it difficult, however, to recruit minority students who are of academically high caliber. As a result, the minority population on campus is less than 10 percent, many of whom are not from the local community. Mission's commitment to academic excellence excludes the overwhelming proportion of minority students who live in close proximity to the university. Minority students from local high schools traditionally do not score well on SAT tests. The relatively high tuition of the private university and reductions in federal student loans preclude most local minority students from applying to or even considering Mission University.

Thus, the clientele from which the institution draws its undergraduates remains similar to its traditional constituency—white, middle-class students from the state who are of the same religion as the institution. An alumnus pointed out the similarity of institutional clientele by saying:

> When I went here most students might be considered lower middle class. That's changed—now students are middle and upper class, but they still have the same orientation. I don't know what it would be like here to be black or of another faith. They're welcome, but it's different.

Because of the low admission rate of academically weak students, the institution has not found it necessary to develop remedial programs for full-time students who may need extra help. At one time the university's continuing-education program provided course work for the local population. In 1981, however, the university discontinued the program due to financial considerations, lack of focus, and uneven quality. What remains of continuing-education efforts are some programs offered through the university's respective colleges.

A second way of viewing the institution and its environment is to note the differentiation between undergraduates and graduates, liberal arts and the professions. Individuals most often identified themselves and potential problems for the university in terms of the difference between graduate and undergraduate programs and clientele. That is, people from different constituencies—faculty, for example—often referred to the clientele they served when they spoke of institutional mission. "It's really the undergraduates who create the mission here," one faculty member in the humanities confided. "We're set up to broaden their education. Professional education is something else altogether."

At a planning conference of alumni and top administrators, an outside consultant remarked on the perceived lack of religious mission in the professional schools: "While the undergraduate program is identifiably Christian, the professional schools—law, engineering, business—aren't Christian in any sense. . . . One would like to know why they do not see the various programs in ethics in these different schools as a part of the mission."

The ease with which the professional community can match the rigor of Mission University's academic standards, as well as

pay full tuition, has made for a comfortable fit between professionals and the university. Nevertheless, key constituencies, including
alumni, see a dramatic difference between the orientations of the
undergraduate and graduate communities.

One central difference is that many individuals saw the professions pursuing research at the expense of teaching. One individual
commented on the IPS, for example: "This institution faces an identity crisis: to be better at what it already is—that is, an excellent
Christian university with a splendid teaching faculty—or to compete in the academic hothouse, where publication and grants are
singularly important."

Even within the undergraduate program one noted the difference between the liberal arts and vocationally oriented programs.
Like many students we interviewed, one student commented, "It's
kind of a strange campus. It says it's liberal arts, but most come
for a skill. Get your grades, interview well, and get a job." An administrator continued in a similar vein: "The professions are running away with the university. The liberal arts are not a strong
presence on campus. In fact, the religious studies and philosophy
departments are a disgrace. You would think in an institution like
ours that those programs would be the core."

The university's "community spirit" related primarily to undergraduates rather than the largely part-time graduate clientele in
business and engineering. An individual in student affairs said:

> Our services are oriented for undergraduates. I don't feel it for grad-
> uate students. The services—dances, forums, retreats—are for under-
> graduates, and the graduates don't feel part of it. The community is
> for the undergraduate population and maybe long-term employees.
> It's difficult for new people entering the institution and part-timers.

Although the past two decades have brought a rough parity in
the numbers of undergraduate and graduate students, many people still think of the institution as primarily undergraduate. The institution still gears many of its services toward the traditional clientele. Further, as might be expected in the 1980s, liberal arts have
lost ground to vocational programs even though many constituencies still see the institution as a liberal-arts university. Indeed, the
goals and guidelines of the university listed as a final point: "The
university shall give priority to undergraduate programs. . . . It
does remind us of our traditional emphasis on a liberal education. . . ."

The university currently operationalizes its mission in a variety of ways. It expresses a commitment to values through reli-

giously based course work and forums on social issues for the undergraduate population. Academic excellence occurs through the recruitment and retention of superior students as well as the development of a quality faculty and superior resources. Community service is often oriented to the business community, while the university community is largely thought of as the undergraduate population. The values the university seeks to promote are those of its religious heritage.

Although the institution has never been considered weak either academically or financially, within the last decade the institution has increased its fiscal resources, become more selective in the recruitment of students, and enhanced its reputation. This first-class regional institution now appears on the verge of pursuing national prominence. The next section outlines the strategies and decisions used to implement institutional ideas and considers how the actors use information and symbols as effective decision-making tools.

Adaptive Strategy as Long-range Planning

Within the past ten years the administration has relied on adaptive planning to pursue institutional goals. Adaptation occurred through the growth of some programs begun in the 1950s and the creation of new programs. For example, in the last decade the university's part-time M.B.A. program has grown rapidly, as has an engineering program that allows working managers to take courses before work in the morning. New programs such as a retail management institute, an agribusiness institute, and a track in international business have also developed rapidly. All of these programs reflect the university's ability to adapt its skills and mission to serve the community in the surrounding area.

The president noted the symbiotic relationship between the university and the business community:

> [A corporation] wrote me a letter recently after the kickoff for the engineering school. We hadn't approached them. We hadn't done anything and they said, "If we could, could we give you $100,000?" I talked to the president of the company and he said, "We want to do it because for us the university is important. It's an important element in the area. You provide us a service and we just need the university. This is our commitment."

The administration's recognition of a fruitful market and that market's eagerness to utilize the university's services have fostered adaptive strategy. Moreover, loyal and active alumni, 80 percent of whom reside in the same state as the university, continue to influence policies long after they have left campus. This entrepreneurial administrative and alumni team has encouraged rapid growth in professional and service courses. In one sense, the university sees its adaptability as entirely consistent with its mission to serve the community.

However, the manner of its adaptation relates more to the rapid-growth industries in the surrounding areas than to the minority populations in nearby cities. The institution's ability to adapt and the awareness by top administrators of which groups to tap into have resulted in fiscal stability, continued growth, and enhanced prominence throughout the region and the nation. As with all institutions that utilize adaptive strategy, the university consistently struggles to develop a coherent perception of its mission as a new focus enters the scene. One individual noted, "We're living a lie, pretending we can have the same mission to encompass the liberal arts and professional programs. We have to make a decision."

Decisions usually occur through presidential initiative and participatory decision-making in committees whose composition is influenced by the president and academic vice president. In addition, departments annually prepare and submit long-range plans. These plans consistently struggle to come to terms with the institutional mission and a department or school's goals. The desire for long-range planning comes primarily from top administration, and many individuals who have done the actual work of articulating the mission and writing the documents express frustration at the process. For example, one individual in a professional school commented, "The constant restatement of the university's dedication to undergraduate education and how our program fits that mission is a waste of time and resources."

Once plans have been articulated, they make their way up a primarily centralized system and receive little or no formal criticism or feedback. A department or school finds out what the administration thinks of its plans by discovering what does and does not get funded. At the same time, the rationale for funding decisions is rarely explained to those responsible for the proposals. One discovers the rationale for administrative decisions primarily through informal contacts either with the academic vice president or the deans of the schools.

The informal communication of decisions both facilitates and impedes the actors' perceptions of their decision-making roles. One individual noted that he had talked about a particular problem with the academic vice president as they walked to the faculty lunchroom, and they had decided what to do within a matter of minutes. The same problem had been left unresolved by a committee. The quick facilitation of the decision left this individual informed and involved about a matter of concern.

Another individual noted that he was often the last person to hear of something he coordinated. A minor irritant such as lack of information about a decision made in one's own area can quickly turn into a problem. If information-sharing occurs haphazardly, individual initiative and input are tacitly discouraged.

Formalized planning can facilitate individuals' perception that decision-making is shared. The two major planning efforts that people refer to are the previous capital campaign and a 1984 retreat for the trustees and regents that involved the vice presidents and president in far-ranging issues. At present, a serious effort to develop a planning process is underway at the instigation of the new vice president for business and finance. More than one individual commented that previous attempts at strategic long-range plans have failed, in part, because of the nature of the individuals involved at the top. One senior faculty member noted:

> Long-range planning is not systematic at all. Somebody has to direct the planning, and the president won't. We have no one to do it, because the president won't step aside, yet he gets involved in the day-to-day affairs of the university, like where will the Ping-Pong table go in the Student Union.

The president acknowledged his reluctance about long-range planning and his desire to know about all activities of the university. The IPS pointed out that executive administrators, by their own recognition, are not actively concerned with long-term planning and objectives. When queried about the IPS findings, the president commented: "I'd say it's right. We really don't know how to plan, I don't know how to plan. It's something we're beginning to take seriously." Earlier in the year the president noted how he became involved in the most minute affairs of the institution:

> If somebody comes to see me and says the wastebaskets in the activities center are full I will call the janitors and tell them to empty the wastebaskets. I can make a comment to somebody that the trees outside the administration building haven't been pruned, and two minutes later there will be one hundred people pruning trees.

Another administrator noted that "long-range planning gets done by whim and individual preference. In one way that's not bad, because individuals really have the freedom to do their own thing."

In a formal sense, however, each dean individually prepares a strategic plan and the academic vice president then drafts a university strategic plan for widespread discussion. Intuitively, the academic vice president has a sense of what he will put into the document prior to writing it. By everyone's recognition he, more than anyone else at Mission, contacts and works with all constituencies of the institution. The academic vice president also develops plans about where he wants the institution to go; his plans, however, do not come from a committee but from his own informal thoughts and conversations. When asked about long-range planning, he said:

> I think in terms of knowing where you want to go and how to get there. I set things down in my own mind; it wouldn't work well if I wrote it down. Our planning has been around physical facilities, and I don't see it that way. Planning revolves around deciding what we want to do academically and figuring out how to get there. . . . I make a distinction between being effective and efficient. I may not be efficient, but I am effective because I accomplish what I want to get done.

When asked how he developed his ideas, he noted that he talked with different constituencies informally and that his consulting work with accrediting agencies gave him food for thought about improving his own institution.

Involvement in the decision-making process remains ambiguous for many actors. The strategic plan developed by the academic vice president is one example of how this role confusion occurs. The normal procedure for developing strategic plans starts with general ideas, concepts, and strategies coming from the top of the pyramid, with plenty of input. Individual units then articulate what they want to do within the general plan. Mission's process, however, has the units autonomously create plans, which will be synthesized by the academic vice president.

In one sense the process suggests a very decentralized structure, yet indications remain that all of the important decisions rest with the president and academic vice president. The president noted that at times there is a need "to manipulate the process" and referred to how he or the academic vice president might pick particular individuals for committee assignments. The process has worked smoothly in transforming a small, liberal-arts institution into a well-regarded comprehensive university. It remains for the president and academic vice president to fully interpret and communicate the university's mission in light of the instrumental changes that have taken place over the last twenty-five years.

The Interpretation of Mission

Interpretive strategy occurs primarily through communicative structures that articulate the university's mission and its historical and religious underpinnings. Actors continually mentioned the president's annual address in the fall as a symbol for where the institution is headed. One individual noted, "The president's talk at the start of the year is always the high point. Everyone is interested and involved, because they know he's spent the whole summer working on the text." The recent addition of luncheon seminars and faculty colloquia have helped create a "university community." The business school has an executive development center that the dean described as a "center for active dialogue on cutting issues."

In terms of interpretation, communication, and symbols, however, one example came to actors' minds more often than any other—the faculty club. The club provides a vehicle for faculty and administrators to sit down and converse with one another in a beautifully renovated building that retained the original architectural design of the institution. Private rooms are available for meetings, and colleagues consistently pack the large common room to dine informally with one another. "It's really brought us together," said a dean. "We are able to sit down with one another in a pleasant atmosphere and discuss issues and ideas in a gentlemanly manner." Students and staff do not attend the club except by explicit invitation of a member.

The "gentlemanly manner" of the institution was yet another of its communicative symbols. The business school hired according to a design when they increased the size of the business faculty. The school's administration articulated its sense of the university's mission and its desire for national prominence to all prospective faculty members. Faculty members arrived at the university with the knowledge that teaching was critical, applied research based on industry-related problems was the preferred form of scholarly inquiry, mature adults were the audience, and multidisciplinary activities were encouraged. "Most importantly," added a dean, "collegiality must exist. There must be scholarly debate amongst us that occurs in a positive manner." He, too, mentioned the faculty club as a perfect setting for conducting scholarly discussion.

The most trenchant symbol of the institution, however, remains its religious tradition and orientation. Although some groups, such as students, were not actively aware of the imprint that religion made on the university, other key constituencies were critically cognizant of the university's religious affiliation. The president and academic vice president have always been members of the religious order. As one individual mentioned, "The religious, even though few in number, run this place." Another individual referred to one recent administrator's troubled tenure at the institution by saying, "He didn't understand the religious culture. It's their school, it always will be. The real decision-making remains with them. It takes place in the evening around the dining room table."

At the trustee's planning conference, a specific recommendation of the group on student affairs was that the vice president for student affairs should always be a member of the religious order. The young, affable incumbent is a member of the order; he replaced a lay person who "did not fit in here." One individual disagreed that the office must be inhabited by a member of the order, but he understood the recommendation: "People think there's a [religious] way of doing things. It is true, too, that [they] do sit around at the dinner table and discuss things. But more than anything else, it's people's perception. People think they hold power and make decisions, so therefore they do."

Although the number of religious who teach is relatively small, less than 10 percent out of a faculty of over two hundred, there is constant reference to a values-based education for the whole person that fits within the religious tradition. Moreover, many members of the religious order who are not connected with the university live together on campus, thereby increasing the order's visibility. The vast majority of the religious faculty teach in the humanities and social sciences, which could account for the juxtaposition of the university's desired emphasis on undergraduate education with the desire of the lay professional schools to create a national constituency even if it does not foster or further the religious role in collegiate education.

The president is the most prominent religious and university spokesperson to external constituencies. However, those inside the university noted the president's inattention to their concerns. One individual characterized what many perceived as the president's and academic vice president's presence:

> You can write him [the academic vice president] a letter and he'll get back to you in two months. He can be inaccessible unless he has something he wants to talk to you about. The president is never present. "Who's he?" people say when he attends something. You never see the president on campus. The AVP does occasionally walk around. He never recognizes me, though.

Most individuals perceived the president's job as articulating the university's mission to external constituencies and raising funds for institutional projects. Given those functions, most people felt the president has been doing a good job. A respected administrator, the academic vice president has provided much of the leadership within the campus community. His tendency not to delegate tasks, however, has only compounded the many burdens of his office.

To embody the university's heritage necessarily demands that the president be a member of the religious order. One individual mentioned, "If the president weren't, this institution would cease to be as we now know it." Another individual commented, "They [the religious order] perceive this as their institution. Would we deal differently with a lay person as president? Undoubtedly. I don't exactly know how, I just know that we wouldn't do things the same way."

As a member of the order, the president felt it necessary to convey the institution's legacy to different constituencies. The president said:

> These clichés I talk about—they are clichés, but they are true. We [the religious order] do believe the ideal of education is service. There's no other reason for my being here if I'm not giving some kind of service. I'm not interested in being a family, but I do think the very nature of the university is to enhance society's awareness of itself. I think in our goals we try to do that—in engineering, in the M.B.A.

Words typically used to characterize the president were "humble," "intellectual," "a renaissance man." These words symbolized what the president—and hence the institution—stood for: academic excellence, and a religious commitment to the notion of a well-rounded educational experience that will foster community service. The president has used his office as a pulpit from which to expound on moral issues of the day, such as nuclear arms and social justice. He points to the institutional requirement of three religious courses, and the institutional orientation toward value-based courses as emblematic of the university's philosophy and orientation.

The president's activities came in for repeated comment by different constituencies of the institution. On the one hand we have mentioned already how many people perceived an invisible presidency—"Who's he, people say." On the other hand one often heard comments similar to the following:

> He gets caught up in the minute activities of the campus. You know he lives in one of the dorms, so he's always walking around. He gets upset if there are posters on doors, or dislikes the color of the carpets. Could you kindly tell me why the president gets involved in things like that?

The point of mentioning this comment is not that Mission's president—or other presidents—should or should not get involved with the color of carpets in the student union. Its significance is that it indicates how constituents perceive both the president and the institution. In one sense the president appeared to be involved more with instrumental activities than with human problems. When contrasted, for example, with the president of Family State, the differences become clear. Family State's president also involved himself in a wide variety of institutional activities, but he addressed problems through a people-oriented approach. Mission's president was more oriented toward things and concepts, similar to the president we shall see at Present State College. Again, the point is not that there is one simple or right way to solve problems, but rather that the internal actors of the institution noticed the president's approach, and it carried symbolic meaning for them.

The president's living in the dorm was noted by all constituents, yet took on different meanings. Articulating a perception held by many students, one commented: "The president is very remote. When they say he lives in the dorms, it's just a promotional thing about the university being a friendly place. All he does is give a talk at the start of the year about why we shouldn't play our stereos loud." Yet an alumnus noted, "The president's living accommodation really stands for what the place is about. How many other college presidents live with the students?"

Presidential involvement in institutional activities at the most microscopic levels was likewise noted by all constituents. It could signal that a standardized hierarchy did not exist, that the system functioned as an informal decentralized structure, or that all activity on the college campus could be considered important. Nevertheless, the manner of the president's involvement tended to re-inforce the perception among many constituents that he willingly deferred long-range decisions in favor of immediate concerns. In seeking to interpret these presidential symbols, many constituencies encountered for themselves the difficulty of articulating the institution's mission as it responds to new and changing conditions.

One individual summed up the tension that many felt about the university's mission and its use of adaptive strategy by saying, "There's a danger of selling your soul to industry. Eisenhower had his military-industrial complex; we're becoming an academic-industrial complex." Although pertinent to Mission University, the comment extends to a large number of institutions that have also sought to articulate their values and goals in times that have required and rewarded institutional adaptation.

The Challenge: Integrating Adaptation and Mission

During a time of upheaval in Spain, José Ortega y Gasset wrote about purposeful change for institutions of higher education:

> An institution is a machine in that its whole structure and functioning must be devised in view of the service it is expected to perform. The root of university reform is a complete formulation of its purpose. Any alteration or adjustment of this house of ours unless it starts by reviewing the problem of its mission—clearly, decisively, truthfully—will be love labor's lost. (1944, p. 28)

Formulating mission is no easy task when one discovers "contradictory trends" that stimulate instrumental growth at the expense of operationalizing institutional purpose. That is, as Mission University utilizes adaptive strategy in short-term planning, different constituencies have pointed out apparent discrepancies between perceived institutional purpose and institutional function.

Twenty years ago people interpreted the mission of the institution through the functions it performed. White, middle-class young men attended a religious institution to enrich their Christian values and help serve mankind. Primarily the religious order taught the young men; religious services and a curriculum geared toward the liberal arts focused students' educational awareness on the distinctive character of the institution. Students applied to other religious colleges if they did not gain entrance to Mission.

Obvious changes have occurred. As a mark of Mission's enhanced academic standing, its chief competitors in the 1980s are a prestigious private and public institution, both secular. Only 10 percent of the faculty are members of the religious order. Over half the student body attends not for religious purposes but to enhance their professional careers. Students comment that religious instruction provides minimal "interference" with their vocational careers. Majors such as religious studies and philosophy receive mention as weak curricular areas, while the engineering school gains prominence and new facilities.

All of these changes have enhanced the institution's financial resources and placed it in the academic limelight. "It's growing pains, that's all," said one individual when asked about the university's mission and its change over time. What do these changes portend for the institution's future? How has the institution incorporated adaptive strategy within its distinctive purpose?

When asked about community service, the president mentioned a "student community action program" on campus that exemplified institutional mission. An institute studying social issues was another example commonly mentioned. Community service also meant serving the business community. However, such programs are neither unique to Mission nor highly representative of it.

At the university convocation in September 1984, the president stated:

> It is important to say that it is not simply because we are a Christian university that we must be concerned with justice. The tradition of our institution provides both an urgency and a transcendent character to our search for justice. It provides a finality: that all things may be one in the Lord. But the search for human justice is a constituent part of the very process of education.

On one level one could argue that adaptive strategy works against the distinctive purpose for which the president speaks. The dysfunction between mission and institutional operations received mention from numerous constituencies. A philosophy major's comments exemplified those offered by many others. He said, "It's very difficult to major in philosophy here. People look at you funny and wonder why you don't major in something practical." This attitude is expressed not only by modern, get-ahead students. A faculty member commented, "There is no longer a clearly defined mission. We say 'quality education,' but everybody says that. I don't know what we really stand for." This apparent dysfunction between mission and operations has served the short-term interests of the institution well; who would not applaud a university with an increased endowment, fine facilities, and healthy applicant pool?

The dysfunction of which we speak is of significant concern, yet it is clearly not the result of an uncaring search for financial security. The tension at Mission University lies in the growing distance between its historical mission and its present circumstances. In this sense the university exemplifies many other institutions that also must adapt their institutional identities to the rapidly changing environment of the 1980s. Mission University highlights how participants in one institution continue to struggle with their identity while at the same time experiencing growth rather than stagnation or decline.

The institution has brokered the difference between mission and operation by the administrative use of interpretive strategy and the centralization of authority in the offices of the president and academic vice president. While Mission continues to adapt to its environment, its unique method of adaptation involves constantly restructuring its saga to fit the domains and niches in which it finds itself. The president and academic vice president have played a critical part in this process. Some institutions need to identify a market, decide to go after the market, and then search for the resources necessary to carry out their plans. Mission, however, had a market—industry—virtually created at its doorstep. The businesses in that market assumed, in turn, that Mission would help them further their own needs and plans.

Interpreting the university's purpose in light of immediate needs allowed Mission to prosper fiscally and academically. Compare, for example, the difference between Family State identifying industrial education as a market and Mission's new professional markets. Institutional saga at Family State never changed in focus or orientation. Its market and clientele remained the same. The challenge for Family State was to identify the market and adapt its programs accordingly. At Mission, little or no market identification was required; instead, the institution had to interpret its distinctive purpose in light of new opportunities.

Interpretation came about in a variety of ways. The top two administrative posts remain in the hands of the religious order. The president and academic vice president personify what the institution stands for. Their actions, attitudes, and personalities acquire symbolic significance. The faculty club came often into discussion as a vehicle that fostered community spirit. The president's address at the beginning of the year spoke of the values of the community. Even the form and style of discourse—gentlemanly, scholarly debate—was a focal point for understanding the true nature of the institution.

The current dysfunction between mission and operations ultimately will be resolved in some fashion. What shape will the institution take in the year 2000? The president stated, "The [next] president has to be a visionary leader—someone who paints for them a picture of what they can do and what the university can be." Inextricably woven in this picture is Ortega y Gasset's challenge to formulate institutional purpose predicated on history and tradition. In the pursuit of academic excellence and vitality through adaptive strategy, the institution has placed considerable emphasis on the rapid-growth industries of the area. Will it last? "I'm not so sure," commented one historian, "that in the year 2000 this area won't be in a depression like Detroit." An engineering professor, outlining his plans for expanding his program, said, "I have no idea if the market will expand or decrease. That's a technical question, and I'm not an economist." Long-range planning needs to answer such technical questions and evaluate them in light of the traditional mission.

The imperative for a future administration is to rearticulate the institution's purpose. This cannot be done by interpretive strategy alone but by including the university's constituencies in the process of articulating mission and operations. The president and academic vice president have played a vital role in the transition from a small college of a simpler era to a multiplex institution in an increasingly abstruse period. Long-range planning, however, must come to grips with the institutional pursuit of short-term adaptation and its consequences to institutional mission. Such a task must be addressed by the entire university community. The current dysfunction between mission and operation was almost inevitable given the confusion surrounding the liberal arts in the 1980s, changes in the religious order, and the new educational demands of growth industries. The complexities of markets, decisionmaking, and ideology point out the protean nature of collegiate systems that force contradictions between historical identity and adaptive strategy. The future lies in ameliorating those contradictions.

———————————— SIX ————————————

Present State College

In times of crisis or chaos, it is said, people turn to individuals with heroic qualities who will resolve their dilemma. The assumption is that a leader can make instrumental decisions that effectively reverse institutional decline. The case study outlined in this chapter suggests such an interpretation, but it would be far too simplistic. We must consider a leader's instrumental decisions in light of an institution's history, culture, and context. What conditions allow for the assertion of presidential authority and power? What are the effects of an autocratic decision-making process on institutional culture and long-term viability?

The point of this analysis is to uncover neither heroes nor villains at Present State College. Instead, we enter an institution that underwent crisis to understand how the actors' interpretations and perceptions of organizational problems involved and influenced a new leader with a mandate to effect change. We analyze how those changes occurred and the consequences such decision-making processes have on the future of Present State. As the institution struggles for short-term viability we consider its interpretive climate and, by extension, the role of interpretive climate in collegiate institutions.

Decline in a Pastoral Setting

Present State's atmosphere, miles from a major city or metropolitan area, is bucolic. As a state college, it followed the pattern of many of its sister institutions. Founded in 1828, it remained relatively unchanged as it gradually transformed itself from a normal school to a state teachers college. The economic boom of the 1960s dramatically increased enrollment and encouraged the rapid construction of buildings. The college took on the trappings of a small,

94

but growing, comprehensive institution. Planning occurred quickly and haphazardly.

As with many other state institutions, the college's mission was to provide educational opportunity for the primarily rural, working-class residents of the area. The rural beauty of the campus and its proximity to major ski areas attracted a population that may not exist at other isolated state colleges. Faculty, students, and administrators mention skiing and outdoor recreation as primary reasons for coming to Present State. Thirty percent of the student body comes from out-of-state because of the state's excellent skiing areas. The physical size of the campus—twice that of other state institutions—together with its hilltop location lend the campus an aura of physical splendor. The college has 14 buildings on 500 acres.

The late 1970s, however, found the institution with problems endemic to the times. A financial shortfall of $300,000 one year pointed the college toward a financial precipice. Largely tuition-driven, the institution saw a dramatic drop in enrollment. By 1980 the state legislature made comments about closing one of the state colleges; lawmakers often referred to Present State as the most vulnerable to liquidation. Although the state legislature has talked about closing one of the colleges for over fifty years, it has yet to shut one down. Nevertheless, individuals on campus perceived that the institution was in crisis and morale was extremely low.

In response to a downturn in statewide enrollment, a new chancellor and the state board of trustees created a three-tiered curricular classification to avoid institutional duplication. Programs and majors became classified as "essential, distinctive, or other." The state informed the colleges that each institution could decide which programs it wanted to keep and which programs the other institutions could have. The faculty at Present State opted for an increased emphasis on distinctive programs in the fine and performing arts and in environmental science. The college dropped majors in English, biology, and history. The state's mandate had the effect of reinforcing an already prevalent image that most of its students were "1960s nature freaks," interested only in nonvocational courses. The effects of curricular change were twofold. First, the traditional clientele of the college—working-class, first-generation college students—did not find the practical courses they wanted, and they applied elsewhere. Second, although the state decreed that these changes were to take place, there was no transfer of funds to cover the higher costs of labor-intensive courses. That is, Present State had opted for courses and majors—drama and art, for example—that cost more than those in business or math, yet they received no additional funds to support these programs.

When the president departed in 1981, the state-level chancellor became acting president until the new incumbent took office. Prior to this interregnum, major staffing changes occurred. There was a new academic dean, director of facilities, business manager, and dean of students. All of these individuals have remained at the institution except the dean of students. The new president, with a law degree from a large public university, came with a general mandate to change the college. The chancellor had created the climate for change during his seventy-five-day tenure as acting president. "The chancellor really shook things up," noted one observer.

Responses in many interviews indicated that the new president has won few friends within four years, and he has made enemies. Yet the institution has turned around, vastly improving its fiscal and enrollment strength. In 1984 the enrollment was up 13 percent over the previous year, the full-time equivalent now being close to 900 students. The budget is balanced again, deferred maintenance has ceased, and the once slovenly institution has been transformed into a manicured campus that accentuates the beauty of the surrounding environment. Thus, from many angles institutional health is high.

Nevertheless, the Institutional Performance Survey and interviews with different constituencies provided mixed signals about organizational health. All recognized that enrollments have increased and that the institution is fiscally better off than it was when the president arrived, yet many perceive a conflict-ridden atmosphere. One individual exemplified many people's comments by comparing the administration to tyranny in the Dark Ages, and added, "He [the president] is shaping the college in a manner I fear that is not in the college's long-term interest." As we explore Present State College, we come to recognize both the benefits and the costs of turnaround strategies within an organizational culture.

Internal Turnaround Strategies

The state mandate for curricular change and the realities of the 1980s student market created a climate that demanded innovation and renovation of Present State's curriculum. This climate helped the new president implement broadly conceived turnaround strategies. The academic dean saw the possibility of programmatic expansion in hotel management, which fit the need of an area with an abundance of resort lodges. Although programs in restaurant and hotel management already existed at other institutions, there were none in small hotelry. The program created a unique niche for Present State that met the academic needs of the student body and the economic needs of the area.

The college also introduced a major in management information science rather than computer science, acknowledging that the math and verbal skills of its student body were not strong. A computer-science major may not have had qualified students for jobs in the local region, where the needs for high-technology computer skills were not great. Further, the development of associate degrees attracted students who wanted a two-year curriculum; these new degree programs now enroll over 10 percent of the student body.

A study of retention revealed that students left the college in part because the curriculum was disorganized. Freshmen and sophomores had been able to take upper-division courses, so that by the time they were juniors and seniors they had exhausted the course offerings in their major. Courses often were not available even though they had been listed in the catalogue, which further confused student advisement and planning. The rapid shift among students toward vocational programs was not balanced by broad liberal-arts requirements. Consequently, when the college introduced general-education requirements and systematized a sequence of course offerings, the attrition rate went down. General-education courses filled the freshman and sophomore years with requirements so that primarily juniors and seniors took upper-division courses.

A writing requirement and standards for admission to freshmen-level programs brought about a renewed sense of institutional quality. The students now have a formal advising process and course requirements that must be met by the end of the sophomore year: the declaration of a major, a GPA of 2.5, and successful completion of three streams of courses in general education.

The increased emphasis on the arts at Present State included a new ceramics studio and new etching and lithographic presses. The college theater is a beautiful facility that serves as a cultural center for the region. Although some have wondered about the wisdom of building such a facility instead of a sports complex, the theater was constructed during the heyday of Present State's interest in the performing arts.

The present administration deemphasized certain programs, demanded the elimination of underenrolled classes, and ensured that faculty members had a full workload. Visible signs that the college supported the arts encouraged undeclared majors to move into the arts and the admissions office to recruit students for the programs. Consequently, Present State doubled enrollment in the-ater arts. The direction and size of the arts program is no longer in question, although the arts will not gain the prominence the fac-ulty desired. As one individual noted, "The arts are here to stay, but we've got to be practical. How many theater majors will come to a rural, isolated town like Present?" Further, the administra-tion deemphasized some arts programs, such as dance. Thus, by streamlining the arts at Present State the programs became viable.

The grounds and facilities of the institution underwent a face-lift. "Deferred maintenance had really made this place look shabby," noted one individual. "The buildings were run down, there was mud where grass should be, and the offices were totally disor-ganized." Consequently, the new president and the facilities man-ager focused on renovating the grounds and buildings; by the fall of 1984 the grounds were beautifully manicured. Faculty and ad-ministrative offices had been scattered throughout the campus; the new plan called for a centralized administrative office and re-organized faculty offices. The previous president had attempted such a change but failed to gain approval from the state chan-cellor. Shortly after the new president arrived he asked for and received permission to consolidate office space by renovating an underused dorm into an administrative facility.

One observer commented:

> Ernie [the new president] had central-office support. It was crucial. The chancellor had no faith in the previous administration. [The chan-cellor] brought in Ernie, the kind of guy he wanted—take charge—and then gave him the leeway to make changes that the previous admin-istration could never get done.

A unified student center also opened, housing the cafeteria, Student Union, student-government offices, bookstore, and a student-run inn that provided a focused place for student inter-action with one another and faculty.

The college closed unused buildings and introduced energy-efficient techniques to cut costs. When faculty retired in underenrolled programs such as education, the administration generally did not replace them. The administration hired adjunct faculty who taught courses and advised students, thereby saving the direct and indirect costs of a full-time faculty member. Adjunct faculty who taught courses that an underutilized faculty member could teach were not rehired. Most importantly, however, the increase in enrollment from 600 to 900, coupled with an income-producing business management institute that provided services to the region, allowed the institution to eliminate its troublesome debt and achieve fiscal stability.

External Turnaround Strategies

The methods used to tell the public about the changes at Present State were manifold. The administration hired a new director of admissions who was well-connected with the state's high-school guidance counselors. Each year he visited every high school in the state and utilized new marketing tools. The communications director developed brochures, pamphlets, and catalogues extolling the virtues of an education like the one offered at the college. A renewed emphasis on rigor and quality no longer brought to public attention an institution that had an open-door policy to all students or an institution that limited the academically weaker student to a poor-quality education. Rather, Present State portrayed itself as an institution founded by the state to provide a quality education, equal opportunity, and a stepladder to the middle and professional classes. The institution extolled its personalized care for students and low student-teacher ratio.

The college hosted events for a variety of groups that brought the institution back into public consciousness. High-school cheerleading squads, hockey camps, high-school theater presentations, and a host of other activities came on campus. These activities provided a casual forum for Present State to highlight its strengths. The president expected faculty and administrators to attend these forums. If a local high-school art department had an exhibit on campus, then the president expected the arts faculty to attend the opening. If a faculty member did not attend, it was not unusual to hear of the president's displeasure. Outreach to local newspapers and presidential speeches to groups such as the Kiwanis and Rotary increased public awareness of the institution.

Present State's promotional efforts were not limited to its local constituents. The institution also established feeder schools outside of the state. When students from out-of-state came to interview at the college, an admissions officer greeted them at the airport one hour away. International students from the Middle East became a small but important market that helped the college meet its enrollment needs. Present State dramatically increased its list of interested students from the Educational Testing Service. Students at the college received promotional brochures to take home with them and give to potential applicants at their high schools. The presence of the admissions staff at regional conferences and college days helped raise institutional visibility. Although the college spoke about its dedication to attracting quality students, the admissions office moved closer toward an open-admissions policy as it tried to increase enrollment. To aid those students not fully prepared for college, a summer program was initiated that provided a "head start" for those who might be lost without individualized help.

When asked about the major techniques he used to increase the external visibility of the college, the president responded by noting informal methods:

> The greatest way to achieve visibility is by getting across to our external constituency the idea that things are happening on campus. Word of mouth. The people who work here—everybody, staff, faculty and administration—are our best promotion. They all live in the surrounding communities and they all can be salespeople in a sense. They're the most effective tools.

The president's impression, then, was that the way to increase visibility to a rural population covering several hundred miles was through concerted oral efforts, including an admissions officer who knew key people in the area. Making outside groups aware of what the college offered and what it did well was one formal method of improving and communicating the momentum of the college. Written brochures and promotional information were a second means of inundating the local population with information about Present State. College members also made their presence known by attending informal events on- or off-campus. Finally, and most importantly, informal contact by college representatives with the local population communicated that the college was on the move. "The best way," the president concluded, "for people to get excited about sending their kids to Present State is for them to sense the excitement of the people who already work here." To stimulate a sense of excitement, the president spent most of his time and energy focusing on the internal clientele of Present State so that they could directly sense the changes at work in the institution and then go into their local communities as ambassadors of the college with an exciting program to sell.

Within the relatively short period of four years, an institution that previously had used few, if any, marketing devices refocused and reemphasized what the institution had to offer. One individual commented, "Ernie has really turned this college around and made it a successful business." The adaptation of new programs and the increased visibility of the institution in a changing environment ushered in a dramatic break from the previous culture of the organization. This shift in cultural dynamic becomes more apparent as we look at the college's mission, leadership, and use of interpretive strategy.

Momentum as Interpretation

In one sense, the success of this institution depends very little on an explicitly stated vision or firmly held belief system. One rarely hears different constituencies speak of mission. The IPS shows mixed, somewhat negative, sentiments about whether people share a common definition of the institution's mission. When the president discovered the IPS results, he noted that faculty identified much more closely with their particular disciplines than with an overall institutional goal. Administrators speak primarily of "markets" and "capturing audiences." One central administrator hoped that the college's typical "pictures of mountains and flowers" would be changed to photographs of good-looking women and men and sports-related activities. The individual commented, "Sex and action sell. We're in a tight market, and if we're to capture the market we've got to get photos that kids can relate to."

The college's tacit belief system, the way things are actually done, comes into direct conflict with the president's attitudes regarding organizational climate. One individual spoke for many by saying, "Not all of us want to work as hard as he does. This place is a job for us, that's all." Institutional mission did not serve as an important symbolic or even tactical means of implementing a turnaround strategy. Turnaround resulted not from binding people together but from presenting a uniquely new face to external constituencies.

On the other hand, the symbolic use of momentum as a strategy for implementing change—perceived and actual—was brought into constant play by the president and chancellor. "When the chancellor became president here he actually spent two or three days a week on campus. You'd see him everywhere. He got involved in everything and you sensed something was up," related one individual.

Another individual spoke of the past in the following way: "We were suffering from a 'do you own thing' attitude. There is still a lack of community. A tendency to cellularize people was engendered by a president some years ago, and it's a legacy that has lasted a long, long time. Faculty still don't see all of this college."

Consequently, actors operated within their own spheres of influence and, as resources became scarcer, they continually vied for specified goods. One faculty member said:

> I advised this one student to take a light load. He was really weak academically. This older professor came up to me, saw what I had scheduled for the kid and said, "I want him in both my classes." Well, it was pretty obvious he was just grabbing bodies so his head count would look better.

The lack of community observed by many individuals appeared on an institutional level, but not within departmental subunits. Respondents to the IPS noted that the institution was predominantly a personal place, yet they also felt a strong bureaucratic and production orientation. A faculty member commented on this seeming contradiction by noting, "The administration—the president—decides things. He's autocratic. But on our own level, day-to-day, it's a very nice place to be. Look, this place only has sixty faculty members. Everybody knows everybody. But we lack institutional community."

The IPS also brought to light that no one except executive administrators felt budget cuts were done on a prioritized basis. Analyzing this finding, the president remarked:

> Sure, that makes sense. By definition, if you cut my area how could you have a sense of priorities? I don't think it should be surprising that people close to decisions know why decisions are made. But if I'm in the arts and I'm not getting all that I want, then yes, cuts could not be done with any sense of priorities.

The foregoing comments point out that institutional community and a unified sense of mission did not exist at Present State.

Different constituencies at the college noted that they did not feel a part of the planning process. The president acknowledged their sense of estrangement by observing that executive administrators prioritize because they "know why decisions are made." When we compare Present State to Family State we observe discrepancies between the way the actors communicate information to one another and how they identify priorities. What guided the actors' consciousness at Family State was their identification with institutional mission. The way they understood this mission was through the information that flowed from the administration and among constituents, enabling all actors to feel well informed about how and why decisions were made. At Present State, with its atmosphere of crisis, decisions seemed to come quickly and often unilaterally from the president's office.

The chancellor's brief interregnum prior to the new president's arrival on campus set the tone for needed change. "We knew something had to be done," said a faculty member. "Enrollments had declined, the place looked bad, and there were rumors they wanted to make this place into a prison." Within six months new personnel had been hired in key positions and the chancellor had hired a new president to "shake things up."

Whether or not legislators actually intended to close the college is a moot point; the actors perceived that a crisis existed. A general sense of momentum developed as different constituencies observed changes in top administration. During the initial years of the new president's tenure, he operated in something akin to a tautological system. The crisis atmosphere at Present State increased the power of the presidency, a development that corroborates recent research suggesting that leader influence increases during the early stages of a crisis (Zammuto, 1985). At the same time, however, the president's confrontational style significantly heightened perceptions that a crisis existed.

The president acknowledged that when he first arrived he made tactical errors in sending memos to people rather than personally talking with them. Because he had come from a large institution, he thought the communicative patterns for getting things done relied on written directives rather than on the congenial powers of oral persuasion. Nevertheless, the president's communicative style was another vehicle whereby people realized that life at Present State would no longer be "business as usual."

Since the president's arrival, participants perceive that he has frequently altered the organizational chart, leaving actors and

roles in constant flux. In fact, the president noted that "the organizational chart has been changed only once per year." The point,
however, is not the number of times a chart is actually changed,
but rather the perception that the organization was in constant
transformation. For example, one individual reported, "He's always
playing musical chairs. Are you pleasing Ernie in your job? Of
course you are. If you don't, you're gone. As long as you produce
things at an acceptable level, he'll leave you alone. His memos,
however, can be never-ending."

Although the president felt he had let up on his written communication, people consistently mentioned that things are done
differently since the new president arrived. One person jocularly
referred to the president's walks through the campus every day:
"Ernie's dictaphone walks are infamous around here. You'll see
him marching around the campus talking into his machine, telling
somebody to clean the leaves under the trees, or that there's a
paper cup in front of a building."

Through his use of space, the president communicated to constituents that he wanted quick change. In addition to his "dictaphone walks," he insisted that administrators and faculty show
up at different functions—recruiting, job fairs, or theatrical pro-
ductions put on by the student body. However, unlike Family
State, involvement in campus activities did not derive from personal friendship and camaraderie. Instead, individuals related with
one another through formal roles and responsibilities. The faculty
member who showed up for an art fair did so not because of
individual interest but because his role as a faculty member demanded that he do so. Likewise, the administrator who visited the
student-run inn did so not because she enjoyed personal compan-
ionship with other administrators or students but because she saw
the functional value of attending informal gatherings as a part of
her job.

The crisis nature of the institution, combined with its rural isolation and the critical tone of presidential communication, created
a perception that morale was low and conflict high. The IPS confirmed both of these findings. One person noted some reasons
why:

> There's been a high turnover in mid-management. Salaries are low,
> and we're in a rural environment, so it's hard for spouses to find work.
> He's [the president] a "hands-on" person. He'll walk through the dorms
> at ten at night and then go tell an administrator to tell a student to
> turn his stereo down. He doesn't trust the people he hires. We feel
> watched, so you can't get excited about this place.

Another individual commented, "He has a tendency to go for the chinks in the armor. He conveys very few pats on the back, and lots of 'Where were you last night?'" Both the substance and style of his communication created a sense that needed change was coming about; the president and many other actors perceived that in a crisis certain modes of communication and decision-making were imperative.

With the use of momentum as a symbolic style for change, the influence of history and the ties of the institution became either muted or uprooted. The president and others spoke of the historical mission of the institution, but they did so not to accentuate an organizational culture, an accepted way of doing things, but rather to delineate how things should be done differently in the 1980s.

A comparison with Family State or Mission University points out the different avenue Present State took to articulate its purpose. The actors at Family State clearly felt that their mission was to provide an education to working-class, first-generation college students. Mission University sought to express its distinctive mission through service and holistic education. At Present State, however, the mode of operation was survival, with actors focusing on marketing strategies that did not concern institutional mission.

As a result, Present State did not hire people because of their willingness to work for an explicit mission or their preference for a close-knit atmosphere. Instead, the institution sought a particular type, and the individual came for personal reasons. "We tend to choose people who will fit Ernie's style," related one individual. Said another person, "I came here because I like living in a rural ski area. I have a higher degree of control over my life now. It's certainly not professional reasons that brought me here." Other faculty members mentioned that they took their positions solely because of the tight job market. They worked on projects and activities outside of the college that fulfilled their needs in ways that Present State did not. Consequently, the fit between the institution and the individual did not depend upon an understanding of institutional culture or historical trends and realities.

Once individuals arrived at the institution, they related to other actors and the institution through their role-related capacities. Noted one long-time faculty member:

> You get rewards in a role here, as a department chair but not as an individual. They never say you're doing a good job. They say, "If everybody worked like you things would be okay." I don't like that. I want to be considered as an individual. It's not just faculty who feel

this way either—it's staff and custodians, too. They must make it less of a job.

The point of this analysis is neither that the institution operated in a Weberian bureaucracy where actors related to one another as defined by roles nor that the institution lacked cultural integrity based upon a shared perception of what needed to be done. Rather, our view of Present State proceeds from the widespread perception that the institution faced practical problems that might have resulted in closure. Combating the problems demanded a new institutional style, a renewed sense of momentum that proclaimed to everyone that "business as usual" was over. The symbolic use of momentum to effect change was initiated by a strong-willed outsider—the new president—unacquainted with the ways of the institution. Attention to the grounds and the search for new staff who were suited to the president's style suggested a new order, prompted by organizational crisis. Administrative personnel rotated and changed, and a fluctuating organizational chart threw roles into confusion. The cultural norms of "doing your own thing" promoted by the previous president quickly succumbed to demands by the new president that each person's organizational role have specified objectives. Role-related activities soon replaced casual conversation and friendship as the recognized vehicle for organizational kinship.

The changes initiated by the president also included firing or reassigning incompetent staff. Although beneficial, these moves carried cultural implications. Two tenured faculty members, for example, were laid off because their "relative fitness and ability" (the union contract language) were judged to be less than two junior faculty who were retained. Although there was general agreement about the professors' lack of skills, many faculty perceived the layoffs to be an attack on a cultural norm of the institution—one that necessitated fiscal compensation. The president disagreed that any cultural norm had been broken and noted that the faculty grievance resulted in a "very modest financial settlement." The issue for the president, then, related to specific provisions of a union contract rather than the organization's culture.

Decision-making procedures enabling rapid change also enhanced institutional momentum. People referred to the present administration as supportive of ideas. However, planning was not a shared articulation of where the college community wanted the institution to be in five years. Instead, planning involved getting the support of top administrators for individually initiated ideas.

"No one says 'Don't' or 'Stop' here," said one individual. "If you get an idea, you can work it out with Ernie or the dean and they'll see it through." The actors viewed the president as the person who pushed ideas through committees once an individual's initiative gained his endorsement. One individual who had a new plan for his department characterized how he got his idea accepted: "You go to the president. Everything else matters very little. I talked with other members in the department, they liked the idea, and I went to Ernie. If he likes the idea, then it will get implemented. The dean? Committees? Sure they exist, but they're after the fact."

Another person noted:

> He's extremely autocratic. There's no question. He pretends to want shared decision-making, but the deans don't make any decision without him. He's impatient. He'll get something done on paper, but it will take a year to work through the resentment. He overmanages because he gets involved in everything. A lot of people say, "I'll just hold on for five years and then he'll be gone."

The IPS pointed out a strong consensus that decisions were very centralized in an autocratic process often based on the power of those involved. When queried about what they meant by centralized, most people echoed the president's own comment: "Yes, I'd agree it's centralized. Authority rests in this office."

It seems paradoxical that individuals at Present State see decision-making as both centralized and responsive to decentralized initiatives. Both views derive, however, from the common perception that, given present institutional constraints, strong presidential leadership was necessary to create widespread impetus for change. One individual summed up the presidential role by saying, "He has had the effect of acting as the catalyst for change." Where the change came from—through individual initiative or presidential directive—was relatively unimportant as long as institutional momentum was communicated to all constituencies within a present-oriented time frame. In this sense, whether one believed the institution was governed through intimidation or individual initiative did not matter. What mattered was that the momentum of change pointed the college away from a past that appeared by all accounts to have failed.

The Future of Present State

When considering the health of Present State, one cannot dismiss the intrusive nature of the state and the environment on the problems and fortunes of the college. The state mandated curricular changes, which the college defined and adhered to. These changes, however, created unique—and subsequently worrisome—niches for the college in the area of the arts and environmental sciences. Enrollment declined not only because of the prior administration's lackadaisical attitude but also because of the real shortfall of college-age students in this sparsely populated region. The state environment created a worried atmosphere on campus, with actors acknowledging the very real possibility that the institution might close due to underenrollment. The chancellor for the state system arrived on campus at a critical juncture and set the stage for the new president to create change.

On a practical level, the institution responded to decline in a multitude of ways. An adaptive strategy encouraged the administration to implement majors in management-information science and hotel management that fit a previously untapped niche. The college expanded its marketing and promotion efforts into new areas, thereby increasing its visibility and prompting the state's population to reexamine an institution it had all but forgotten. Curricular and programmatic changes attracted students who previously would have gone elsewhere. New programs, such as the business management institute, generated needed income.

Aware of the consequences that the college faced if it did not change, constituents willingly accepted the confrontational style of an autocratic president who used momentum as a symbolic tool. The process created anger or disappointment on the part of different actors, but it had short-term results. Present State had bottom-line goals that were clear prior to the president's arrival; his success depended not on being a crowd pleaser or a consensus-oriented leader but rather on achieving fiscally oriented goals. In the words of one individual who had been critical of the president, "There's no room for nice guys here now. The bottom line, though, is that there are students. The image of the college has changed and the deficit has been eliminated."

The president, too, was aware that end results had been accomplished at the expense of the process. Acknowledging the disquiet on campus, he commented, "There is a certain level of tension that can't be dissipated while I'm here. No matter how nice I am this year it can't dissipate itself. But people need to feel a little bit more secure again. Not just yet, though."

As with all institutions, questions remain. To what extent does mission, a sense of identity and purpose, alter the configuration and long-term success of the college? How can one balance goal-achievement and institutional or cultural process? Can certain administrative styles achieve temporary gains that ultimately spell long-term trouble? What happens when a strong leader moves on? One individual closely associated with the president stated:

> The thing I fear most is what happens when those of us who have been working sixty or seventy hours per week finally peak out. You can only maintain a certain level of energy for a time. We're all getting tired. I'm getting tired. I'm waiting for new people to come in and take charge, but I don't see it yet. And new people here who don't know the recent past won't understand. So it's really possible that a lethargy, a complacency, can seep in—especially when Ernie leaves.

Many top administrators privately admit that it is time for the president to move on. Actors throughout the college expect that the president will leave in the near future. As noted, one individual said he'd "hold on" until the president left. The president acknowledged that he would eventually exit, saying that for him, "Problem solving is fun. The problems weren't difficult to identify here, and I would like to continue at an institution where I can solve more problems."

What kind of institution will Present State be in the future? This question will loom increasingly important as a presidential succession draws near. The college has successfully weathered a difficult crisis. But while the institution has emerged more secure, it is not clear that participants have developed a sense of institutional identity and history. Although solving short-term problems, the use of adaptive strategy has posed other, more fundamental questions. The institution appears in need of collectively deciding its purpose and mission. Questions need to be raised about increasing the percentage of out-of-state and international students to meet enrollment demands at a state college. Retention continues to be a problem, in part because the institution accepts widely diverse students: foreign, out-of-state, local working class, community college–oriented, curricular-oriented, low achievers and high achievers, to name but a few such subgroups.

The curriculum, untied to any institutional identity, appears to be a free-floating object with which many groups are unhappy. The chief success of the curriculum is its ability to adapt to market demands. As one individual noted, however, "Hotel management won't grow forever. We can't simply continue to create curriculum by interpreting what students think they need for jobs."

Moreover, students and faculty alike often expressed considerable dissatisfaction with general-education requirements and programs. One general-education professor commented:

> I have to spend the whole semester convincing students why what I'm teaching is worthwhile to them. They say—just like in the 1960s—that general education lacks relevance. Their criticism is borne not out of open-mindedness, but out of ego and self-centeredness. I wonder if we aren't reinforcing their ideas because the curriculum lacks coherence.

Like its curriculum, the college's social and community activities remain unfocused, bearing little clear relevance to an as yet insufficiently articulated mission. In articulating its identity, Present State must reflect on its historic, long-term educational role in the state. One individual noted:

> I see this as a community that is in sore need of having an ethnography done on itself. I'm not sure the college has a mission that's clearly understood. We come from a time when it wasn't necessary to think about it, but now it's vital. Part of it is simply geographical. Our very existence, our raison d'être, is to serve a rural, isolated, poor part of the country. But we've got to articulate that. The crisis is over. Let's get on with it.

Because "the crisis is over," Present State needs to consider organizational health and morale in a new light. If morale was once low because of poorly made instrumental decisions, morale is low today because constituents feel divorced from the institution. Many constituents lamented the absence of a team spirit. One faculty member complained, "You learn quickly that when the president says to a group that something is open for discussion, that's not the case. He'll present the idea, let you talk for a minute or two, then you'll find out everything's been decided." While individuals with ideas went directly to the president, formalized decision-making processes appear to have been underutilized during the crisis.

Many participants speak of the need for a process-oriented person as their next leader, while acknowledging that the lack of attention to process was necessary given the college's immediate problems. Few people speak of the college in terms of historical roots or a common mission. Nevertheless few would disagree that the institution is now much better off—academically, fiscally, politically—than it was in 1981. Present State's greatest challenge lies not in ensuring immediate viability but in defining its identity and charting its future course.

SEVEN

Covenant University

Organizational culture is so basic to and pervasive in an educational institution that when an existing or original culture grows weak, members search for a surrogate by which to understand their organization and interpret its actions. In many cases a surrogate involves what might be termed a "governance culture," a widely understood way of doing things, a way of surviving in the organization. In the case of Covenant University, this surrogate culture grew out of the creation of a faculty union. The arrangement has brought a degree of stability to the university's internal working relationships. Nevertheless, crucial issues that have an important bearing on the institution's future continue to go unaddressed.

As a nearly hundred-year-old religious institution, Covenant has benefited from strong values and beliefs for much of its history. However, its cultural coherence became diluted as environmental changes and an increasing proportion of new lay faculty and administrators gradually transformed the dynamics of university life. At a time of crisis in the mid-1970s, Covenant sought stability not in its now much-weakened roots but in the formal, bureaucratic solutions that unions bring. Although confrontational, a symbiotic relationship between faculty and administration has since developed that has allowed the university to function in an orderly if rather unimaginative way.

The question that this and similar arrangements pose is whether they provide the basis for a new cultural order or whether they are merely convenient, though sometimes necessary, coping mechanisms that cannot address underlying issues. For Covenant, these issues concern reevaluating its mission and responding to environmental change and opportunity. These tasks require both leadership and considerable cooperation from members of the university community if the institution is to effectively interpret and communicate its purpose to its many constituents. Perceptions vary on whether the union has bought time for the university or merely marked time. Respondents agree, however, that the ghosts of problems past haunt the institution's present, rather unsettled circumstances.

A Cosmopolitan Religious University

Covenant University, founded in the mid-nineteenth century, is a religious comprehensive institution with 5,400 students. It is located in a major city. Nineteen percent of the students are minorities, and another 25 percent are international students. About half of the students at Covenant are members of the sponsoring religion, 56 percent are undergraduates, and the mean age of students is twenty-six. Seventy percent are full-time students. Tuition comprises 82 percent of the budgeted revenues of the university. Students are enrolled in colleges of liberal arts, business, education, nursing, and law. The university also offers a lively continuing education program. Many students find the city in which the university is located to be a major positive factor in their decision to attend Covenant.

The university president must be a member of the religious order, whose members live together in a residence on campus. Until the mid-1960s, all of Covenant's trustees were members of the religious order. The board has since been expanded, however, and members of the order now constitute about 30 percent of the board. A decline in the size of the order inevitably has meant that fewer members are serving on Covenant's administration and faculty. Twenty-five years ago, members served in all administrative positions at the level of dean or above. Today, all the deans, the vice-presidents, and over 90 percent of the faculty are lay people. University constituents often refer to the influence of the religious order and its relative decline. Overall, as one faculty member remarked, the university is "thoroughly secularized now." But the order remains influential in university dynamics. Because the president wears many hats—as a brother in the order, nominal spiritual leader of the college community, and chief executive officer of the institution—his influence can pervade the campus. "From a large portion of the institution, the president elicits a kind of obedience that can be amazing to an outsider," reported one administrator.

Given the character of the institution, one would not expect to encounter a faculty union on campus. To understand its formation, we must first consider Covenant's traditional mission and why in recent years it no longer acted as a cohesive force that held the institution together.

Mission

Covenant's mission for its first century was to provide good-quality liberal-arts education in the religious tradition. It sought to emphasize moral and ethical values and foster a strong sense of community. Students were predominantly white, eighteen-to-twenty-two-year-old members of the sponsoring faith. For many years it remained a small urban college with academic and cultural advantages. Although the institution was designated a university some fifty years ago, it continued to retain its original focus. In recent years, however, the mission and character of the institution have changed. The curriculum now focuses more on professional programs and the university offers continuing education throughout the state, using part-time faculty members. The student body also has changed. It includes more commuters, more part-timers, more adults, more internationals, more minorities, more women, and more members of other faiths than it did twenty years ago.

Faculty, administrators, students, and civic leaders frequently refer to Covenant's mission, but it does not seem to be well-understood or consensually agreed upon. As one administrator put it:

> We finally have at least a foundation for university-like activities. We're still a slightly overgrown liberal-arts college. It doesn't have a university mentality, and it's not sure it wants one. It's a drifting spirit of the trustees, the religious order, a few of the old-time faculty.

An alumnus said, "The university sends no clear messages about its identity. People know it's a religious school, sort of out there somewhere. Probably teaches liberal arts, has a big church, lots of lawyers and government types went there."

A sense of mission at Covenant does not pervade a broad range of activities; rather, its memory is invoked as circumstances dictate. What persists is its rhetoric. Individuals have used references to the mission to support or refute controversial positions on diverse institutional issues, to the point that several respondents on campus independently stated that appeals to the mission had been used as weapons in arguments. The problem seems to arise from two sources. First, some of the key, long-time leaders of the university prefer the historical mission and clientele. Sometimes they act or speak as if, in their minds, the historical mission were still alive as a hope for the future if not as an actuality. Yet one long-time leader, a member of the religious order, said, "To give way to nostalgia for the old mission would be to extinguish the institution." Second, the university's programs and clientele have changed markedly over the years, but leaders have not undertaken a clear, purposeful reassessment of its mission. In the absence of such a fresh evaluation, what remains is essentially rhetoric.

The president stated: "I try to convey the institutional identity to people—that's needed. When I talk to people, I emphasize the religious tradition and sponsorship, the liberal arts at the core of all our programs, individual caring for students, and quality as a hallmark of our kind of education." He is conscious of the need for leadership in defining and proclaiming mission. But his statement is at odds with the university's increasing secularism and vocational-professional education. More than one administrator disagrees with the president about quality. As one put it: "This university has no concept of or commitment to excellence. . . . We don't have an 'electric' leader, we don't have an obvious commitment to excellence—or even the rhetoric. Most places at least quack about how excellent they are."

Faculty Union

The gradual erosion of a once-coherent culture set the stage for an institutional crisis in the early and mid-1970s that prompted the formation of the faculty union. The existence, development, and leadership of the union have since played central roles in determining many features of the university, including its governance, decision-making, allocation of resources, and organizational climate.

The union was formed in 1975, at a low point in Covenant's history. Enrollments and finances had been troublesome since at least 1969. Considerable turnover in management positions hastened the loss of a shared identity. Moreover, faculty and administrative positions steadily turned from religious to lay incumbents. This diminished the proportion of faculty whose choice of life-style required deference to the administration and reduced the number of administrators who had the religious position to command such deference. But the presidency was and is a religious position, and the tone of top administration continued in the traditional vein. Paternalism and centralization prevailed. Top administration sought to cope alone with external pressures, unable to involve the faculty in the effort. One observer commented:

> The university brought the union on itself, I suspect—the usual cavalier attitude. Here you have an institution of limited resources, and the members of the religious order dedicate their lives to it, and they wonder, "What do you guys want money for?" They don't understand real life—never did.

The president who served from 1968 to 1974 permitted operating deficits that were small at first but then accumulated to several million dollars. Enrollments declined. As at other schools at that time, the president yielded to pressures for a less-structured curriculum and a relaxation of academic regulations. The move alienated those among the university's constituencies who valued the traditional approach. Although people who knew him say that the president was exceptionally bright, the trustees eventually sought a replacement for him.

By all accounts, the new president was bright too, but he came from a different city and never was accepted fully by Covenant's religious leaders. He and the university operated in difficult circumstances, and his actions only made the situation worse. He announced an across-the-board salary increase of 10 percent in 1974 to help compensate for a salary freeze the previous year, but he yielded to pressures from the blue-collar and clerical unions and the twenty faculty members in the law school, giving them 15 percent. When the remaining employees—two hundred thirty non-law faculty members—protested the favoritism, the president responded that if they wanted to deal with him they should unionize. The remark is thought to have been flippant rather than serious, but the president got what he asked for.

Until 1974, the university senate included representatives of administration, faculty, and students. The faculty's first move in response to the president's remark was to establish a faculty senate. When the president made it clear that he felt no obligation to listen to the group's recommendations, the faculty saw no alternative but to form a union. The several faculty votes that were held on the way to unionization consistently showed that about three-fourths of them supported the idea.

As if to justify the faculty's belief that nothing short of unionization would be effective, the president made another arbitrary
move at Christmastime, just three months after the certification
election and before a contract had been negotiated. He sent termination notices to all 111 nontenured faculty, planning to rescind
some later in the year. The faculty vigorously protested. Ultimately,
the terminations were negotiated and fewer than a dozen faculty
left, some of their own accord. The president seemed unaware of
how badly the situation had deteriorated. The trustees fired him
in 1976, just as the first five-year faculty contract took effect.

Having no strong voice in university decisions, and seeing the
leaders unable to prevent financial difficulties, many faculty felt
that not only their interests but the welfare of the university itself
were in jeopardy. As one faculty member put it:

> Before the union, the university senate was a sandbox. Furthermore,
> with respect to "collegiality," administrators would ask certain faculty
> members for their opinion over coffee. That made those faculty feel
> good, but there was no accountability, and no responsibility to a
> constituency. . . . The union arose out of the economic crunch. It
> was a symptom of the economic situation. You have to ask what this
> place would have been like without the union. The salary of the typical
> faculty member has more than tripled in the past ten years. There'd
> be no tenure, no due process. We can attract good faculty here, with
> our salaries. General education is good here.

The current university president took office in 1977. Although
the faculty accept him far better than his two immediate predecessors, his administration has only recently shown signs of willingness to work with the union. Strictly defined allocation of authority and strongly adversarial relations seem incongruous in a
university with a long tradition of community spirit, service, and
deference to administrative authority.

In 1975, unions were a rarity on college and university campuses. Neither the union leader nor anyone else on the faculty
had union experience. The union relied in its early stages on outside advisers who were not specialists in higher education. The
same was true for the administration. Such circumstances led
administration-union relations to develop along unusually adversarial lines, described variously with pride, indifference, or horror
as an "industrial model." In the first four years, the parties twice
reached an impasse over faculty salaries. Later, they disputed over
retaining their arbitrator.

At all levels, Covenant's administrators abhor the adversarialism of the industrial model. Many find reason enough for that feeling in the sheer difficulty of having ordinary day-to-day conversations with faculty. Lines of communication between the two groups, never well-developed in the university's recent history, became highly formal. The absence of easy interchange reinforced the suspicions of each group regarding the other.

The union has made decision-making easier for administrators in some ways. At many institutions, it takes months or even years to move academic decisions through the committee process. One individual commented: "Here, as an administrator, I could design a curriculum and submit it to the faculty. After forty-five days, I can implement it, no matter what the faculty say. All that matters is that I follow the procedure. I don't have to pay any attention to what the faculty say."

Faculty members have noticed that

> we're outside the mainstream of decision processes. For instance, the dean proposed a language requirement. The council of science chairmen wrote a letter denouncing the notion—it was instituted. Decision-making is done up there and they tell us what it is. If you yell loud enough, sometimes it makes a difference.

Although administrators have relatively wide latitude for making decisions, some of them believe strongly that the faculty relinquished vital prerogatives in curriculum and peer review. One said:

> The faculty also gave up peer review. When I give a promotion decision, I use the language of the contract—no adjectives about the person's performance. The faculty get no feedback about how they're doing, because whatever we say could be used against us in a grievance. We have no damn business making these decisions at all. The faculty has abdicated its power to the administration.

Another negative aspect of the situation as seen by some administrators is their perception that it adversely affects students. One administrator said, "The students get left out in the cold with the union." Another elaborated:

> Students are a means to an end here. The leaders of the faculty association use students individually and collectively to harass administrators—they don't really care about students. We say we're doing things for students, but really we're just getting rid of the negatives so they won't get fed up and transfer to a state school. If they leave us, we won't get paid. There's a real problem here with minimization. People do as little as they can.

Some administrators also feel that unions are out of place in a university. Said one, "The union puts a silly emphasis on collectivism. A good professor is an individual. He or she has precious little interest that can be represented collectively. The good faculty tend to ignore the union."

Although not all faculty are happy with the union, most seem to accept it and to be glad for their threefold salary increase in the ten years since the union began. One who earned less than $15,000 in 1975 now makes $43,000. By rank, Covenant faculty now earn an average of 22 percent more than the national average for comprehensive, church-related universities. For the three professorial ranks, the average is 26 percent. The difference from national averages is diluted by the fact that the cost of living in Covenant's region is among the highest in the country. Nevertheless, gains made by Covenant's faculty are impressive.

Faculty who complain seem less likely to target the union than the administration or issues that fall in the administrative domain. One described a meeting in November:

> The faculty were angry about having no overhead lights or bookcases in some of the offices. [The academic vice president] came to the meeting to hear the problems. He took notes, said he'd do something; awhile after that, we gave him a tour. Then they asked us to give a tour for the director of facilities. Then a tour for the financial vice president. Here we are, four months later, and nothing has happened. The faculty get fed up when this kind of thing happens. They withdraw from the university. They figure ten or fifteen hours of work each week is a fair exchange for their $40,000 a year, under the circumstances. I certainly understand that. They come here wanting to perform, but the situation seems to promote their withdrawing.

More generally, an associate dean commented on the difficulty of hiring new faculty:

> It's a real moral dilemma, the hiring process. We get good applicants. You have to keep things to yourself, you can't be realistic with them. They come, and we all hope it'll work out for them. I'm sold on the idea that there's plenty of opportunities here, but it's totally frustrating to try to take advantage of them.

Richard Windham, president of the union since its inception, speaks strongly on its behalf. Asked whether the union brought a change from an academic "cultural ideology" to a "class ideology," Windham replied:

> Relations are always adversarial between employers and employees, but that does not necessarily mean that they are hostile. One person

has power, the other doesn't. It's true for janitors, and it's true for college professors. It gets sugar-coated in higher education, but it's there. Tragically, in "collegiality" faculty have a greater incentive to be loyal to administration than their colleagues. That's how they get their rewards. Collegiality is being in cahoots with management, often to the detriment of your colleagues. For instance, the mistakes of peer review go away. Faculty victims leave when they are denied tenure or promotion. No one is held accountable for them. At Covenant, the sugar-coating was stripped away. No more rose-colored glasses. People began to see their interests clearly.

Windham believes that the adversarial model used at Covenant works for higher-education organizations:

Yes, I'd recommend the industrial model for other colleges. It gives the faculty the power to organize themselves. If I were an administrator, the first thing I'd do is tell the faculty to get themselves organized, set their agenda, then come sit and we'll talk it over. Collective bargaining is a way to broaden areas of agreement.

The diversity of opinion on unionization at Covenant is great, but many seem to agree on one issue. An administrator put it this way:

This university does not have a history of behaving like a university, such as faculty participation in collegial decisionmaking and peer review. We grew too quickly. The union was a symptom of problems. It did not eliminate those problems. In fact we're just beginning— maybe—to understand the problems.

A plausible interpretation of what happened at Covenant begins with the acknowledged fact that decision-making at Covenant before 1975 was highly centralized. The faculty had no tradition of collegial participation. The union gave them reasonable— ultimately generous—salaries, a vehicle for participation (albeit in the union, not directly in university issues), and guaranteed due process. All of the benefits from unionization at Covenant are available to faculty at many nonunionized universities. It is conceivable that unionization receives the credit for phenomena that faculty at other institutions take for granted as part of normal functioning. Alternatively, as Windham's statement suggests, faculty elsewhere are deluded if they believe they have standing equivalent to that of Covenant's faculty.

Relations between union and administration have improved dramatically in the past two years. The administration has accepted the union. The union president and the academic vice president respect one another. The union is working with administration on recruiting, retention, academic planning, and developing a new general-education curriculum. The parties have begun to discuss some of the issues that will be involved in negotiating a new, five-year contract in 1986. One leader reported, "We're doing prenegotiation now. We haven't run into any major problems yet. But we're still in a honeymoon period this year."

Leadership and Decision-making

The faculty union/administration dichotomy is only one of many dimensions affecting Covenant's decisions. Covenant is exceedingly complex for its size. Many respondents characterized it as "a series of contained entities," or "duchies and fiefdoms," engaged in "turf warfare."

The law school has its own faculty union and "might as well be on another planet." The college of continuing education is not unionized at all. Blue-collar and clerical workers each have their own union. Among the faculty, some individuals continue to regret unionization and differ with union actions. As is true on many campuses, the liberal-arts faculty and the professional-school faculties sometimes find themselves with different, even opposing, points of view. Courses are offered and faculty are housed at a variety of sites: the main campus, an acquired campus two blocks away, and extension offices throughout the state. Some students attend full-time during the day, others on evenings and weekends. Many are single young adults, but many others have families and careers to manage. Consequently, groups with exceedingly diverse interests influence decisions. Moreover, many such decisions are likely to have unintended consequences unless they can somehow accommodate the needs of very different constituencies.

Referring to the turnaround president of Chrysler, one person called the current president "the Iacocca of Covenant University." Others, however, are less generous, and tend to portray the president as indecisive, especially when it comes to internal affairs. By all accounts, the president is extremely effective with external constituents and relates well with key figures and groups in the city. He has completed one major fund drive ($27 million) and is embarking on another. He has supported the financial vice president in improving financial controls. Although his attention has begun to turn toward academic affairs, the deans have been largely responsible for academic development. It is too early to tell whether or how the president's attention to academic issues will translate into organizational changes.

Complementing the president is an academic vice president who was a special assistant for planning at Covenant from 1979 until he became vice president in 1983. He earns higher marks in academic and faculty affairs than his predecessors. His current priorities include establishing a viable planning process and improving relations with the faculty, through its union. He created two new positions in his office. The associate vice president for planning took office late in 1983. An associate vice president for faculty relations took office in the middle of 1985.

Although all agree that the president is, in fact, in charge of the university, the financial vice president who arrived in 1980 is clearly a powerful actor. Financial concerns have taken center stage for the past decade, and financial decision have been centralized in the vice president's office. Although some order has been introduced into the once chaotic financial situation, many believe that the time has come for nonfinancial considerations to have a more powerful role in decision-making. But as one administrator remarked, "The business vice president runs the place because everybody lets him. I don't blame him. He's doing his job. Everyone else's abdication of decision-making gives him a significant hunk of the academic side as well."

If there is a problem with abdication of decision-making, it may be due partly to the high turnover rate of vice presidents and deans. The rate has recently declined, with nearly all incumbents having served at least two years. In addition, the number of associate deans and other midmanagement positions has grown in the past ten years. One administrator attributed the increase to the union (associate deans do what faculty department heads once did), the larger size of the university, the implementation of more complex management systems, and rising student expectations for university services. The growing number of associate deans and other midmanagers may help buffer the adversarial relations that have prevailed between faculty and administration. It has also occasioned high resentment among some faculty, who believe that the positions waste funds that should be used for academic purposes.

Although the collective bargaining agreement has defined many features of decision-making, the process at Covenant is far from straightforward. Continuing difficulties with finances and enrollments compound matters, however much those areas may have improved since the early 1970s. One administrator said: "Our management team promotes paralysis with their standard answer, 'We don't have the money.' A little more discretionary financial aid from institutional funds would go a long way toward helping the enrollment problem. But it's seen as risk capital—which it is not."

The university has been characterized as lurching from crisis to crisis, with the urgent need to make a decision often precluding adequate consultation before it is made. For example, by sheer oversight, incremental changes over the years in the academic calendar brought the length of a semester down to only twelve weeks. When the administration noticed the problem they decided to remedy it immediately by eliminating the January intercession. According to some individuals, the move was reasonable and acceptable to the faculty. However, because it was made without faculty consultation, the faculty protested. Intercession was reinstated.

Decision-making is still centralized, even with the union. A midlevel administrator reported:

> Everything is done centrally—the colleges have no autonomy at all. Admissions, faculty development, alumni, fund-raising—they're all centralized. We can't even raise our own money—not even with some kind of split with central administration. We could easily make up the deficit, but the president just does not want restricted funds.

Others fault top administrators for indecisiveness. Another midlevel administrator added, "The old-boy network is strong here. And there's an enormous reluctance to do anything. They sit on it ... and it isn't going to hatch." The composite view from these comments is that decision-making is stymied by a top administration that retains authority but does not exercise it.

Lack of adequate communication about decisions has produced bad feeling. Another midlevel academic administrator believes that top administrators explain decisions, but only after someone openly challenges them. He explained that recently the administration spent thousands of dollars to prune trees and install a sprinkler system. The faculty believed that those funds had alternative uses with far higher priority, and they grumbled about it. The administrator sympathizes with their reaction, but he has information that top administrators never shared with the faculty about the reasons for those expenditures. He believes that the decision would have been generally well received by the faculty if they had been told those reasons.

Another example of communication breakdown occurred with the decision to spend $100,000 in advertising for new students. Only three weeks elapsed from the day the admissions director proposed a modest version of the idea to the first appearance of radio and newspaper spots produced by a professional ad agency. The decision was made and implemented without mentioning it to the recruitment committee, whose members are leaders of the union and administration. A union member complained, "We just spent $100,000 for ads. We pushed the panic button. There was no consultation with the joint union/administration committee."

The key decision-making groups on campus are three administrative bodies and one special new group. The president's council, the budget development committee, and the financial management group do not allow for faculty or union participation. However, a special new group, called the academic forum, reflects the recent commitment by administration and union to work together. Its members are top academic administrators and key leaders of the union. As its name suggests, the group's primary function is to provide a forum for communication rather than to make decisions. After less than one year of monthly meetings, the forum has received mixed reviews. Some participants retain the cautious optimism that accompanied the forum's first meetings. One member, new to Covenant from a more collegial institution, said, "I go to the academic forum, and sometimes I just want to scream. Don't people see how foolish this all is? I thought the forum would make things more rational—just the opposite."

Although welcomed as a vehicle for greater cooperation, the academic forum must still prove itself. The confrontational relationship between the faculty union and Covenant's administration has highlighted, and in some respects resolved, a certain set of significant issues. Nevertheless, this same adversarial relationship has kept many other important concerns pending. Covenant's future depends in great part on the degree to which both the union and the administration can now address key strategic questions in a consensual, unified manner.

Strategic Management

While Covenant recalls its sense of identity from the past, it has yet to successfully interpret remembered ideals to present realities. University leaders have had a difficult time communicating a coherent sense of the institution's mission and goals to both internal and external constituents. As a result, strategic management has remained a challenge. In the last decade, the administration has sought to develop goal-oriented strategies as well as adaptive ones that will respond to environmental changes and opportunities. The success of these strategies, however, has been hampered by uncertainty regarding the institution's overall direction and purpose.

The predominant strategic mode at Covenant has been goal-oriented or linear. This approach is particularly apparent in activities pertaining to finances, planning, and the physical plant. The stringent financial measures that have been taken since 1980 constitute an effort to gain managerial control over vitally important yet heretofore unruly forces. One such measure for some years was to forgo the development of physical facilities and equipment; another was to establish procedures for controlling expenditures. Consistent with linear strategy and partly in response to the accrediting association's strong recommendation for better academic planning, the current academic vice president places planning high on his priority list.

Covenant also has engaged in adaptive strategy, thanks in part to the strong influence of financial issues on decision-making. Two of the major elements in Covenant's environment are its potential students and the leaders of the city, some of whom are Covenant alumni. Potential students are very diverse, with the two most readily identifiable sources of applicants being graduates of parochial high schools and residents of the metropolitan area. The number of parochial high school graduates in the area has declined, and the city itself is not growing. As one administrator put it, "We don't have a buffer of acceptable students beyond those that we admit."

Covenant has attempted to extend its applicant base by contracting with an outside agency in the mid-1970s to provide off-campus and weekend courses for adults. Covenant soon took over the operation to ensure quality control, and eventually it became the College of Continuing Education. It is now a viable, revenue-producing facet of the university, though not fully accepted by the regular faculty for several reasons. The continuing-education faculty constitute a separate group, because they are part-time and because they are not unionized. Moreover, the college's tuition rates are lower, and its off-campus courses and the location of its offices on an acquired campus remove this operation from Covenant's traditional community. Nevertheless, the college succeeds as a semiautonomous operation that generates revenue and visibility for the university.

Covenant's profile in the city is considerably lower now than it was twenty or more years ago. At that time it was common knowledge that a large share of city and judicial officials were Covenant alumni. Although city leaders remain an important source of legitimacy and funds, the community at large seems to be growing more uncertain of Covenant's role in its educational and civic affairs. Likewise, the university seems to be uncertain about the challenges and opportunities of being an urban institution in a cosmopolitan city.

In establishing the College of Continuing Education, Covenant found a market with untapped potential and adapted its educational services to satisfy that market. As students' interests have shifted, so have faculty positions and other resources. The business school has grown rapidly, but the liberal arts have shrunk, as is true of many institutions across the country. In some respects, Covenant has adapted to the changing racial, ethnic, and international composition of its student body. The university, however, is not known as a true melting pot. Members of identifiable groups tend to socialize among themselves rather than intermingle with others, but there have been no hostilities.

Although useful and important, Covenant's initiatives in linear and adaptive strategy suffer from a lack of cohesion that comes from being uncertain how to communicate its identity to its constituents and in today's educational marketplace. Although blessed with many positive attributes, among them its location, Covenant seems to be an institution adrift and unsure of its bearings. It tends to interpret change in terms of outdated images of itself. As a result, it often experiences its environment as a liability rather than an opportunity.

Interpretive strategy, the process by which institutional leaders communicate goals and ideals and thereby marshall support for its mission, is less in evidence at Covenant. One exception is the stance taken by the president about five years ago in response to charges of improprieties in the conduct of the athletic program. Over the course of several years, the university tolerated agonizing and highly publicized inquiries into the behavior of some members of the athletic department. Ultimately, the president took drastic action. He terminated a major sport, in what was widely hailed as a courageous move to protect the integrity of the university. One observer commented:

> The scandal did a great deal of damage to the university's reputation generally—more than has been detected. How the hell was it permitted to get to the state that it did? The university gave the impression that it was unable to understand and control what was going on. The president said he had no knowledge . . . that's hard to believe. The result was a severe credibility problem. See, you're selling something special, a religious education. It has a certain mystique, mostly misunderstood.

Although many on campus would agree that the incident was damaging, they believe that the president's decision and his accompanying statement went a long way toward repairing the damage.

Although the president's stance on athletics and the rationale he offered to justify it indicate an awareness that difficult situations can be managed through communication, this awareness is not often implemented in the institution's daily activities. The president is regarded as being quite effective with external constituents, but many in the college community wish that he would provide more effective interpretive leadership within the institution. Institutional leaders are reworking the mission statement and appeal to Covenant's identity in discussions, but these actions have yet to move beyond the stage of rhetoric in the eyes of many constituents.

Covenant's current mission has not crystallized and the historical mission maintains but a ghostly presence. At the same time, however, the administration has undertaken initiatives during the past year that have potentially great symbolic value. For example, it conceded a faculty grievance that was high on the union's priority list. Moves such as this signaled to the union that the administration was serious about working cooperatively. Such actions may help set the stage for a new management style and provide the institution with a greater sense of identity and direction.

Governance Culture Without Community

In the last two decades, Covenant's traditional bonds weakened as the educational environment itself simultaneously grew more diverse. Religious membership among the university's trustees and faculty decreased, and the interests and philosophical orientations of students in general became less conservative and more vocational. Many facets of the university became disparate and uncoordinated. Covenant's enrollments and financial condition deteriorated, and the faculty lost confidence in the administration. To protect their own interests and ultimately those of the university, the faculty took dramatic action to change the course of events by establishing a union. Bargained agreements replaced more traditional, though at that point highly ineffectual, cultural bonds.

For the next seven or eight years, university leaders attended primarily to conditions of faculty employment, relations with external constituencies, building the revenue stream, and controlling expenditures. Although the union established order in internal working relationships, it could only address directly a relatively limited range of issues. A number of crucially important tasks have long remained pending and are on the agendas of both the administration and the union. These tasks include renewing and rationalizing the academic program; building an institutional sense of purpose, including clear priorities and implications for action; developing a spirit of cooperation among diverse groups in the university; improving the admissions office and expanding its target audiences; and improving the quality and efficiency of physical facilities.

The emphasis on financial considerations in all decision-making has left the impression that the university will do anything if it makes money. The nonpecuniary interests of the university have been neglected, and morale remains low. Divergent factions on the staff make decisions in isolation, without telling anyone about them, telling them just a little, telling them long after they needed to know, or telling them only after they have insisted upon being told.

Perhaps most revealing about Covenant is the relative absence of shared values and goals, apart from what we have termed a governance culture. On the campus of a religious university, one normally hears spontaneous remarks about caring for students, devotion to academic quality, and affection for the university. Sometimes such comments are passionate, other times perfunctory. At Covenant, they are not made. Spontaneous comments most often relate either to the faculty union and administration or to bureaucratic matters—bad management in the bookstore, pervasive theft and inadequate security measures, malfunctioning elevators, or erroneous records. Frustrated by a widespread inability to freshly interpret the traditional mission, one administrator commented:

> Look where we are. We have a fantastic location. The state schools are defined by their stateness—we can certainly zig between their zags. For the undergraduate program, I think we should strike out, move

forward. This is a great training ground for future leaders of an intercultural and interethnic society. That idea creeps around here, but I think we should seize it affirmatively as consistent with our religious mission—instead of sending missionaries out, the corners of the world come here. Our students can deal not just with ideas but with people—very diverse kinds of people. . . . There are tremendous opportunities here—opportunities for growth, off-campus development, opportunities to inspire the undergraduate curriculum. Yet the institution limps around, constantly dropping its crutches.

Covenant is now beginning to address existing problems and develop beneficial new initiatives. The administration has recently developed a summer registration program for new students to increase the rate of matriculation. It also has tightened the advising system, established on-line computer systems, reviewed the curricula, and so on. Nevertheless, while these incremental adjustments and improvements are welcome and necessary, what is really needed, in the words of one administrator, is "a spark that'll ignite people, that'll galvanize the place." Without consensual agreement on the institution's mission and its implementation, initiatives such as those mentioned above provide little momentum and still less direction for substantive change. Covenant remains an institution in search of itself. If it is unable to develop a sense of identity and purpose, its moment of institutional crisis may not lie in the past, with the formation of the faculty union, but in the future, with diminishing credibility and support among its many diverse constituencies.

PART FOUR
Culture and Identity

A founder of a business once remarked that "creating a culture is like surfing. You cannot make a wave. All you can do is wait and watch for the right wave, then ride it for all it's worth."

While cultures cannot be created ex nihilo or engineered according to a fixed design, they can be nurtured. The two institutions that we explore in this final section are each searching for cultural identity. Yet the wave each seeks to ride will not come from without. Unique to each institution, the dynamics of organizational life present sufficient critical mass for a coherent culture to emerge.

At Triad University, governance structures render cultural coherence a difficult challenge. The president is paddling, making linear management improvements, while waiting for a wave that shows no sign of coming. More precisely, the president is waiting for the convergence of three waves, heretofore independent waves of the three colleges within the university. Triad is a clear example of structural gridlock. Without convergence, the three colleges can and do develop their own strategies, making any university-wide strategy nearly impossible. The dominant theme of university management is and has always been fiscal conservatism. This theme, coupled with relatively freestanding colleges of law, business, and liberal arts, could make for a relatively healthy circumstance in which each college adapts to meet its own needs, none to the financial detriment of the others. Yet the university has adapted less during recent years in geographic and programmatic terms than others we have seen. One current idea to draw students from a wider area is to establish a residence hall for the first time. This is a response to the major environmental change facing Triad, its increasing competitive pressure from other institutions in the area.

At R&D University, operational concerns and inattention to process inhibit the growth of a shared culture. R&D is a relatively young institution that was founded on academic ideas that are unique to this university. Its identity depends on its ability not only to differentiate itself from other universities, which it has done, but also on its ability to express its aims coherently and consistently in everything it does. Such expression has yet to emerge. The very uniqueness on which it is built handicaps the university because most of its faculty and staff bring with them the images of a university that are common to American higher education. They lack an image of what R&D wants to be, so they have difficulty knowing what they can do to support it.

The president of R&D is similar to the president of Mission in his personal style—a strong academic orientation yet a personal remoteness from the academic community. Unlike any other president in this study, R&D's president and his vice presidents are located in offices that are physically distant from the rest of the campus. This constitutes a dramatic example of the effect of space on organizational culture. The president here is oriented largely toward the external environment, which is increasingly common and necessary in higher education but stands in sharp contrast to the presidents at Rural State and Family State.

Common to both Triad and R&D is a need to reflect on long-range issues such as mission and goals in terms of the immediate realities of daily institutional life. In the end, this question is not unlike that faced by the other institutions in this study. On each campus, leaders are looking for strategies that will help them comprehend and communicate what holds their institution together and what allows it to make a special contribution to the educational process. What each requires is leadership attuned to the dynamics of culture and willing and able to interpret and communicate shared values to the campus community.

EIGHT

Triad University

Previous chapters have considered organizational cultures in conditions of both continuity and change. Even in instances of considerable dissension and rancor, the presence of a widely perceived and mutually held cultural identity at these institutions provided a common organizational denominator. Triad University differs in kind from these other institutions. Its distinctive feature is not the presence of one shared cultural paradigm but the presence of four—three subcultures and a relatively weak institutional culture. This prompts us to ask what holds the institution together.

When ties to a nominal culture become distant and attenuated, strong subcultures tend to form within and even dominate an institution. Given the loose structure of many colleges and universities, the presence of subcultures is both natural and appropriate. Undergraduate programs have different needs and interests than graduate programs, as do liberal-arts and professional programs. Nevertheless, most institutions have a shared culture that links diverse activities and concerns. Although subcultures may exist, they usually partake in and contribute to a common frame of reference.

At Triad, three largely autonomous subcultures fragment the institution. In the place of widely shared beliefs and a common mission there exists a governance culture that provides members of the institution with an understanding of management procedures—"how things get done"—but offers little cohesion regarding institutional values, purpose, or identity. This situation has its historical roots in the institution's powerful board of trustees, who have exerted considerable operational control since the 1940s but have not provided leadership to coalesce the three subcultures into one institutional identity. A competitive but nevertheless favorable environment has blessed Triad with short-term operational success but also has masked the consequences of its fragmentation. Impending changes in the environment, however, may have a serious impact on the institution as it is known today.

An awkward but nevertheless functional "holding company" for diverse constituencies, Triad prompts questions about whether operational success can be sustained in an uncertain environment without the institution having a widely shared cultural identity. The case highlights the extent to which the trustees have permitted fragmentation among the organization's several subcultures and the degree to which the president has attempted to remedy the cultural vacuum that persists.

A University for the Working Class

Triad University was established as an urban law school in the early 1900s. The founder's life exemplified the Horatio Alger rags-to-riches story: His goal was to provide equality of opportunity for working men who wanted to share in the American dream. During the next forty years the founder and his family, supplemented largely by part-time faculty, built the school by offering a complete law curriculum in the evening. They kept tuition exceptionally low. In 1934, the founder established an undergraduate college of liberal arts in response to a state law adopted under pressures from the professional law associations, requiring two years of undergraduate work prior to admission to the bar. Journalism and business programs were added in 1936 and 1937, respectively. Women were first admitted in 1934. The college became a university in 1937, incorporating all the programs. The founder thereby was able to ensure that low-income area students in the law school could satisfy the new state requirement and national norm for undergraduate education before entering the legal profession.

The founder initially resisted the new requirement, which he believed would restrict equality of opportunity for low-income working students. However, by the 1940s the founder had come to believe that the future of the university lay more with the College of Liberal Arts than the law school. The trustees, who gradually assumed powers once retained by the founder, strongly disagreed. Many were lawyers themselves, and they believed the law school should remain the heart of the university. A fierce battle ensued, won by the trustees. The president's forced resignation in 1948 remains a watershed event in the institution's history.

In a published and widely circulated history of the institution, a faculty member recounts the drastic actions taken by the trustees: "A veil was drawn over [the founder's] portrait. His name was expunged from the university's catalogues and, as much as possible, from its consciousness. As the founder's name faded from awareness, however, so did a sense of his achievements; [Triad University] forgot its roots."

Twenty years after the founder's forced resignation and two years after his death, students led a campaign to restore his presence to institutional memory. Only in the last few years has Triad sought to recover and integrate its heritage. The effort is made extremely difficult by the fragmentation that has developed in the intervening years.

Triad University is located in a transitional, residential neighborhood in the heart of a major city. Approximately half the students are undergraduates; most graduate students are in law or management. Enrollment is about 6,000, 55 percent attending full-time. Nearly half of the students are in the College of Management. The remainder are distributed equally between the colleges of liberal arts and law. The average age of students is twenty-six. Nearly half of all undergraduates enter as transfer students from area community colleges, over 80 percent work, and half receive financial aid. Half the student body is female and 6 percent are minorities. Students attend from 14 states and 48 countries, including 200 undergraduate international students. Most students from outside the university's metropolitan area attend the law school. Over 80 percent of total enrollments come from the city and its closest suburbs.

The university's urban location offers distinct advantages. Not only do many students work full-time nearby, but the proximity of government agencies and businesses enables many students to find internship experiences related to their course work. The central meeting point of the city's transit system is two blocks away, making Triad readily accessible for students from a number of city neighborhoods and suburbs.

The disadvantage of the location is that university buildings are dispersed over several blocks among nonuniversity buildings. There is neither a campus in the traditional sense nor a multipurpose student center, making spontaneous informal gatherings difficult. The university does not own a lawn mower, a vehicle, a parking lot, or a dormitory. It is considering leasing residential space and other measures to help attract undergraduate students from a wider geographic area.

The original mission of the college was to provide equal opportunity for low-income Americans, many of whom were immigrants, the first in their families to attend college. The initial vehicle for this mission was low-cost evening instruction for a profession in law. As the school expanded, the schedule, curriculum, and tuition rate emphasized easy access, flexible attendance patterns, and uniform standards for day and evening students. An observer of the university said:

> [Triad] defined its own goals, and it meets them. Its goals are different from the goals of other schools in the area. It's practical, not esoteric—very down to earth. [The original leaders] were pioneers, really. They psyched out the market long ago. [The 1970–80 president] was shrewd; he knew how to market schools. The school is convenient, cheaper than the other privates—it's the poor man's alternative. [Triad] educates "the public." The president sold it on the basis that it was an affordable, easily accessible ticket to a credential.

The university depends on tuition revenues for over 90 percent of its operating budget. Its endowment is $9 million, generated primarily through annual budget savings over the years. The administration puts the proceeds of the annual giving campaign in the plant fund, and it has set aside $1.5 million as an enrollment-stabilization fund.

Offsetting the high tuition dependency and relatively small endowment is the university's near-freedom from capital debt. The trustees have a reputation for fiscal conservatism. As one administrator put it: "Triad is known for strong financial and operational management. We have no debt, a relatively healthy endowment. Our return-on-investment record is clear. The stature of the treasurer in the community is very strong. We're known as the 'no frills college.'"

In some respects, the fiscal conservatism that characterizes Triad's management was once in keeping with the first-generation immigrant experience that the institution was designed to meet. Fiscal conservatism has since become a key mechanism by which the trustees attempt to keep costs down and tuition low. However, as the link with the founding mission has become more distant with the passing of time and prolonged banishment of the founder's memory, bottom-line management has asserted itself as a strategy in its own right. Operational concerns, not visionary leadership, have guided the institution through the last forty years. Although Triad has enjoyed the prudent if rather tight-fisted control of an active and concerned board of trustees, it has also lacked a forceful leader who could interpret the institution both to itself and to the community. As a result, the three chief components of the institution—the School of Law, the College of Management, and the College of Liberal Arts—have each pursued their own distinctive agendas. We soon discover that fragmentation is the board of trustees' chief legacy and cultural integration their most important future challenge.

Three Subcultures

The lack of an overall sense of mission is apparent in university publications. The current stated mission describes the location of the school, the intended clientele, and the intent to provide "quality education." It includes three additional paragraphs, each describing the programmatic thrust of one of the three colleges. A 1981 draft of the mission statement included a general description of university-wide educational content, but the final version in 1983 deleted it. This was Triad's first attempt to articulate a university-wide mission, but it appears that the three colleges are sufficiently different to make a general statement infeasible.

Daily operational differences provide an even more difficult obstacle. An administrator said:

> I'm worried about the linkages between law and the other two colleges. That's a nice big split in the mission. And a lot of people would like to talk about three missions—one for each college. I'm grateful for the good reputation of the law school, but law also provides a model for the other colleges' aspirations for autonomy.

Law schools are traditionally relatively autonomous entities and usually function at an institution's periphery. In Triad's case, however, the law school has consistently remained the central most influential factor in the life of the institution. This renders autonomy more of an accepted norm than would be the case at most other institutions.

Although rooted in the history of the university, the differences between the three schools are perpetuated by deans who wield considerable influence with the board of trustees. The role of president—potentially a unifying, interpretive force—is all but eclipsed by this arrangement. As a result, the president's attempts to introduce university-wide initiatives have not enjoyed the success they might have. Important strategic questions tend to be addressed not at the institutional level but rather by each of these three, largely autonomous subcultures. This contributes to a certain schizophrenia both within the institution and in its relations with the community.

THE LAW SCHOOL

Among the three colleges, the law school's preeminence remains unquestioned. It has consistently been the historical focus of Triad and a key factor in its successful operation. Traditionally, the law school most clearly exemplified the original mission of Triad, which focused on a working-class clientele, the teaching function, and professional training for those historically denied access. This mission lingers on in Triad's institutional memory and its rhetoric is still invoked. A trustee reported, "There's a strong feeling on the board to reach people who wouldn't otherwise go to college."

In the past decade, however, the law school has successfully raised its standard of admission and instruction, earning a regional and even national reputation. Tuition in the law school has risen faster than in undergraduate programs, and so has its capacity to provide financial aid. Its primary clientele is no longer lower-class city residents. Day students come from all over the country; evening students include many who are earning their second professional degree. Thus, the school has broadened its role to include new and different constituents.

However, not unlike the first-generation immigrant it was originally designed to serve, the law school may now be distancing itself from its roots as it makes a successful mark on the world. In this respect, the law school lies both at the heart of the institution and at its periphery. Concerned about claims that the changes are contrary to Triad's historic mission, the law dean stated: "You don't admit people of inferior academic quality and argue that that's in tune with the past mission. It was discrimination, not good quality, that we were against. We still give people who have to work a chance to study, especially in the evening division."

The law school has been able to respond to changes in its environment in part because it has enjoyed forceful leadership from its deans and the close cooperation of the trustees. More importantly, it has addressed strategic questions that have not been adequately posed, let alone answered, on an institutional basis. A distinct cultural identity has developed, yet it differs from the ethos that characterizes the College of Management and the College of Liberal Arts.

COLLEGE OF MANAGEMENT

The cultural identity of the College of Management has been formed in many respects out of a desire to emulate—and compensate for—the preeminence of the law school. Founded in 1937 as Triad's "newest professional department," the management program was designed to provide another door of opportunity to the university's working clientele. For many years it operated under the umbrella of the College of Arts and Sciences. The perception that it remained a stepchild within the university prompted its supporters to upgrade the program in the mid-1960s. This effort led to the creation of the College of Management as a separate entity. Its autonomy has grown ever since, as have its enrollments. By 1980 the college had become Triad's largest academic unit in terms of number of students, though by no means had it eclipsed the law school in reputation and influence.

In the last several years the management school again has engaged in an effort to upgrade its programs. It is now seeking professional accreditation to compete more successfully with prestigious management schools in its immediate area. This initiative represents an effort to bring the management school into the academic mainstream. As a result, the college seems to be headed toward both a more affluent and more geographically diverse clientele, particularly in its graduate programs. Its faculty, in turn, is assuming more of a research and theoretical orientation in response to accreditation requirements. In these respects, the management school is becoming more like the law school and less like the arts and sciences. Like the law school many years ago, the management school sees accreditation as an important legitimizing factor as it competes in a tight, rapidly changing market. Some observers believe, however, that unfortunate trade-offs accompany this initiative. The effort to meet accreditation requirements can inhibit the development of specialized programs that would attract more students, particularly from the immediate area.

As a distinct subculture within the university, the management school is now grappling with important strategic questions. What is its place in the university and in the environment? To what extent can it adjust its traditional mission when seeking out new clientele?

It is not yet clear whether the course pursued by the management school will provide workable solutions to these questions.

COLLEGE OF LIBERAL ARTS AND SCIENCES

Established in 1934, the liberal-arts college was designed to serve wage-earning men and women for whom full-time college attendance was impossible. As professional law associations increasingly urged state legislatures to require two years of college for admission to the bar, Triad's founder came to believe that an undergraduate program was vital to the university's future. Not only would it guarantee continued professional access to the working man, it also would provide necessary organizational and financial support for the law school. Both spiritually and practically, the law school has been the parent organization for the liberal-arts college throughout its history. The dominance of law-school alumni on the board of trustees often relegated the liberal-arts college to second-class status within the university. The college experienced considerable growth in the 1950s and 1960s, and improved the quality of its faculty in the 1970s. However, this was due more to general economic and educational conditions than to any coherent initiative on the part of the university.

Today, the college continues to serve primarily lower- and middle-income students. The lack of university-level strategic planning before 1980 and its slow development since then have made it increasingly difficult for the college to maintain its traditional clientele or to tap new potential markets. IPS results indicate that Triad tends to develop current programs but not add programs in new areas. Enrollment trends in the liberal-arts college are toward more full-time study and daytime classes. Recent figures indicate that 56 percent of all Triad students attend full-time, while 75 percent of liberal-arts students do so. In the absence of data on potential markets for continuing education, the college of liberal arts has not offered new evening courses to offset declines in its evening enrollments. A university task force recently discovered that numerous student services were not available in the evening. Broad issues such as student recruitment, retention, tuition, financial aid, housing, and student services now occupy the attention of the college's administrators.

As with the law and management schools, the college of liberal arts has developed into a distinct cultural entity within the university. Unlike the other two schools, this identity is not governed by a disciplinary focus. Because of its broad educational and operational charge, the undergraduate college discovers its coherence more through commonly perceived needs and grievances than through commonly shared aspirations and goals. While the College of Liberal Arts and Sciences embodies Triad's traditional mission more than its other schools do, operational concerns inhibit the college from implementing this mission in an effective, long-range manner. Like the other two subcultures, the liberal-arts college now recognizes that it must address important strategic questions. A committee has been formed to develop a strategic plan. New initiatives, however, have yet to alter long-held perceptions that the college of liberal arts, like the university at large, remains uncertain of its bearings.

CULTURES IN ISOLATION

The presence of subcultures within an organization is a natural occurrence. Triad, however, has a much stronger tradition of relatively autonomous schools than do most other institutions. Recent attempts to develop a shared culture must necessarily confront long-standing tendencies. Many factors contribute to what has been a lack of cohesion. Development efforts direct considerable attention to law alumni, further strengthening their already powerful influence. Law graduates make up 40 percent of all alumni, yet give 80 percent of contributed funds. However, they are quite unlike undergraduate students at the university. They come from a much wider geographic area, more well-to-do families, and higher ability levels. Moreover, the self-contained curriculum they pursue allows little contact with the rest of the university community. Although Triad's liberal-arts college once supplied three times as many Triad law students as any other undergraduate college, the university's undergraduates now face much stiffer competition to gain admission to the law school. The law school typically brings in more revenues than it spends, while the liberal-arts college does not. With three hundred fifty full- and part-time faculty on a campus providing scant opportunity for informal gatherings, faculty tend to know few others outside their own college.

In the absence of shared values and concerns, self-interests tend to guide the actions of the three colleges when dealing with each other. Those whose self-interests are not jeopardized

by declining enrollments are unlikely to defend the less popular areas on academic grounds. For example, a strong statement
by the liberal-arts dean protesting any further encroachment on
the liberal arts went unsupported by the dean of the management school, even though his students take 40 percent of their
course work in the college of liberal arts. Only the liberal-arts
dean strongly objected to another top administrator's proposal to
leave vacancies unfilled that constituted nearly half of the English department faculty. Although the faculty is now developing
strong, university-wide educational policies, skirmishes to defend
one's own turf still dominate day-to-day activities.

Trustees

At Triad shared values and goals tend to be eclipsed by a governance culture dominated by the board of trustees. The board has
twenty-three members, about half of whom are lawyers and Triad
alumni. Relatively few are key business leaders or come from families of great wealth. The bylaws now provide for the election of
one trustee from alumni of each of the three colleges, which has
diluted somewhat the dominance of lawyers on the board. Nevertheless, nearly half of the trustees are graduates of Triad's law
school, nearly half have served for more than a decade, and many
are members of the same ethnic group.

The trustees are known for their attention to detail and their
fiscal conservatism. The university has virtually never taken on
debt, in part because it would require future students to pay for
current projects. The trustees are unwilling to assume that the
university will have enough students to repay debts. When the
state subsidized very low interest rates for computer acquisition
in 1984, the trustees reluctantly accepted $1.2 million, but only
on the condition that it be repaid early. When they bought a
major building, they borrowed from endowment at 10 percent
for ten years. The trustees seem to measure success in terms of
the bottom line and appear unwilling to make changes or take
initiatives that could improve long-term effectiveness if short-term
efficiency might be affected adversely.

The trustees have long taken a strong interest in operational
issues. Into the 1960s a trustee, acting as chief fiscal officer, went
so far as to require his signature on every book order. He allegedly
censored some orders on the basis of the books' content. The

trustees still attend closely to detail, as in reviewing the vitae of faculty members applying for a leave of absence. As one faculty member explained:

> The trustees have a running distrust of presidential power. They want to be in charge—have wanted to ever since 1948, when they forced out the first president. He was a genuine CEO; he called the shots. But then they completely reconstructed the role to prevent another one like that. They want him dependent on them. Well, they filled it with their own cronies right up until 1980. And even so, they gave them one-year contracts with a review every June.

One administrator further described the effects of trustee involvement in daily operations:

> In the early 1960s, when I came here, all the faculty had desks in one big classroom—and they shared one telephone. The whole university consisted of one old building. That was when we had a trustee as treasurer. In 1966, when the president died, three people turned down the job because they didn't want to be president of an institution where the trustees were so involved. Finally, they offered the job to one of the trustees, and he took it. He held the position three or four years, then resigned for health reasons. The trustees didn't conduct another search. A businessman from the board became president, and he stayed for ten years. He was very well liked, and ultimately retired at sixty-five. This time the trustees conducted a national search, following all the guidelines, and they ended up hiring [Doug].

Although intimately involved in daily operations, the trustees preferred for many years to keep a discretely low profile in the community for the institution, the administration, and the trustees themselves. Moreover, the lack of internal cultural coherence tended to result in a diffuse public identity dominated by the law school. In the last several years efforts have been undertaken to improve Triad's visibility in the community. The university now utilizes the same graphic design for all signs posted in and on buildings, public relations activities have improved, and better coordination and a more aggressive posture have enhanced student recruiting.

The trustees are very close to one another, and some devote a great deal of time to Triad. As with many such groups, they work informally. A faculty member commented:

> At the heart of everything is a small group of people who have a lot in common and who talk mainly to each other. They will listen to an outsider, but only if they know and respect you. So you find someone individually and talk to them. They'll feed good ideas into the system for you.

According to one trustee, the board works hard because "we're achievers, we want to be involved, have an impact. Here, what we say and do has a very direct effect on the university." The trustee added, "For many years, there was a bias against us in the city. So, people who got their degrees here, including most of the trustees over the years, were determined to make it last and succeed."

Commenting on the reason why the board retains control, a trustee commented, "It works! The school has grown, its reputation has grown, alumni are pleased, students do well when they leave here. It works." Indeed, if one defines success in operational terms, few can argue with this trustee's assessment. However, while bottom-line management can help ensure efficiency, it does not necessarily guarantee effectiveness. Because the trustees cannot truly fulfill the interpretive role of a president and have been hesitant to take forward-looking strategic initiatives, success remains fickle—a matter of enrollments, job markets, and end-of-year financial reports. Without roots in an organizational culture, this kind of success is easily influenced by a variety of factors and could change for the worse in a relatively short period of time.

Administration

Regarding the structure of Triad University, one administrator commented, "We'd never do it this way on purpose." A colleague added, "When we have the right people in the right places and no crises, it works okay." The president of Triad heads a loose federation of colleges whose strong deans and isolated faculty members see little advantage in greater coordination. The university has no chief academic officer. Recent initiatives to develop greater overall coherence within the university are a notable departure from the past. Their success remains uncertain in an administrative environment that has long permitted decentralized control.

THE PRESIDENT

Caught between powerful deans and control-oriented trustees, Triad presidents play unusual roles. Until 1980, the presidents were insiders, often trustees, with known convictions and habits of relating to other key players. The current president, named in 1980, is not. One respondent sympathized:

[Doug] is in a bad situation. He's not "of the institution." He's not even an insider—wrong ethnic heritage, wrong geographic roots. He still has to prove he's one of them, to trustees, alumni, everyone. He can't establish control. It's not even clear that he wants to establish control. Maybe he just wants to show that an outsider can last here.

Old-timers tended to compare Doug with his predecessor, Fred. Fred was seen as a father figure who had keen but low-key political savvy. Said a faculty member:

[Fred] was immensely effective with the trustees. He made it appear that what he wanted wasn't really his will, because he worked behind the scenes, networking. He showed them how it was in their interest, rather than saying, "Do this because I believe it's the right thing to do." [Fred] had been a trustee for years before he became president. He was their equal and he acted like one—not first among equals. Just the one who happened to sit in the president's chair. [Doug], on the other hand, is not a crony. He doesn't play this system very well. He says, "Do this because it should be done." He's very bad getting the faculty to do things with that style, and it's totally alien to the trustees. He's strong-minded, he's stubborn, and he thinks he's right most of the time. What's worse is he shows it.

An administrator, however, saw the president's orientation rather differently. "[Doug] was trained by the book. He asked why people were doing things. They'd never been questioned before, and some of them resented it."

Under the circumstances, some wonder why the board selected Doug as president. According to a trustee:

In 1980 we were looking for a president who cared about the institution, who wanted to learn about it if he was new here. Someone who would preserve what we are and who we service. Someone who was familiar with educational institutions, looks at changes and trends in the field. And someone who had a background with urban institutions, who understood what it meant to be urban and have funding limitations. [Doug] had all that.

Many of the difficulties experienced by the current president have to do with the extent to which the trustees identify themselves not only with but as the institution. Soon after Doug's arrival, the trustees invited him to review the structure of the board. Among his proposed alternatives was that an executive committee be formed to do much of the work, but trustees were quick to reject the idea. A faculty member remarked:

The move would have helped take the institution out of the 1950s and 1960s, where in many ways it has been stuck. But that wouldn't do at all. The trustees don't give power to anybody—even each other. Some of the problem [between the board and the president] is due to personality differences, but most of it is due to history.

Personality conflicts notwithstanding, most segments of the university have a high regard for the president's persistence, attention to detail, and hard work. He has made some progress toward coordinating institutional functions by reactivating a long-range planning committee, a broadly representative body that meets bimonthly. He also holds weekly administrative council meetings with the deans and his executive staff. Previously unheard of at Triad, these meetings have proven useful in spreading information and in instilling some sense of unity. Unlike his predecessors, the president develops an annual report for presentation to the faculty and trustees, convenes an annual all-faculty meeting, and has encouraged the development of documents that attempt to provide, for the first time, a unified perspective on the university that covers all those academic units.

Noting that the president is very conscious of long-range planning and sharing information, an administrator commented, "He got us thinking ahead more." Another faculty member agreed, "[Doug] seems to have a plan. He's trying to involve us, but you see—we had plans, too. And we were disappointed that he didn't come in to implement ours. But he hasn't ignored ours. He's merging them with his as he goes along." He added,

> [Doug] has the experience to guide us to our proper place as an academic institution. His mind is always on track, always probing. It's a credit to him that we are where we are, in spite of the old guard. He brought us something we weren't looking for . . . because we didn't know we needed it.

In most institutions, planning and sharing information are vital functions which, when performed by the president, tend to indicate strong and effective leadership. In the case of Triad, however, the trustees have fostered a tradition that severely limits presidential decision-making power and organizational influence. As a result, recent initiatives have met with some resistance. In spite of moderate progress, the possibility remains that these initiatives can become little more than "treadmill" exercises that have little bearing on the present and future condition of the university. Commenting on this situation, a faculty member remarked:

> Many of us want the president to have more authority vis-a-vis the trustees. But they show no sign of falling in line with that. . . . What are the costs to the university? I guess all I can say is, the opportunities we've lost. We never had a different situation, so it's hard to imagine what those opportunities might have been. I'm just not sure.

DEANS

The autonomy of the deans and their respective colleges presents a major challenge to the president's persistence and a considerable obstacle to the university's organizational effectiveness. Although the deans report to the president, they also work closely with a committee of the board—one for each college. One dean commented, "I deal with my committee of the board much more than with the president. I keep him informed, of course, and certainly try to obtain his support, but I wouldn't hesitate to present an item to the board if the president disagreed with me about it."

Deans are seen as managers of internal politics, not leaders, and central administration is almost invisible to the faculty. The deans were described as "barons with fiefdoms" and as "minipresidents." The interests of the university as a whole depend largely on the extent to which college-level actions benefit the university. For important, university-level decisions, swift action often depends on agreement between the deans and the president. When consensus is lacking, the president brings people together to talk about the issue on the chance that eventually something might happen. Ideas or issues are not pushed to closure if agreement is not forthcoming.

The university has no policy-approval process that spans all institutional segments. Although some committees have broad representation, there is no university faculty council. The university has no integrated admissions philosophy; no policy that relates financial aid to mission, tuition price, and recruiting; no rationale for faculty promotion, tenure, and salary decisions; and so on. Each college may or may not have elements of such policies and its actions may or may not be consistent with the other two colleges. When proposed changes require cooperation among the colleges, the process can take years.

MIDDLE MANAGEMENT

Problems at the level of middle management further hamper decision-making. According to one faculty member, "Our whole midmanagement is in disarray." People described some midlevel managers as inept, untrained, entrenched, recalcitrant, and uncoordinated. Internal promotions and reassignments have produced some incumbents who know the university far better than they know how to perform their current tasks.

Others see the problems as structural. Midlevel managers are, they say, too few, too overburdened, too poorly organized, underpaid, and underappreciated. The structure of the university has tended to produce redundancies and gaps in job responsibilities, and it has precluded the efficient flow of information and communication among middle and top administrators. Some reforms are underway, but they are slow in taking root.

In many respects, the problems at the level of middle management are symptoms of broader concerns. Entrenched and uncoordinated, faculty, staff, and administration can often find it difficult to work together. The slow development of any shared cultural identity may only accentuate these divisions.

Managing Change

By most accounts Triad is a very successful institution. Although it faces stiff competition from other colleges and universities in the area, it has managed to take advantage of generally favorable market conditions. Its success, however, has tended to mask the absence of a strong, broadly shared culture. Although some attempts are underway to develop cultural and operational coherence, impending changes in the environment could challenge the institution's ability to cope.

Potentially ominous clouds on the horizon include demographic change that is likely to hit Triad rather hard. Moreover, the current ethnic mix in the institution reflects a long-standing inability to adapt to a new environment or to take advantage of new opportunities. Current recruitment and retention problems reflect this situation and serve as warning signals that troubled times may lie ahead. Although some nominal progress is being made, strong, diverse subcultures can promote at times an organizational gridlock that makes it difficult for the university to deal with changes in its environment or even to institute internal reform. On the other hand, strong subcultures may enable each college to adapt to its own environment. The result could be a collection of successful colleges under one umbrella. However, considerable risk is involved. This course could further fragment the institution and dilute its overall institutional image.

Highly dependent on tuition revenues, Triad considers its environment largely in terms of the student market. The undergraduate market consists primarily of Catholic residents of the city and nearby suburbs, but it is broader for the school of management and broader still for the law school. The university's minority population, at 6 percent, is far less than the city's proportion of minorities, but Triad remains ambivalent about actively recruiting them. Half of the university's new students transfer from other colleges. With so many geographic, economic, and ethnic variations in its actual and potential clientele, Triad's market for students is difficult to define. Given its dependence on students, one would expect Triad to pay close attention not only to recruiting but also to the satisfaction of those enrolled. Some comments indicated that the university does so; many indicated that administrators have neither analyzed nor assertively managed student recruitment and retention.

Recent initiatives are attempting to remedy these problems; nevertheless, they tend to remain discrete and could benefit from broader, university-wide support. As our study ended, a new position, dean of enrollment management, was filled with a highly respected professional in the field. A heightened awareness of equal opportunity is manifest in the appointment of a new director of minority affairs, who also serves as a presidential assistant. Likewise, a new committee now considers cultural diversity in the curriculum. Relatively low tuition and free tuition for senior citizens also help improve access. In addition, federal Title III funds have established a sophisticated, highly regarded learning resource center to assist underprepared students and have also supported other student-centered programs. The administration has been working diligently with zoning authorities and neighborhood groups to clear the way for improvements to the student center.

As one might expect given Triad's administrative and academic structure, coordination of these and other activities remains difficult. Systems for supporting students could be improved so that the university presents a consistent, responsive, warm demeanor to them. For example, until recently the functions of admissions, financial aid, and registrar were only loosely coordinated and the individuals involved reported to diverse senior officers. Likewise, many on campus have targeted academic advising for major improvements. Because the university has no dormitories of its own, housing remains a topic of concern. University assistance in locating housing in the city comes from scattered, uncoordinated corners, sometimes as an unstated fragment of someone's job description. Administrators expect that improved referral services will alleviate the problem.

Although positive, these initiatives may not represent change sufficient to the widespread transformations that many foresee in the institution's environment. Projections show that the state will be hard hit by a 40-percent decline in the number of high-school students by 1992. The eight local public high schools that provide Triad the greatest number of graduates anticipate a 29-percent decline from 1983 to 1988. In one respect Triad is somewhat insulated from these changes by the fact that over 80 percent of its students are Catholic. Parochial feeder schools provide nearly 40 percent of Triad's freshmen, and they expect far less decline than the public schools. This same insulation from the general community, however, limits Triad's capacity to respond to environmental change and to take advantage of new opportunities and student markets on both college and institutional levels.

Within commuting distance of Triad, the city is 25–30 percent black, with Asian and Hispanic residents growing in number. In 1982, 55 percent of the city's public high-school graduates were black and Hispanic. Triad has admitted black students throughout its history. The first recorded black law student received his degree in 1915. Although enrollment of minorities has never been higher than it is today, the current 6-percent rate is still well below what it might be, considering the university's location and potential student market. A 1982 accrediting team commented on apparent widespread racism among students. A university task force subsequently repudiated the charge but described official behavior as "benign neglect"—the same phrase chosen by a 1975 task force on the status of women. A faculty member commented, "We don't in any sense make minorities feel welcome. We have more blacks here from foreign countries than from the United States."

Despite demographic changes in the city, Triad has continued to serve the white ethnic groups that lived in its locale when the law school opened. On that dimension, the student body has changed very little. An administrator said:

> I want to see us stay with the historic mission. We want minorities, we want first-generation college kids. We could be a real [city] school. Right now, we're too lily white, too neighborhoodish, too clannish. We're shortsighted not to take action to change the university's image as a white immigrant bastion that occasionally allows minorities in. It would be easier if this were Ole Miss in 1962 in that the racism there was so obvious. Here, the people are really nice, and I assume they don't realize that the effect of their inaction is to keep minorities out.

Attempts to address these issues are hindered by what many respondents perceived to be ineffective, reactive decision-making. This renders environmental change more ominous than it might be at another institution. Decision-making in each college and at the university level differs in the particulars but tends in all contexts to baffle faculty and others. In one college, faculty have encountered unwritten rules of unknown origin with unspecified consequences. Most respondents were not sure how decisions get made. Speaking of a university procedural decision, one dean remarked, "It's not quite clear who could say 'Let's do it' and have it happen." Decision-making is seen as prompted by crisis situations. Sometimes, as in the case of minority affairs and enrollment management, the crisis culminates in the creation of a new administrative position to oversee the troublesome area.

Efforts by the current president to institute some measure of reform are hindered by several factors, among them the dominance of the trustees and the autonomy of the deans. These factors are manifestations of the history and evolution of the university; they are intrinsic to it and are unlikely to yield to the force of personalities or pressures that might be applied for short-term major changes. The conservative shadow cast by the trustees forestalls risky or innovative ventures by administrators and reinforces the primacy of the law school. Most major initiatives presented to the trustees have been rejected, including proposals to move the university to the suburbs, invest in land in the area, and become a residential institution.

The president encourages strategic planning, something unheard of at Triad only several years ago. A dean remarked: "The last president was a guy who focused on 'learning to cope with the downward slope.' Each dean had a disaster plan. The whole concept was that our enrollment numbers were totally out of our control. Not this administration—we're planning for alternate futures."

Some scenarios rightfully envision a bright future: The university has virtually no debt, its expenditures are firmly controlled, facilities management is highly developed, and the current president places high priority on long-range planning. Preparing a comprehensive strategy, not to mention implementing it, is undercut by what has long been Triad's fragmented culture. Lacking effective central authority for many strategic concerns, the administration devotes attention primarily to collecting information and creating opportunities for improved communication. Both functions are relatively new to Triad and potentially quite important. They could set the stage for more effective decision-making and greater cultural coherence. At present, however, obstacles make progress difficult. More often than not, new members of the university are socialized to existing norms by running into political forces that teach them what they cannot do. Any sense of community is localized to departments or colleges.

With the president hindered by severe structural and cultural constraints, interpretive leadership remains difficult at best. Many respondents support the president's attempts to develop a shared culture, but they also note that new initiatives are sometimes surrogates rather than effective tools for real change. One faculty member said:

> What bothers me and a lot of others about [Doug's] style is his emphasis on appearance over substance. As long as it looks good, there's no attention to making it be good. Like his interest in spiffing up the physical plant—that's a metaphor for a lot of his priorities. I guess that's a plus, but significant resources are diverted away from things that would improve the experiences of our students.

Whether recent initiatives will be successful or ineffectual remains unclear. Much depends on the support that the president can garner and on the willingness of the trustees to give the university's administration a freer hand. Time is also crucial; although culture can be fostered, its growth cannot be forced. Given Triad's history, it is doubtful whether the trustees and deans will accommodate significant change and encourage presidential leadership.

Needed: A Vision of Unity

At its founding, Triad was animated by a distinctive mission: to provide upward mobility and educational access to working-class students in its area. Over the decades, Triad has evolved as an institution, but its ability to articulate and implement its mission in a changing environment has diminished. Actions, policies, and procedures have instead come to reflect the trustees' conservatism and the law school's power. Strong subcultures have formed within the institution, contributing to a contentious political atmosphere and hindering the development of common values and goals. The potentially unifying and interpretive role of the president is hindered severely by these structural and cultural constraints. Recent attempts to develop cultural and operational coherence at the university level have enjoyed limited success while encountering many obstacles.

This is not to say that Triad is qualitatively lacking. The faculty are reasonably well paid, dedicated, good teachers. The reputation of the university for educational quality and fiscal responsibility is well founded. Its location and physical facilities are strong assets. But much of what Triad does is uncoordinated and inconsistent, and administrative structures provide few vehicles for remedying the university's problems in any orderly fashion.

A coherent, consensual new view of what Triad is trying to accomplish has not come with modifications to the original mission. The mission statement adopted in 1983, with its three independent pieces, one for each college, is but a symptom of divisions that have long fragmented the university. Triad's several subcultures are widely perceived as moving at different speeds and even in inconsistent directions. Some favor building and diversifying the student body by recruiting from a wider geographic area, others by attracting local minorities. There are few if any university-wide priorities on which to base actions to improve the institution. Likewise, there is little basis for rationally adjudicating internal political struggles.

Because Triad operates in a tentative, short-term fashion, its success also cannot be otherwise. The trustees' conservatism reflects a fundamental, pessimistic insecurity. They have raised funds to a minimal degree and only for capital projects. They scrimp and save in the expectation that enrollments will decline. They maintain almost a one-to-one correspondence between tuition revenues and total expenditures, a procedure that assumes no institutional momentum from one year to the next and reflects a businesslike, profit-and-loss mentality. Consequently, Triad enjoys a good physical facility, a relatively strong financial position, and a track record of adapting to fluctuating resources in spite of tenure, specialization, and other structural barriers to adaptation in higher education. The cost, however, has tended to be insularity. Triad has adapted to resource levels but not necessarily to environmental opportunities.

With the trustees as the dominant force in decision-making and the fragmentation of the three colleges, Triad has little incentive or capacity to reexamine and revitalize its mission. Most unsettling, perhaps, is not the thought that Triad cannot manage a changing environment in a coherent fashion. Rather, it is the possibility that it has lost the capacity to manage or institute thoughtful, institutional change internally. Triad may lack not only a coherent culture but perhaps also the capacity and will to create or reconstruct one. The president's recent attempts at reform notwithstanding, strong voices extolling inconsistent scenarios for the future still prevail.

NINE

R&D University

Many top administrators inherit long-standing institutional traditions and norms when they enter their positions. These cultural factors can either aid or thwart their efforts to move a college or university in a particular direction. Yet even when an institution has a long history, it is not uncommon for both leaders and constituents to feel unsure of its identity and mission. Facing such difficulties, many administrators may nourish the secret hope for a fresh start, a clean institutional slate. Given the often invisible yet tenacious web of organizational culture, the thought of entering a situation unencumbered by established norms can become an exceedingly inviting prospect. This freedom is not always an asset. At R&D University we discover the pervasive influence and support that an established culture can provide by noting the effects of a relative absence of culture on this campus.

Founded only fifteen years ago as a public institution, R&D lacks many of the cultural foundations found on other campuses. Because organizational cultures develop and change slowly, this relatively new institution faces special challenges. Through well-developed strategic planning, R&D has sought to provide direction and purpose to its activities. This form of cultural engineering has its drawbacks, however. Instrumental ties may hold the university together but not its people; it may provide constituents with a rational understanding of its actions but not a shared, intuitive sense of its identity.

The relative absence of a common culture influences all aspects of organizational life at R&D, including various dimensions of leadership, decision-making, and strategy. Administrators and faculty members often describe the institution in terms of its differences from others but seem to have difficulty in articulating a mission in their own terms. Rhetoric about world-class quality abounds, but in the face of institutional realities, it tends to promote as much cynicism as excitement. Thus, the slow development of organizational and cultural processes and lack of consensus about the institution's identity may inhibit the university from meeting its high goals.

Because R&D University is located in a growing region of the country that continues to attract many high-technology companies, it enjoys a very favorable environment. Indeed, the institution's performance, narrowly defined, is extremely good. Because R&D is in a period of sustained growth, and will remain so for the foreseeable future, a sense exists that the university cannot do anything wrong. The real test of the institution—and its nascent culture—will come when growth slows or stops and when real strategic choices must be made. The 1960s have taught us that growth itself can present a number of problems. R&D's long-term success will depend as much, if not more, on its willingness to nurture an organizational culture as it will on factors in its external environment.

The Birth of a Research University

Although now a public institution, R&D University traces its roots to private enterprise. Three men who led a major high-technology firm founded a scientific research center in 1961. They attracted excellent scientists from all over the world—a talent influx they believed was vital to the continued growth of business in the region. However, by 1969 the center needed a broader base of financial support. Center authorities gave the organization to the state that same year as the core of a new unit in the state university system, R&D University. It would offer graduate degrees for its first six years and then extend its curriculum to include the last two years of undergraduate education.

During the early 1970s, the university completed a major construction program, "invented" an academic structure, and hired about 130 faculty members. In 1974, R&D had 700 graduate students. It doubled to 1,400 graduate and undergraduate students in 1975 and nearly quadrupled to 5,200 in 1976. The student population grew steadily through 1983, when it reached its current total of about 7,500 students. In full-time equivalent students, enrollment is 4,200. About half the students are working adults who attend part-time, and half the student credit hours are taken from 6 to 10 P.M. The average age of undergraduates is twenty-nine, of graduates thirty-one. About 40 percent of the students are at the graduate level, and many special students are taking classes but not working for a degree.

The university is located in the rapidly growing suburbs of a major city. It has no residence halls or athletic program. Most of the students live in the upper-middle-class area around the university. As the founders foresaw, the city has become a national center for high-technology firms. Their employees are a natural clientele for R&D because they recognize the value of higher education for both personal and professional development. These factors correctly imply that although R&D is considered an urban university, it has few students who are low-income, minority, or poorly educated.

The original research center staff became the core faculty for what is now the college of science and mathematics. By 1975, additional colleges included business, social science, arts and humanities, human development, and general studies (individualized degree programs). Business now enrolls approximately half the undergraduate students. The university offers 30 baccalaureate degrees, 20 master's degrees, and 12 doctoral degrees. The configuration has changed only marginally since 1975. Except in science and math, the colleges are not organized in disciplinary departments but function instead as single units. The university also includes a major Center for Communication Disorders (CCD). The center is a well-endowed clinical, research, and teaching facility located fifteen miles from the university campus in the downtown area, near major medical facilities. The CCD was autonomous until it was given to the university in 1975.

Collectively, a number of factors constitute valuable assets for R&D. Prospective students enter the area as many information-based and professional firms relocate or expand their offices. The firms themselves take an active interest in R&D as a means of attracting top employees, developing current employees, and sharing in research. The faculty are of high quality, built around a core of top scientists. The university attracted new faculty who valued the opportunity to establish new programs and to emphasize graduate-level work as well as R&D's prestigious level and type of education. Yet of those hired in 1974, only one-third remain at R&D. About 50 percent of those who apply for tenure receive it.

The state tuition rate is exceptionally low, and the university's market for students consists of education-oriented people who can easily afford it. R&D attracts about half of its undergraduate transfer students from area community colleges. Many of these students face academic adjustment problems when they enter R&D's sophisticated academic environment. Nevertheless, R&D attracts about half of the city's qualified community college graduates. The amount and nature of growth in the area also indicates a continuing supply of graduate and special students.

The university began with research facilities and 325 acres of land from the research center. Five hundred additional acres donated in 1975 constituted an endowment for the university. Currently, the university owns 1,100 acres, 400 of which constitute the campus itself. The university sold 139 acres in 1981 for $14 million. The balance has an estimated current value of $50–$70 million. The university's senior vice president oversees the development of the area by firms carefully selected for their potential relationships with R&D. The large land endowment promises to provide both intellectual and financial capital. Endowment funds from land sales could reach $100–$300 million within twenty to thirty years.

However, the university also operates under serious constraints. Much of its well-being depends upon satisfying area employers that its educational programs are relevant to their interests and that its leadership is sound. Furthermore, its status as a public university constrains R&D. Although state regents are said to remain quite flexible regarding how their policies are implemented, the state coordinating board and the legislature exercise tighter controls. The coordinating board must approve course inventories, degree plans, and plans for major capital development. The board's staff is extremely sensitive to the prospect of possible duplication of programs. Their sensitivity is reinforced in the case of R&D by the influences of older, powerful, public and private universities in R&D's metropolitan area. These institutions do not welcome competition from R&D for students or support.

The state's funding formula also helps shape the institution. The formula provides a special allowance for the added costs of offering only upper division and graduate courses. If R&D were to extend its curriculum to freshmen and sophomores, it would have to enroll two thousand such students to offset the special allowance it now receives for not teaching courses at that level. Nevertheless, some believe that R&D should extend to all four undergraduate years. The current arrangement is awkward, given the overall decline in transfers from community colleges and the unlikely prospect of attracting transfer students from other four-year schools. Entering undergraduates, who must enroll as juniors, may be deficient in some ways that the high-level course offerings cannot easily remedy. And although the R&D curriculum requires and encourages students to take courses outside their major, the lack of introductory courses in some fields constrains their choices. However, the negative incentive of the funding formula, the opposition of other four-year schools nearby, and the current emphasis on winning approval for a new engineering school have led the administration and most faculty to consider the freshman-sophomore question as a moot issue.

In one sense, R&D University seems guaranteed success by advantages and constraints over which it has little or no control. It is located in one of the fastest-growing metropolitan areas in the country, and projections estimate that its potential student market will grow by a factor of five in the next fifteen years. The university's key constituency, high-technology business, is also growing rapidly, and its leaders take an active interest in R&D's welfare and programs. Any tendency that might encourage R&D to grow too fast for its long-term stability is held in check by stringent controls from the state coordinating board and legislature.

This could lead one to argue that R&D's welfare is far more dependent on its environment than on anything management could do to affect it. Yet individuals on campus expressed the view that while R&D was likely to grow no matter what management did, management would determine how much it grew and its qualitative condition. One pointed out that R&D's success required maintaining a very delicate balance among many important constituencies. As he put it, management must deal with "a large number of benevolent forces moving in similar directions at different speeds."

Mission

As a research center, R&D's precursor sought to perform basic and applied research that would support the development of high-technology industry by attracting top scientists to the region. As a university, R&D produced a 1971 document stating its three major goals as

1. disciplinary integrity within an interdisciplinary context

2. strong relationships between a student's curriculum and the entire world of work and ideas

3. reduction of the scale of the undergraduate program, so that personalization occurs in a process which has elsewhere undergone severe depersonalization

R&D was to be "an institution of the first class," and it was to meet and work through local problems, rather than bypass them. From 1969 through 1975, the mission expanded to include the training of new researchers in an expanding number of fields. To this day, however, an administrator reported that "advanced scientific research is what this place is about—the roots for its sense of itself." A top administrator explained how he and others conceptualized the growth of R&D:

> The principal commodity in the academic marketplace is prestige. We were new, so we were at the bottom of the heap, and the academic market for doctoral graduates was shrinking. The only way to advance was to be different. There was no future in doing what everybody else was doing. So we started by knowing what we didn't want to do. We decided to emphasize equipping doctoral students for nonacademic as well as academic employment. We created programs in unorthodox ways to suit that purpose, to give our graduates occupational choices. And we're succeeding at it.

With the introduction of undergraduate students in 1975, albeit only at the upper-division level, the mission changed in subtle but important ways. The target audience shifted somewhat from businesses and industries in the area to the potential students themselves, many of whom happened to be employees or spouses of employees of the firms. Those students wanted more training in diverse fields and had more diverse prior education than their earlier peers. Moreover, the university began to seem less like "the new think tank" and more like a typical university. Issues arose that challenged the decisions not to admit lower-division students, not to offer lower-division coursework, and to focus attention primarily on scientific and technical fields.

When the current president took office in 1982, he immediately established a bottom-up process to prepare a six-year strategic plan for the university. One consequence of this strategic-planning process was to clarify the university's mission. The mission statement in the strategic plan emphasizes continuation of a relatively narrow program focus and defines the possible extension to the lower-division level as a "nonissue." The extension would create a great deal of controversy, and the administration has chosen instead to focus its energies on establishing an engineering school.

Several respondents stated that the university's mission is now "clear, but not consensual." Results of the IPS survey support the statement. The average response of faculty and administrators to a question about mission agreement was the lowest of the cases in this study. Administrators ranked mission agreement much higher than faculty did. Proponents of a full, four-year program and other moves that would make R&D more like a typical university continue to believe in their value.

Administrators want R&D to be known as "a good, tough university that is doing a few things well," or as "a graduate research institution with programs conducted in unorthodox ways, where students can enter at the junior-year level." They do not wish to be a comprehensive university, either in terms of program offerings or in levels offered. They are proud of the fact that, unlike most major research universities, they aim to prepare graduate students not only for academic employment but for nonacademic jobs as well. About two-thirds of their advanced graduates go to work for government, business, and other research positions outside academia. Recently, a university system official suggested that R&D could become "the new UCLA." He was promptly informed by the R&D deans that if they wanted to be at UCLA, they would go there. The deans and others see R&D as distinctively different in desirable ways. They also prefer developing the university's high potential over working at an established university.

The belief that R&D is different is widespread and proudly held, but expressions about what constitutes that difference tend to be diverse and particularistic. Mentioned were the lack of lower-division work, the lack of dorms and other student-based accoutrements, the focus on business and industry, the university's history and evolution, the relative preponderance of graduate and night students, the narrowness of academic program offerings, the interdisciplinary course requirements, the university's location in a high-growth area, the organizational structure of the university, and the quality of the faculty. More generally, a faculty member noted, "This place has a great deal of potential energy. . . . A lot of state universities are spent—their potential is used up." People comment freely about what the university is *not*—not another UCLA, for example—but their vision of what the university *is* remains fragmented.

Given the difficulty of establishing a new form, especially when it closely resembles well-established cousins, it is not surprising that one long-term faculty member asserted that the primary

achievement of the past ten years has been to sustain and develop
the basic ideas on which the institution was founded. Several faculty members and administrators pointed out that its "uniqueness"
caused many problems because people do not understand what
the university is. Visiting the campus in the daytime, newcomers
wonder where all the students are. They ask why it enrolls what
they perceive as "many" foreign students (7 percent, plus about 5
percent immigrants) and why the alumni are relatively inactive.
The university only recently graduated its first alumni, many of
whom did not establish strong bonds with the institution because
they were on campus only to attend classes.

Many people also question why the university is asking for
money, because they assume incorrectly that it has unlimited access to the fortunes of the founders. An administrator asserted that
maintaining the university's uniqueness "requires daily vigilance"
to prevent lapses into typical research-university patterns. Finally,
one administrator stated that the university "pays for its ambigu-
ities and uniquenesses every day." He said that its aspirations are
impossibly high, and that its resources will be unable to support
those aspirations in the foreseeable future. Therefore, people are
called upon to do more than it is possible for them to do under
the circumstances.

Indeed, one of the phrases often heard on campus is "world
class." Achieving world-class stature is a short-term objective for
the CCD and a long-term objective for the university as a whole.
The steps by which the university will achieve world-class stature
are not spelled out in terms that everyone in the institution under-
stands. As a result, the message sometimes comes through that
they are expected to be world class, right now. As one respondent
put it, "This creates large amounts of tension for those who take
it seriously, and a lot of cynicism when we fall short."

Comments about the scarcity of resources relative to institutional purposes were frequent. One administrator observed:

> We can't run a library with legislative funds and still meet the high
> goals of this institution. It's madness to think we can run this institution
> as if we were a small Carnegie Mellon or Stanford at our present
> level of funding. That's where our morale problem comes from—the
> rhetoric doesn't match reality because of the gap in resources.

A faculty member illustrated one consequence of the shortage of
library funds, saying:

> The library never got a reasonable level of resources. I spend $4,000
> a year myself in order to even pretend to be a practicing scholar.

There are no sabbaticals in the system, no recognition for scholarship. There's minimal travel money, and nil or minimal funds for research assistants. There isn't a word processor in my whole school. Most of us have our own; it's the only way we can get anything done.

A faculty member in another area concurred. "What's at odds with institutional purpose here isn't the academic culture—it's the resources available. They're killing us. We set national standards for ourselves; we want to produce. But we have no resources to do it, and a lot of barriers." He illustrated the gap between expectation and reality by recalling a recent meeting on tenure standards:

> The question was asked during the meeting, "What schools do you think we're comparable to?" People have a tendency to name the top ten, maybe top twenty, schools in the country. Yet our resource level puts us several levels down. People don't want to hear we're comparable to someplace like [the secondary state university in a neighboring state], but their teaching load is probably very similar to ours. The ideology here is "We're a very good, research-oriented university." But deep down, our faculty records are probably more like second-tier state universities.

The mission incorporates some apparent contradictions or paradoxes. For example, the emphasis is on graduate education, which inherently is highly specialized study, usually based on traditional academic disciplines. Yet the university also emphasizes its determination not to organize into academic departments. As a long-time administrator pointed out, "Having [academic] departments would have been self-defeating. Departments exist to advance the discipline—an entirely academic pursuit. So again, we knew what we *didn't* want."

The university requires faculty members to teach and students to enroll in interdisciplinary course work. Said a dean, "We promote interdisciplinarity in a number of ways. For one thing, the money goes with the faculty member, not the department. That gives the faculty more freedom as independent entrepreneurs to find a place for themselves in the institution." Some of R&D's programs take what one administrator called "new forms," interdisciplinary emphases more often associated with small, private, liberal-arts colleges than larger, graduate and upper division, public universities.

Faculty members also noted the inherent tension between the university's world-class aspirations and pressures to do research on local problems. "There's a clash between [R&D's] uniqueness, working with corporations and the community, and ideas of academic excellence and autonomy. The university committee on

qualifications looks at the traditional academic criteria [in promotion cases], yet the administration often wants you to get local
contracts and build community ties." Similarly, some people stress
R&D's mission in graduate education while others believe that the
university should pay more attention to undergraduate education.
Similar tensions exist between technical and liberal-arts programs.
Moreover, the university is in the city, but it is fifteen miles from
downtown in the midst of its most affluent suburbs. Although it is
technically an urban university, it thus serves a very atypical urban clientele for very atypical purposes. Some faculty members
believe that R&D should do more for lower-income and minority
residents. Finally, although the university aims to be world class,
a very high proportion of its students are local residents. This is
likely to continue as long as the university is located in a high-rent
district and has no residence halls.

These circumstances, as well as the university's own uncertainty about its purpose, help fragment its mission. Because the
ways in which it differs from other institutions do not follow an
easily recognizable pattern, few people have an adequate frame
of reference for comprehending the university's identity and actions. This situation is at least partly responsible for the widespread
conviction that the university needs to convey a clearer, stronger
image to both its internal and external constituents.

Leadership and Decision-making

The first university president, who held the job on an acting basis
for two years, had been a researcher in the original center and
subsequently returned to the university faculty when he stepped
down. A dynamic, sociable, politically well-connected president
led the university from 1971 to 1981. He enjoyed the challenge
of building the university in its early stages and put most of his
effort into making friends for the university downtown and at the
state level. He left R&D to become a leading officer of a statewide
system.

After another acting presidency, the current president took
office in 1982. He came from a major state university, where he
had been vice president for research and graduate studies and
acting president. A noted scientist, he remains active as a scholar.
People say the president is a "straight shooter" who says what is on
his mind. Whereas the first president paid close attention to the

prime movers in the downtown area, the current president has built increasingly strong relations with those in the neighboring suburbs. His top priority is winning approval for the proposed engineering school, and he has spent the majority of his time and effort toward that end for many months.

The current academic vice president has served in that capacity since 1974. During his first year in office, he was largely responsible for the massive recruitment of faculty that preceded inauguration of the undergraduate program. Faculty say that the academic vice president is brilliant, the intellectual center of the university, and dedicated to implementing its mission. However, some disagreement exists about his methods. Many believe that occasional lapses in communication or apparently contrary procedures are due to simple misunderstanding or oversight, but some attribute less charitable motives. Remarks by faculty members dramatized these differing points of view. One said:

> [The academic vice president] is the focus of legends and myths. He has never once treated me unfairly. Even if I disagree with him, he always has had good reasons for his decisions. He's just a damn good academic vice president. People say we're overcentralized. Compared to what? We're a small school. Small schools are centralized. What they're talking about is defining administrative prerogatives versus faculty prerogatives, and that's a traditional schism you'll find anywhere.

Another faculty member said: "[The academic vice president] is an exceedingly political person. I had a new insight about what that meant when I heard an interview with Richard Nixon. He said, 'Well, that's politics—you reward your friends and punish your enemies.' And that's our vice president."

Communication between faculty and the academic vice president receives mixed reviews. Communication problems certainly are exacerbated by the fact that the administration building lies half a mile across the prairie from the rest of the campus. In the minds of many university constituents, this physical separation has become a telling symbol of alienation. The academic vice president commented:

> Tensions and misunderstandings between faculty and administration are endemic in academic institutions, that doesn't bother me. A happy shop is not necessarily a productive one. It's nice if you can have both. . . . [A colleague elsewhere] thinks the purpose of administration is to make the institution healthy internally—high morale, good will, cooperation, collaboration. I think that's important. But the purpose of administration is to realize institutional purpose.

A former vice president for business who has been associated with R&D since it was a research center now holds the title of senior vice president. His primary responsibilities relate to managing the university's endowment land and overseeing its gradual development into a research park. Three other vice presidencies are vacant. The vice president for development resigned in 1983, and the search for his successor had not been completed by mid-1985. The university created a vice presidency for student affairs in 1984, but that search also had not been completed by mid-1985. The vice president for business resigned in 1984, and a search was underway in mid-1985.

One of the problems in filling high-level vacancies is that middle management is thin. A faculty member saw it this way:

> The administration is lean and mean. Maybe we'd be better off with more layers of administrators. Where I was before, my department and my school protected me. Leadership here has the potential to exercise power that affects me personally at any time. I have tremendous control over a lot of academic decisions in my area, but I can be second-guessed at any time without even being told, much less asked.

As an indication of a lean administration, in 1982 R&D spent 9 percent of its budget for institutional support, compared to an average of 13 percent for the other cases in this study.

In academic leadership, three of the six deans came to R&D within the past two years. Faculty and others on campus generally view these changes as successful efforts to improve leadership in those areas. The deans hold a good deal of decision-making authority, including authority to allocate resources within the colleges, subject to legislative guidelines and lump sums determined by top administration. In addition, the university contains elements of a matrix form of organization. Individuals whose responsibilities cut across the academic divisions lead both the graduate and undergraduate divisions. The academic senate and academic council, both of which are led by the president and academic vice president, handle governance issues.

The university has recruited faculty largely at the junior level, so a relatively high proportion of them are young and have taught at one or no other universities in their careers. The university attracts faculty who want what was often referred to in interviews as "a clean slate" that is relatively amenable to their efforts to implement new research and curricular ideas. Although one sometimes hears about the "unreconstructed scientist" who was part of the original research center and has not fully accepted the broader mission of the university, membership in that group is diminishing both due to retirement and due to acceptance of the mission among those who remain. Many now see the group as the "stable core" of the university. That group teaches in only one of the six colleges, so any campus-wide effects of their presence and their preferences have been diluted. Top administrators see a need now for the infusion of some very senior faculty members who can act as leaders and mentors.

Decision-making is highly centralized at R&D. Survey respondents rated it higher than respondents at any of the other cases in this study. Some faculty see centralization as a problem, others as a natural reflection of the facts that R&D is relatively small and under tight state control. All agree that faculty involvement in governance is minimal. One reported that only twenty-two candidates could be found to run for twenty-three seats on the academic senate. The agenda items are trivial. Many committees meet frequently, but with limited effect. One faculty member mentioned the activities of a faculty committee responsible for formulating important policies relating to curricular matters. Despite the important purpose, most of the committee's time was spent editing policy documents. Even so, many changes (often minor) were inserted as the document moved up the chain of command, some for no apparent reason, giving the appearance that the faculty committee's deliberations were a waste of the members' time. A faculty member's conclusion: "We have strong personalities at the top who don't want to share power with the faculty."

Another faculty member said:

At [R&D], there are very few processes whereby conflict can be resolved. We have a committee on paper that deals with faculty grievances. In other places, the grievance committee is extremely powerful. It has the very top people on the campus on it. Normally, they make a recommendation on a matter and that ends it. It clears the air. People trust the results. Here, [the academic vice president] is extremely hard-nosed in dealing with people—autocratic. He told people who had complaints to take them to the dean—when the dean and academic vice president made the decisions to begin with.

The research orientation of R&D is evident in its administrators' collection and analysis of institutional information. For example, the self-study for accreditation in 1976–77 included relatively sophisticated statistical analyses of students and programs. The level of institutional knowledge among faculty and staff is relatively high and downward flows of information seem to be frequent. Participants use all of the key internal groups—president's council, council of deans, academic senate, and academic council—for information-sharing, but decision-making by those groups remains limited.

Although most people see R&D's leaders as strong, competent individuals, systemic factors lead to the conclusion that, as one respondent put it, "organizational challenges are greater than academic ones." More pessimistically, another described the university in terms of "organizational pathology" and wondered aloud, "What holds this place together?" Structural factors that tend to fragment the organization include high turnover among deans, high turnover and relatively junior status among faculty, ambiguous lines of academic authority, physical separation of academics and administration, and vacancies in key administrative positions. R&D has not had the time or pervasive senior faculty leadership to develop patterns of interaction, policy, and behavior that constitute a clear definition of what the university is and how things are to be done here.

The IPS confirmed these difficulties. Among these case studies, R&D ranked lowest on many dimensions, among them mission agreement, innovation, morale, credibility of top administrators, system openness and community interaction, and organizational health. Although extremely favorable environmental conditions contribute to the university's relatively good performance, its future success will depend on the willingness of its leaders to address these issues.

Strategic Management as Cultural Engineering

Fostering organizational culture is a slow and difficult process, replete with unforeseen challenges and little understood even by those leaders who have succeeded in developing an institution's values and mission. R&D's approach has been to use strategic planning as something of a surrogate for organizational culture. This form of "cultural engineering" requires that leaders plan and execute their actions along lines that constituents can understand. This entails two tasks: planning and executing well and interpreting plans in a way that will foster constituent support for the shared values and norms that underlie them. Although R&D does extremely well at planning, it has yet to translate instrumental actions into a shared sense of purpose and identity that pervades all aspects of daily life on campus.

Of the several forms that strategic management can take, linear (or goal-oriented) strategy and adaptive strategy are most in evidence at R&D. The key element of linear strategy at R&D is the six-year strategic plan developed in 1982–83 and undergoing revision in 1984–85. Although the state mandated the plan, R&D was ready for the exercise. Faculty and staff participated widely in its development, and the resulting five-point program seems to have constituted a clear foundation for what has transpired since it was written. Those interviewed on campus often mentioned the plan, and the administration has taken major steps to implement it. At most other institutions, including those in this study, planning is rarely undertaken in a serious manner, or when it is, the results soon gather dust. Not so at R&D. The continuing salience of R&D's plan may constitute evidence of keen foresight, the recognition of obvious needs, or both.

The university's strategic plan focuses on five key goals. The first goal, and certainly the one most often referred to, is the creation of an engineering school. The need for a premiere engineering program motivated the original founders of the research center in 1961. They had originally hoped that the city's private university would meet the need, but they were not satisfied with its capacity or commitment to the task. These founders, and the business leaders who have moved into the area in the intervening years, remained convinced that R&D should offer engineering. However, effective political opposition from the private university and the other state university nearby (both of which offer engineering) have thwarted R&D's efforts, as has the coordinating board's determination to prevent program duplication. The founders put up millions of dollars to endow the school if it is established, and local business leaders mounted a campaign to win its approval.

R&D collected a great deal of national and local data on projected needs for and costs of the program, and it commissioned studies by outside groups to legitimate and document its position. Having won the approval of the state university regents, the plan is now pending before the coordinating board. At this point the decision is a political one. Although R&D has marshaled an impressive array of political forces on its side, powerful constituencies remain opposed to the move. Participants rated its prospects at better than fifty-fifty in mid-1985.

Four other key goals are mentioned in the strategic plan. R&D wishes to develop the affiliated CCD to national preeminence. The center's personnel, facilities, and independent financial support are such that it will cost the university little to make it into the best such operation in the country. Another goal expressed in the planning document focuses on improving several key program areas. R&D has little interest in establishing new majors or changing existing ones, but rather intends to make current programs qualitatively better and procedurally more attractive to students. The remaining two goals concern improving the number and quality of graduate students and improving maintenance and developing more instructional, research, and office space.

Much of the action specified in the plan's five points is subject to managerial control. Developing the CCD is more a matter of taking actions consistent with that priority than seeking resources or permission to act. Likewise, increasing the quality of graduate students is largely a matter of policy-making and consistent internal decisions. Two of the five points, however, are more dependent on uncontrollable forces than the others—establishing the engineering school and expanding the physical plant. The coordinating board must clear both and the legislature must appropriate funds if these goals are to be realized. Including these goals in the strategic plan was as much a signal to external audiences regarding what the university was willing to fight for as it was a statement of managerial intent. In the plan, the president deliberately downplayed other, possibly controversial, issues, such as admitting lower-division students. Likewise, the document does not mention establishing a law school, which had been discussed in other circles.

R&D's use of adaptive strategy has aligned the university with its environment by enabling it to respond to constituents' demands, such as those of students for programs or employers for trained staff. In a sense, R&D is an adaptation. From its very origins as a research center, the university has developed along lines that will meet the requirements of local business and industry. The most pronounced change in local demand has been quantitative, not qualitative, and R&D has grown to meet this expanding challenge. Likewise, the pool of students has grown since 1975, but interests have not changed markedly. Curricular reform has been limited since the research center became a university because changes in programmatic configuration must pass muster in a highly controlled and competitive political arena. Paraphrasing one respondent, the countervailing forces are so strong that there is virtually no incentive for curricular change. The faculty committee on educational policy handles curricular issues, there being no curriculum committee per se. Change is often driven by the need to revise the catalog biannually. Any substantial changes tend to occur as discrete events rather than continuously or incrementally, as in the decision to establish an engineering school.

Overall, R&D has adapted relatively smoothly to clear demands for growth. Attention to detail has contributed to its success. For example, one of its smaller colleges revised its sequencing and scheduling of course work and was rewarded the next year with a 50-percent increase in graduate students and a 14-percent increase in undergraduate students. Similarly, R&D permits students to register before their final application and supporting documents have been processed. They may register by telephone and pay with charge cards. This process makes R&D far more accessible to working adult students than is true of most universities.

Through its linear and adaptive strategies, R&D has succeeded in planning and implementing instrumental decisions that have enhanced its performance. However, many respondents indicated that little consensus exists regarding institutional values and little cohesion is evident in day-to-day activities. Although strategic planning at R&D is widely viewed as successful, it cannot serve effectively as a surrogate for organizational culture. While the plan is a coherent view of R&D's desired future, the fabric of daily organizational life has yet to reflect its concerns and aspirations.

Culture and Interpretation

Organizational culture has its roots in perception and communication among people within and without the institution. It is the means by which people come to understand and interpret what the institution is about. The results have a good deal to do with morale and the capacity of diverse constituents to recognize common goals and values and contribute to them in a unified manner.

Because of its emphasis on communicating and interpreting institutional mission, interpretive strategy can help articulate institutional values, thereby providing a framework within which to incorporate and orient linear and adaptive approaches. At R&D, however, general phrases and broad concepts often are used to communicate desired institutional values, but the reception within the organization is often cynical. No unifying theme has gained wide acceptance, and people tend to discount suggested themes as mere public relations efforts.

People at R&D believe that the university is distinctive, but they do not fully understand or agree about the nature of its distinctive-

ness. They are aware of the university's history and acknowledge
that history affects its current direction, as in the continuing emphasis on research and graduate study. But when one asks, "Who
are you collectively and where are you going?" the responses reflect different priorities and divisions. Under such circumstances, it
is difficult for faculty, administrators, and friends of the university
to pull together. They are largely unified, if not completely enthusi-
astic, behind the drive for an engineering school. Beyond that one
issue, however, no broad, unifying, long-range vision is available
to keep the momentum going. The aim to become a "world-class"
institution is widely shared, but its implications for action are not
clear and institutional constraints that thwart the realization of
this goal often elicit cynicism.

The university has little institutional tradition. Although it experienced a large infusion of new faculty in 1975, few of them were
midlevel or senior scholars. Nearly all of the existing senior faculty were in only one of the six colleges. During the next ten years,
faculty turnover was high and replacements were generally hired
at the junior level. High turnover was also common among deans.
A large proportion of the faculty who are active in institutional
affairs have limited experience at other campuses and many of
the active faculty do not have tenure. The two most evident con-
tinuities were the first president, who served through much of the
1970s, and the academic vice president, who has held the position
since 1974.

These factors tend to centralize decision-making in the academic vice president, who has the longest tenure among top administrators. He is in a position to set the direction and tone of
internal affairs at R&D. His primary method for setting R&D's
direction has been the selection of deans and, to some extent, faculty members who believe in the primacy of applied research at
the upper division and graduate levels. Apart from the discretion
he exercises in appointments, the academic vice president seems
to have little interest in organizational culture at the institutional
level. He commented:

> We don't have, or don't promote, an organizational culture. That de-
> pends on the deans. We need strong deans, and we have a better
> chance of that without departments. The deans have to please the
> academic vice president and the president as well as the faculty. It
> may appear autocratic to some, but the programs are successful only
> if the deans are.

Having a relatively junior, high-turnover faculty in a new university also mitigates against the emergence of anything resem-

bling an organizational culture at the institutional level. As one top administrator reported:

> Given that the culture of incoming faculty members is that of a traditional academic university, and given our unique institutional purpose to produce nonacademic graduates, the absence of a strong culture here may actually help the university achieve its institutional purpose. Nevertheless, the institution could be more successful if the culture were strongly committed to its purpose.

A faculty member saw nothing unusual about the lack of an organizational culture:

> This university is just like any other—some factors pull it together, others tear it apart. We have not one organizational culture, but many. The physical plant guys have a culture, the secretaries have a culture. The disciplines are a variable, the fact that we're in various buildings, the size of the place. One of the functions of management is to keep them operating so that they're not at cross purposes. What the institution is depends on linking strategies—between schools, between faculty and administration. People who occupy multiple roles are links. They relate to different kinds of people.

It appears that a small number of faculty act as linking agents through serving on multiple committees and taking roles in academic administrative affairs. Their efforts, however, have little apparent direct effect on the lives and attitudes of their peers. Most faculty conduct their research and teaching with an autonomy typical of most research universities.

Faculty and administrator responses to a survey question rated R&D's morale the lowest of the cases in this study. An administrator expressed the belief that the faculty are disillusioned. He said, "I'm happy with our progress—but I'm a historian, you see. I take the long view. The faculty thought they were coming to an institution that was already *there*." He believes that many feel low commitment to university life and have withdrawn into their disciplines. In his opinion, this is happening "on a grand scale." A faculty member, asked whether it really mattered if morale is low, replied:

> Does morale matter in terms of the university's ability to do what it has to do? Not in the short run, but having low morale is counter to substantially advancing the institution. A lot of us do things that are not in the faculty job description, but they help the university. How long would we do that if we weren't getting any strokes? I feel I'm contributing and [one dean] recognizes it. He's an exception. There are strong incentives for the faculty to be selfish, not to contribute to the university—that's a structural fact of higher education. A lot of people here who are in a poor mental state are people who have contributed as much as anyone, but they didn't get supported for it.

So you risk losing the best people. The mood is grim. If you're mobile, why put up with it?

Another faculty member agreed and gave specific examples:

There are a great many ways in which morale affects whether the institution can achieve its ultimate purposes. Grant and contract work is volunteer. I don't have to lift a finger in that direction, though clearly it would help the institution if I did. But I'm not evaluated on that. Whether I do it depends on how I feel and how my colleagues feel. Or take courses. I can put one together and teach it over and over. How I approach students and get interested in them has impact on how they feel about the institution and whether they will be long-term friends of the university. [One of the teaching tools I use] takes an incredible amount of time to set up. Why should I bother to do it? Take faculty recruiting—what's more important that that? If morale is low, I could refuse to participate, or participate halfheartedly. Then I go to professional conferences and someone asks me how it's going. Word gets out. That's what kills you. You get known as a place good people don't want to go to. It's not a massive hemorrhage that'll kill you, it's all the little pinpricks.

A dean and a faculty member expressed their views on what the university needs to do next. The dean said:

We need to get the structure correct—clean up management, make sure each of the colleges have found who they are. Then we need to clean up our image with the public, get employers downtown to know us. We need to find our comparative advantage, our niche, what we want to be when we grow up. Unless we can look at the faculty and not feel that they're apologizing for working here, we're not there yet.

According to the faculty member, the university should take a number of steps:

First, hire a president and vice president who know the demands of academic life, how to choose faculty, how to reward them. They should have proven administrative experience but not have been pitched toward the administrative career ladder as early in life as the ones we have. They should know something about how to communicate, both on campus and off. Then, I'd move the administration onto the campus. And we need more competent people in other places. We need people who are willing to take some risks—secure people, both personally and professionally. We need a larger vision than we've had before.

He continued:

We should have been located in the center of the city. Too late now. The powers that founded the university owned land here, and they wanted to be in a nice, white, middle-class neighborhood. You can't even take a bus here from downtown. Raising money—that's critical. We can't go anywhere on state funding levels. We should also cut out our pretentiousness and take a good, hard look at who we are and who we might be, given our realities. We need to do a real self-study.

Where You Are Going Versus Who You Are

Institutional goals have been the moving force throughout R&D's existence. From its beginnings as a private research center, the institution has set high goals for itself and has developed a sophisticated planning process to meet those goals. Moreover, R&D's favorable environment has permitted it to meet the vast majority of those goals. The university's success is compromised, however, by the relative absence of shared cultural norms and processes. As a relatively new institution born out of a scientific think tank, R&D inherited the disciplinary culture of the sciences but not the broader institutional culture that could nurture endeavors and shared values across a variety of fields. In the years since it became a university, R&D has yet to translate ideas about the uniqueness of its mission into the fabric of daily organizational life.

The relative absence of an organizational culture produces different priorities for action among members of the university. Leadership is there for an inherently difficult task. These challenges are compounded by current structural conditions, such as key vice presidential vacancies, a thin layer of middle management, the physical separation of administration from campus life, and the lack of a university-wide core of senior faculty to promote socialization at the institutional level. Moreover, state control circumscribes decision-making, as does the importance of meeting the needs of local business and industry.

Although R&D University clearly must continue to plan and adapt, its greatest challenge lies in fostering belief and commitment among its constituents. Indeed, divorced from an interpretive context, strategies of planning and adapting have actually reduced morale and consensus. Confidence in R&D and its mission and a commitment to shared values and processes thus emerge as strategic issues in their own right. To ensure the university's long-term success, R&D's leaders should count among their goals the development of an organizational culture that will help translate institutional values from occasional rhetoric to daily activity and widespread, active support. Otherwise, the slow pace at which organizational processes develop will undermine institutional goals, no matter how appropriate they may be.

PART FIVE

Conclusion

TEN

The Challenge
to Leadership

We turn now to the challenges a cultural view of organizations presents to organizational leaders. Once leaders understand what culture means and see it at work in a set of case studies, how should they respond in their own settings? Answering the question requires that we look briefly across the cases, using the cultural framework depicted in Chapter 2, reproduced here as Figure 10.1. We then suggest effective leadership strategies that arise from a review of the cases.

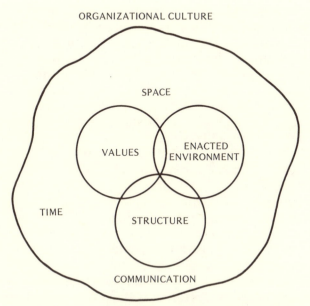

Figure 10.1. Dynamic Equilibrium in Organizational Culture

Matches and Mismatches in Cultures

We suggested earlier that the dimensions of culture—structure, enacted environment, and values—exhibit varying degrees of congruence with one another. The framework provides a means of diagnosing the points at which an institution's progress toward dynamic equilibrium may be hampered by dimensions that are out of balance. When they are incongruent, one dimension undermines the other instead of reinforcing it. The institution cannot develop momentum toward equilibrium when it is headed in diverging directions. The cases contain areas of both congruence and divergence; it is to eliminating the latter areas that we recommend leaders direct their attention.

VALUES AND STRUCTURE

Triad University provides a good example of congruent values and structure. Organizational values for the autonomy of each college are reflected in the structure of decision-making—separate trustee committees for each college, acceptance of direct dealings between trustees and deans, and the coordinating role of the president. Rural State College values informality and conversation, and these values are facilitated by structural elements such as its small size, rural setting, and collegial governance.

We have also noted situations in almost all the cases where values and structure are incongruous. Rural State and Family State both strongly emphasize service to local students and the importance of good teaching, both of which aims could well be diluted if they achieve their aspirations for university status. Rural's informality and collegiality contrast sharply with the authoritative way the president recently decided to hire a new dean. The value of the liberal arts and value-based instruction at Mission is not especially evident in its current emphasis on vocational and professional programs.

Triad provides a linked chain of diverging values and structures. Its historic clientele, the working poor of the city, constitutes a decreasing share of enrollment to the extent that each of the colleges seeks to upgrade its standards and extend its geographic markets. The colleges' autonomy to make moves in these and other directions, valued throughout the university's history, undercuts the president's efforts to establish university-wide planning and governance.

When values and structure are not mutually supportive, the organization is saying one thing and doing another. The disjunction may be an inevitable phase in the process of change, a small hypocrisy, a temporary aberration, or a source of mounting frustration and anger. In the late 1960s and early 1970s, Covenant was oriented toward personal, value-laden instruction, but its president was seen increasingly as a distant, unfeeling autocrat. This incongruous juxtaposition of values and structure ultimately helped spawn the faculty union. But not all incongruities carry sufficient weight to create major problems—if they did, organizations probably could not grow and develop. They might not even exist.

Similarly, Mission University once experienced a clear congruence between structure and values. As a parochial institution for the region's Christian families, the university offered a postsecondary education geared toward Christian values. The administration and faculty were predominantly from the religious order. Yet during the last twenty years the university has grown into an institution of enhanced prominence and academic excellence. Diversity of student clientele, faculty, and administration has flourished. Some would say that growth has come at the expense of institutional values. The point is not that leaders must always maintain equilibrium, but instead that they must recognize incongruities and then assess their significance and likely consequences.

VALUES AND ENACTED ENVIRONMENT

The rural northwest quadrant of a rural state is a perfect setting for Rural State College. The intimacy of the two means that Rural State requires no numbers to assess its environment—what moves the region moves the college. Similarly, Family State College echoes its small, working-class town through strong personal relationships and devotion to developing local talent and serving local needs.

The situation is similar, if more diffuse, at Mission and R&D. Both the universities and their environments embody newly formed values of growth and the salience of area employers, although Mission's historic values are less pragmatic, and R&D's world class aims are subject to limits imposed by state funding and controls. Triad's fiscal conservatism sits well with its city's political and philanthropic leadership, as well as with the law alumni, who are oriented toward fiduciary responsibility.

Mismatches between values and enacted environment also occur. Present State has adopted a highly aggressive marketing
stance in the midst of a slow-paced context of farms and resorts.
The environment at Covenant is a cosmopolitan city, and Covenant
serves a cosmopolitan clientele. However, the university also has
created a new environment for itself through an aggressive outreach program. As long as the program is kept entirely separate
from the main campus, this new environment may not prove troublesome to the main campus. Even so, it is a minor irritant in
that the extension faculty are not unionized and, far-flung and
part-time, they could never be part of any sense of community
the university may rebuild eventually. Furthermore, in Covenant's
case it is less that the environment has moved away from institutional values than that the values have nearly disappeared. The
university is missing a prime opportunity to link values with environment by building a global community right on campus.

Triad's governance illustrates an interesting twist in values-
environment congruence. Triad values a strong board, strong
deans, and subunit autonomy. The arrangement clearly does not
match Triad's environment, if that environment is defined as
Triad's peer institutions—other private, mid-range, comprehensive
universities of moderate size with a strong teaching emphasis.
However, that is not the environment that Triad's trustees and
deans enact. When asked about their "unusual" governance, they
respond that it is not unusual because it resembles the governance
of large prestigious private research universities. The fact that in
most ways Triad is more like any of a dozen other institutions in
their city is, to them, relevant when it comes to recruiting but not
when it comes to governance.

One could argue that matching values with enacted environment is as important as matching structure with enacted environment, although most attention in recent years has gone to the
latter. The behavior that arises most naturally, comfortably, spon-
taneously, and profusely is behavior that springs from values.
When values are not consistent with structure or environment,
behavior is to some degree limited and artificial, which in turn re-
duces an institution's capacity for effectiveness. We do not argue
for dogged adherence to entrenched values, nor do we claim that
change in values must precede change in structure or enacted environment.

If values are to adjust to environmental demands, then institutional leaders should be aware of what such adjustments entail.

Conversely, if an institution adheres to its values in light of a changing market, leaders need to be aware of the consequences. Mission University broadened its mission in order to accommodate a rapidly expanding environment. Present State College abandoned its primary goal of service to the local people because of a decline in the local population.

We mean to point out that change in all three areas is inevitable. When multiple changes are compatible, the organization approaches dynamic equilibrium. An organization is in balance not because it has settled into a static state but because the pot is bubbling evenly. Every change acts back on us. Organizational leaders shape the culture and it, in turn, shapes the leaders.

STRUCTURE AND ENACTED ENVIRONMENT

Values and structure seem often to be at odds, but we find structure and enacted environment to be more congruent than otherwise. This may be largely a reaction to the same forces that gave rise to strategic planning as a popular function in higher education. With the end of the military draft, rising inflation, and declining demographics, colleges have learned to change their structures as needed to cope with hostile environments or, for the fortunate few, to take advantage of favorable ones.

Both R&D and Mission universities have had high demand for professional and technological programs, and they have responded accordingly. R&D not only established academic programs, but also encouraged its adult clientele with phone-in registration, credit card tuition, and evening course schedules. Covenant reached out for new students through its off-campus instruction. Present State adopted an aggressive marketing stance to offset declining demographics and increased competition.

On the other hand, Present State's initial endorsement of its arts program was out of step with its depressed rural economy. Some people at Family State would say that its curriculum has drifted for a decade and, if left unattended, may become a mismatch with the environment in the near future. Others would say that Rural State College's goal of university status is incongruous in its present environment. Mission University's requirement to have a religious president may also be incongruous if the institution has fundamentally reoriented its perception of the environment and its role.

If we were to list the three relationships—values/structure, structure/environment, and values/environment—in the order of their intrinsic importance to most colleges today, we would place structure/environment in third place. College leaders seem to concur. Their attention to mission, fundamental purposes, and other components of institutional values has increased dramatically during the 1980s. They may be responding to a prior overemphasis on achieving congruence between structure and environment with too little regard for values.

A MATTER OF PERCEPTION

A central theme of this discussion is that how people perceive the organization and its environment deserves far more attention than it often receives. People construct their realities as they attend selectively to countless stimuli, as they assess what events mean to them, and as they communicate among themselves. The message is that leaders need to pay attention to these processes. Before turning to specific suggestions on how to do so, we need to point out that serious negative consequences can arise when perceived reality does not match undeniable fact. The organization is then deluding itself.

Most of the cases contain at least an element of this phenomenon. Some examples are foreboding; others may pass without causing harm. Many key people at Covenant and Mission universities maintain their image of a close campus community that stresses liberal arts, ethics, and personal relationships. Yet both universities have become highly entrepreneurial, larger in size and scope, building professional or off-campus programs. The religious presence on both campuses is a slight shadow of its former self. One campus is strongly influenced by area employers, the other by adversarial faculty-administrator relations.

R&D aims at world-class status as a research university. The argument has been made that R&D is on the right road to achieve that aim, but it has a long way to go with limited resources. But the world-class image is so strong that it creates frustration when juxtaposed against the faculty's needs for equipment, books, and space, or their expectations about their role in governance. A demoralized faculty is unlikely to form a world class research university.

As these examples illustrate, perceptions can construct a reality that is contradicted by other forms of reality, such as the perceptions of others, the pattern of academic programs and enrollments, and resource levels. Such contradicting valences can create serious problems in the long run. Leaders who are aware of contradictions are in a position to prevent those problems.

Culture, Strategy, Leadership, and Identity

The tensions that arise from mismatches in the dimensions of organizational culture suggest the worth of seeking not only a dynamic equilibrium within the culture but also a coherent identity with regard to culture, strategy, and leadership. We illustrated three levels of coherence in Figure 2.2 and in the three sections of cases—continuity, change, and identity.

Several important organizational benefits arise when culture, strategy, and leadership overlap. When identity is clear and coherent, all who are involved with the organization have a star to navigate by in their efforts to contribute to the group. They see what the organization is and, with consistent strategic leadership, they see where the organization is headed. People generally will choose to leave an organization that they do not find comfortable and to contribute actively to those they believe in. The organization with a clear identity and direction attracts those with similar aims and encourages them to find ways to help.

As this dynamic unfolds, participants in the organization develop a sense of worth both for themselves and for the organization. They feel competent and needed. Their commitment and loyalty to the organization increase, often bringing ever-greater efforts to contribute. In other words, a coherent identity can create an upward spiral of achievement and satisfaction.

The risk, of course, is that the organization will become so change-resistant that it calcifies. The environment is less likely to permit this is modern times than it was when change was slower and tradition stronger, but organizations can forestall the impact of external change by enacting an interpretation of the environment with which they feel comfortable. It seems reasonable to suggest, however, that organizations will either filter in enough environmental information to permit evolutionary change or eventually face a crisis that forces precipitous change. The former is usually preferable, and leaders can foster the kind of vigilance this requires.

Coping with change in an evolutionary fashion requires at least three ingredients. First, leaders need to understand the historical roots of the organization, the themes that echo from its founding to the present. Leaders need to draw on these themes and seek new interpretations of them that can respond to new challenges. Second, organizations need to keep their eyes on the present and look into the future, both inside and outside the organization. The literature on strategic management has been especially valuable in raising questions about the environment and the future that are often neglected in the comforts or pressures of the present. Third, leaders need to understand the limits of organizational identity—what the organization will do and what it will not do. This is not to say that identity is static, but leaders must recognize when they are asking for change of this magnitude and proceed accordingly.

Much of the literature on leadership and strategy in the past has dealt with how to make rational choices in what we have called the linear and adaptive modes. It has focused leader attention on quantifiable, analyzable phenomena. That is useful, but it is not enough. Triad University is effective in those domains. R&D University has a very strong, very "correct" strategic plan. Not one of the institutions in this study is experiencing significant decline in enrollments or finances. What these cases show is that some organizations that are effective on these dimensions are ineffective in eliciting the full powers of their human resources. They lose the capacity to be all they can be. The textbook on the nonlinear, nonadaptive components of leadership and strategy has yet to be written, but we believe the cases imply some suggestions.

What Leaders Can Do

We offer here some suggestions to leaders, components of a diagnostic frame of reference, a way of living in the collegiate managerial environment. While other authors may offer how-to-do-it suggestions, we are less instrumental and more strategic. We want to suggest instead how to see it. We propose ways for leaders to identify what they need to do and how they need to do it, given the unique organization in which they find themselves.

Our philosophy is that leaders are catalysts for chemical change, more than producers of physical change. We assume that change is not linear and predictable, and that it has complex, often spontaneous, ramifications. We will outline some important leader behaviors, but the state of the art is too primitive to permit assertions about their sequence or their importance relative to one another. However, we have learned from these cases that the following tasks are important relative to other things leaders might do.

Find internal contradictions. Looking for contradictions has several virtues. First, it alerts leaders to potential sources of future difficulties. Second, it identifies areas where desired change has been implemented only partially. Contradictions also reveal where additional efforts are needed to enhance widespread understanding of institutional purpose or direction. Finally, the search for contradictions can be used to test whether the far-reaching ramifications of a proposed change will be as desirable as its expected local or short-term effects. One reason this simple activity has so much power is that it runs counter to our natural inclination to make orderly sense of our experiences, often by minimizing or ignoring contradictory evidence.

To find contradictions, leaders can simply listen and observe daily institutional life, asking themselves whether their experiences are compatible with one another and with their understanding of institutional values. "Why?" and "Why not?" can be key questions. Why are we thinking of changing the core curriculum? Why don't we have a fall faculty convocation? Why are the faculty unhappy about the increase in foreign student enrollment? Why don't we have more minority students?

A more general approach, one that could be a productive group exercise for a leadership team, is to discuss three questions: How does what we say contradict what we do? How does what we do in one area contradict what we do in another? How does what we say in one way or in some settings contradict what we say in others?

Contradictions between what is done and what is said are often incongruities between values and structure or enacted environment, as shown in the previous section. Those between what is done in one area and what is done in another area may be structure-environment incongruities or disjunctions between certain elements of either one. For example, some colleges recruit adult students, but they offer limited evening courses and do not provide night registration, night services for students, or child care. Similarly, a college may say that it takes pride in the teaching skills of its faculty, but it may also say that the road to tenure is paved with research publications.

Leaders can extend this approach to test the decisions they plan to make. If the decision relates to structure, consider how it will fit with other aspects of structure as well as with values and environment. When leaders cannot be certain of an answer, they need to ask what would be the consequences if they were wrong. What assumptions does a leader make in formulating the decision? Given that the institution is like a river—a person cannot step into it a second time and expect it to be the same as it was the first time—assumptions based on past experience require reconfirmation before they can be reapplied with confidence.

At times, it is helpful to set up a situation that is explicitly dialectical. Ask one person to prepare and present a case for one course of action, while one or more others do the same for very different approaches. Their debate clarifies what is at stake and can generate creative new solutions.

Leaders should certainly seek out people they do not normally see and ask them for opinions about the institution. Although some malcontents are self-serving or do not fit the organization, others have legitimate concerns that merit attention. People tend to speak with those with whom they are most comfortable. Senior administrators in a large institution are most apt to confer with other senior administrators or senior faculty, even if the discussion concerns junior faculty development. Uncovering a broad array of opinion helps leaders reach sound decisions.

When leaders have recognized an internal contradiction, they must exercise judgment. The appropriate response may range from a shrug of the shoulders (perhaps accompanied by a notation to revisit the issue in the future) to a massive curriculum overhaul. Whatever the response, the institution and its leaders will have guarded against the kind of self-delusion we saw in many of the cases.

Develop a comparative awareness. Often administrators grow intensely attuned to their own institutional problems and solutions, unaware that alternative solutions to similar problems have arisen at other institutions. Sometimes critically important differences in response arise from the way one defines the problem. Administrators at Covenant University treated collective bargaining as a necessary evil, while the administration at Family State College saw the collective bargaining agreement as a healthy way to clarify roles and responsibilities.

Family State College thought it needed to hire faculty members from prestigious institutions, yet Rural State College hired faculty with a closer fit to its own culture. The presidents of Present State and Covenant could learn much about ways to rebuild and strengthen academic culture from conversations with individuals at Family State.

Our point is not that one institution should copy another's solutions; indeed, a central premise of this book has been for institutional leaders to understand the uniqueness of their own culture. However, tunnel vision on one's own organization aids no one, especially leaders in crisis.

Comprehending another's reality requires reflective thought. As a trip to another country often brings about insight into one's own values and assumptions, administrators gain from visiting other campuses. Institutions often want to know who their competitors are, or how much College X raised its tuition this year. We contend that administrators also need to understand their cultures in comparison to other institutions. A comparative perspective gives the introspective administrator a clearer view of the processes and decisions of one's own institution.

Clarify the identity of the institution. Identity begins with mission but goes beyond it to include vestiges of history, traces of the personalities of many current organizational participants, and effects of leadership and strategy. It includes certain capacities that are inherent in how resources are arranged and the configuration of values, structure, and enacted environment. Identity includes all such elements that define what the organization is and suggest what it could become.

The mission expresses core values, many of which are the same among all higher education organizations. The importance of developing student intellectual abilities is a value they all share. Other mission elements tend to be common to one type of institution more than another. Service to the local student and economy was common to Rural State and Family State. Providing access and opportunity for "forgotten" students at one time characterized Triad. Among these cases, only Mission and Covenant, the religiously affiliated universities, had an expressed commitment to fostering students' values—a function that the other institutions may well perform, but not as part of their manifest purposes.

Despite their similarities, subsets of the case-study institutions differ sharply from one another in key features of their identity. Rural State lacks the highly personal, affective climate of Family

State, but it has a momentum for curriculum development that would be helpful at Family State. Present State's climate is the least personable of the three, but it has good information on itself and the most well-developed marketing process. Covenant is unusually adversarial in its governance while at Mission, its closest counterpart in many ways, governance is a process of interactive discovery.

A strong sense of identity serves two important purposes: It focuses efforts to maintain dynamic equilibrium in culture, and it directs organizational action, including strategy and leadership. In effect, it ensures that everyone is on the same boat, and they know where the boat is headed. Just as an international visitor tends to see a strange culture as incomprehensible, requiring the visitor to expend great effort to function effectively, the organizational member in an inchoate culture lacks a regularized backdrop and guiding principles for his or her activities. Identity provides the framework that allows participants to deal with existential issues of the worth and meaning of their participation in the organization. They can see how they can contribute to the organization's welfare and thereby achieve personal satisfaction and organizational rewards.

Because new people join the institution every year and the institution itself changes constantly, a strong sense of identity must be cultivated, tended, and frequently revised. The institution needs an identity that has roots in institutional history, yet it also needs one that relates specifically to current conditions. Triad has a firm, clear set of roots as a nondiscriminatory urban university, but the lack of integration of its component parts and their common service to students leaves Triad unguided as it attempts to make plans and set priorities for the future. Mission University has strayed from its historical underpinnings as a liberal-arts college in order to deal with current economic conditions, but the lack of interpretation of current events in historical context has left a good deal of ambiguity on the campus about the university's identity. As such examples of difficulty illustrate, organization members need to recognize both how they are carrying on tradition and how they fit in current conditions.

Communicate. Members have only one way of understanding the organization's identity—through communication. They listen to speeches and read policy manuals, but they also receive messages from behavior and events. A president who walks around campus, occasionally pausing to play cribbage, says something different than one who walks around with a tape recorder or one who is rarely seen on campus. Many times, actions communicate more than words, and when the two conflict, actions usually have more credibility than words.

For that reason, we propose to modify the advice that often arises in the management literature: "It is important to do the right things and to do things right." Without denying the truth in that, we add that it is important to say the right things and to say things right—whether one speaks with words or deeds. Saying goes beyond doing in two ways. First, it is incomplete unless it has been perceived and comprehended by others. Second, saying can take place as effectively when one key word (or symbol-laden deed) goes unuttered (undone) as when another is spoken.

Organizational life exists through human interaction. Human interaction is interpretation between speaker and listener. An effective leader must be aware not only of what he or she wishes to say or do, but also how institutional followers will interpret what the leader says and does.

Elsewhere (Chaffee, 1984a and 1985a) we have shown that effective leaders engage in interpretive strategy, meaning that they use high levels of communication to convey messages about what the organization is, what is happening within and around it, and where it aims to go. In effect, interpretive leaders convey a cohesive point of view about organizational life. The idea is essentially the same as knowing the organization's identity and communicating it.

Act on multiple, changing fronts. Since organizations change constantly in complex ways, they need to foster activity in many areas of the organization. In one year, that might mean focusing on recruiting, student services, fund-raising, and board development; in the next year, promotion policies, the classics department, management information systems, and financial aid. While some areas are targeted for special attention, the more lively each area is, the better. The cases suggest some guidelines for approaching all such activities.

• *Treat every problem as if it had multiple solutions.* It's a safe assumption which, if made, encourages searching until the best possible solution is found. Organizations typically search only in the neighborhood of the problem and only until an acceptable solution materializes.

• *Treat every solution as a fleeting solution.* When conditions change, yesterday's solution can easily become part of today's problem. But solutions get reified in many ways. The champion who was credited with a solution may be emotionally attached to it. Implementing a solution may have meant large expenditures, new buildings, new faculty, or large investments of hard work. Successful contemporary organizations do not eject such solutions on a whim, but they are prepared to consider the possibility that the former solution is part of a major new problem.

In this context, we note especially the formation of the adversarial faculty union at Covenant as a temporary solution to a patronizing, unsupportive administration. It worked, but it has also become part of major new problems involving campus climate, availability of university resources for nonsalary needs, and curricular fragmentation. The new solution that is evolving at Covenant could include significantly less adversarialism between the union and the administration as they seek new solutions together instead of ignoring problems while they duel.

• *Look for consequences in unlikely places,* both when contemplating taking an action and after taking it. One might not expect that devotion to accomplishing the university's goals would undermine faculty morale, but it did at R&D. One might think that presidential leadership to ensure hiring an effective dean would be welcomed, but it was not at Rural State. One might not expect trustee dominance and decanal autonomy to yield an adaptive, financially healthy institution, but they do at Triad. To the extent that leaders think through the possible ramifications of their actions, they are in a better position to choose and, having chosen, to recognize and ameliorate any undesired consequences.

• *Beware of any solution that hurts people or undermines strong values.* People constitute the primary vehicle through which any college functions and responds to its challenges. As far as we know, hurting people was never the intention of any current or former actor in these case studies. We are not talking about good or bad intentions, we are talking about results. True, someone will be hurt at some point in the life of every institution. We are not talking about organizational utopia, we are talking about human consideration.

Solutions that undermine strong values will be resisted, perhaps to the point that they are not feasible solutions after all. They can be tempting, however, when it seems necessary to send a message to a truculent group or establish a major new institutional direction.

We advise caution in these areas, but there are times when such moves are necessary. Recognizing the special difficulties that accompany them can prepare leaders to carry them out successfully. As they do so, we urge them to seek new ways that minimize their harm to the individual and the organization.

A Final Note

The courage these seven institutions showed by participating in this study and their contributions to a new understanding of institutional life should not be underestimated. In 1962, Riesman and Jencks wrote that they had studied

> only relatively excellent institutions; it would be too much to subject the poorer ones to this kind of searching analysis, however enlightening the contrasts might be. . . . The inner workings of institutions, like those of individual personalities, are best revealed when the whole system is under strain. (p. 8)

Without either claiming to have produced an equally searching analysis or asserting that these seven institutions are in any sense poorer than others, we note that most of them are under strain of some kind and that they can teach us a great deal about life in mainstream higher education in the late twentieth century.

Although this is the final chapter of the book, it is not a conclusion. We will continue our efforts to learn from their experiences, and we trust that the reader will, too. As we do so, Rural State and Present State probably will be looking for new presidents, Covenant and Triad will be negotiating relationships among faculty and administrators, Mission and R&D will be developing or not developing a stronger identity, and Family State will be finding or not finding compatible faculty. Their stories would be different if we revisited them today. But then and now, they are stories of people, not heroes or villains, not programs or clientele. Effective leadership in organizations arises most often from those who appreciate human abilities and needs.

References

BECHER, T. (1981). Towards a definition of disciplinary cultures. *Studies in Higher Education, 6*(2), 109–122.

BECKER, H. (1963). Student culture. In Lunsford, T.F. (Ed.), *The study of campus cultures* (pp. 11–26). Boulder, CO: Western Interstate Commission for Higher Education.

BENNIS, W. (1984). Transformative power and leadership. In Sergiovanni, T., & Corbally, J. (Eds.), *Leadership and organizational culture* (pp. 67–71). Urbana, IL: University of Illinois Press.

BLACK, M., & METZGER, D. (1964). Ethnographic description and the study of the law. *American Anthropologist, 67*, 141–165.

BURNS, J. (1978). *Leadership.* New York: Harper & Row.

BUSHNELL, J. (1960). Student values: A summary of research and future problems. In Carpenter, M. (Ed.), *The larger learning* (pp. 45–61). Dubuque, IA: Brown.

CALLAHAN, R. (1962). *Education and the culture of efficiency.* Chicago: University of Chicago Press.

CHAFFEE, E. (1984a). Successful strategic management in small private colleges. *Journal of Higher Education, 55*(2), 212–241.

CHAFFEE, E. (1984b). *After decline what? Survival strategies at eight private colleges.* Boulder, CO: National Center for Higher Education Management Systems.

CHAFFEE, E. (1985a). The concept of strategy: From business to higher education. In Smart, J. (Ed.), *Higher education: Handbook of theory and research, 1,* 133–171. New York: Agathon.

CHAFFEE, E. (1985b). Three models of strategy. *Academy of Management Review, 10,* 89–98.

CHAIT, R. (1982). Look who invented Japanese management! *AGB Quarterly, 17,* 3–7.

CLARK, B. (1970). *The distinctive college.* Chicago: Aldine.

CLARK, B. (1971). Belief and loyalty in college organization. *Journal of Higher Education, 42,* 499–520.

CLARK, B. (1980). The organizational saga in higher education. In Leavitt, H. (Ed.), *Readings in managerial psychology.* Chicago: Chicago University Press.

CLARK, B. (Ed.) (1984). *Perspectives on higher education.* Berkeley: University of California Press.

DEAL, T. & KENNEDY, A. (1982). *Corporate cultures: The rites and rituals of corporate life.* Reading, MA: Addison-Wesley.

DENZIN, N. (1978). *Sociological Methods.* New York: McGraw-Hill.

DILL, D. (1982). The management of academic culture: Notes on the management of meaning and social integration. *Higher Education, 11,* 303–320.

FELDMAN, M. & MARCH, J. (1981). Information in organizations as signal and symbol. *Administrative Science Quarterly, 26,* 171–186.

FOUCAULT, M. (1973). *The order of things.* New York: Vintage.

FREEDMAN, M. (1979). *Academic culture and faculty development.* Berkeley: University of California Press.

GADAMER, H.G. (1979). The problem of historical consciousness. In Rabinow, P. & Sullivan, W. (Eds.), *The interpretive social science.* Berkeley: University of California Press.

GAFF, J. & WILSON, R. (1971). Faculty cultures and interdisciplinary studies. *Journal of Higher Education, 42,* 186–201.

GEERTZ, C. (1973). *The interpretation of cultures.* New York: Basic Books.

GEERTZ, C. (1983). *Local knowledge.* New York: Basic Books.

GRANT, G., & RIESMAN, D. (1978). *The perpetual dream.* Chicago: University of Chicago Press.

GUBA, E., & LINCOLN, Y. (1981). *Effective evaluation.* San Francisco: Jossey-Bass.

HENLEY, N. (1977). *Body politics.* Englewood Cliffs, NJ: Prentice-Hall.

HIGHAM, J. (1974). Hanging together: Divergent unities in American history. *Journal of American History, 61,* 5–28.

HIRSCH, P., & ANDREWS, J. (1984). Administrators' response to performance and value challenges: Stance, symbols, and behavior. In Sergiovanni, T. & Corbally, J. (Eds.), *Leadership and organizational culture* (pp. 170–185). Urbana, IL: University of Illinois Press.

LINCOLN, Y., & GUBA, E. (1985). *Naturalistic inquiry.* Beverly Hills, CA: Sage.

MALINOWSKI, B. (1922). *Argonauts of the western Pacific.* London: Routledge.

MARCH, J. (1984). How we talk and how we act: Administrative theory and administrative life. In Sergiovanni, T. & Corbally, J. (Eds.), *Leadership and organizational culture* (pp. 18–35). Urbana, IL: University of Illinois Press.

MASLAND, A. (1985). Organizational culture in the study of higher education. *Review of Higher Education, 8,* 157–168.

MEAD, M. (1928). *Coming of age in Samoa.* New York: W. Morrow.

ORTEGA Y GASSETT, J. (1944). *Mission of the university.* New York: Norton.

OUCHI, W. (1981). *Theory z.* Reading, MA: Addison-Wesley.

PACE, C. (1962). Methods of describing college cultures. *Teachers College Record, 63,* 267–277.

PETERS, T., & WATERMAN, R. (1982). *In search of excellence.* New York: Harper & Row.

PETERSON, M. (1985). Emerging developments in postsecondary organization theory and research: Fragmentation or integration. *Educational Researcher, 14*, 5–12.

PONDY, L. (1978). Leadership is a language game. In McCall, M. & Lombardo, M. (Eds.), *Leadership: Where else can we go* (pp. 87–99). Durham, NC: Duke University Press.

PUTNAM, L., & PACANOWSKY, M. (Eds.) (1983). *Communication and organizations: An interpretive approach.* Beverly Hills, CA: Sage.

RABINOW, P., & SULLIVAN. W. (1979). *Interpretive social science.* Berkeley: University of California Press.

RIESMAN, D., & JENCKS, C. (1962). The viability of the American college. In Sanford, N. (Ed.), *The American college* (pp. 74–192). New York: Wiley.

RIST, R. (1980). Blitzkrieg ethnography. *Educational Research, 9*, 8–10.

SCHEIN, E. (1985). *Organizational culture and leadership.* San Francisco: Jossey-Bass.

SMIRCICH, L., & STUBBART, G. (1985). Strategic management in an enacted world. *Academy of Management Review, 10*(4), 724–736.

SMITH, A., & ROBBINS, A. (1982). Structured ethnography. *American Behavioral Scientist, 26*, 45–61.

SPRADLEY, J. (1979). *The ethnographic interview.* New York: Holt.

SPRADLEY, J. (1980). *Participant observation.* New York: Holt.

TIERNEY, W. (1985). Ethnography: An alternative evaluation methodology. *Review of Higher Education, 8*, 93–105.

TIERNEY, W. (1988). Organizational culture in higher education: Defining the essentials. *Journal of Higher Education, 59*(1), 2–21.

TIERNEY, W. (forthcoming-a). *The web of leadership: The presidency in higher education.* Greenwich, CT: JAI Press.

TIERNEY, W. (forthcoming-b). The symbolic aspects of leadership: An ethnographic perspective. *The American Journal of Semiotics.*

TRICE, H., & BEYER, J. (1984). Studying organizational cultures through rites and ceremonials. *Academy of Management Review, 9*, 653–669.

TRUJILLO, N. (1983). 'Performing' Mintzberg's roles: The nature of managerial communication. In Putnam, L. & Pacanowsky M. (Eds.), *Communication and organizations: An interpretive approach.* Beverly Hills, CA: Sage.

ZAMMUTO, R. (1985). Managing decline in American higher education. In Smart, J. (Ed.), *Higher education: Handbook of theory and research, 2,* 43–84. New York: Agathon.

Some Thoughts on Method: Procedures for Validating Qualitative Research

In order to investigate how higher education management makes decisions, utilizes different strategies, and determines and achieves institutional effectiveness, the research team studied seven colleges and universities. The guiding principle of the research was to construct a multifaceted approach to the study of organizations. The team did not assume that perception is always reality, but we gave credence to the idea that organizations are socially constructed. We assumed that participants' perceptions of problems, solutions, and culture go a long way toward determining organizational health.

Although each member of the research team had extensive experience in management and governance in higher education, we did not enter the field with preconceived notions about institutional effectiveness or what constitutes good decisionmaking. In large part, we borrowed Malinowski's (1922) concept of "foreshadowed problems."

> Good training in theory, and acquaintance with its latest results, is not identical with being burdened with "preconceived ideas." If a man sets out on an expedition, determined to prove certain hypotheses, if he is incapable of changing his views constantly and casting them off ungrudgingly under the pressure of evidence, needless to say his work will be worthless. But the more problems he brings with him into the field, the more he is in the habit of molding his theories according to facts, and of seeing facts in their bearing upon theory, the better

> he is equipped for the work. Preconceived ideas are pernicious in any
> scientific work, but foreshadowed problems are the main endowment
> of a scientific thinker, and these problems are first revealed to the
> observer by his theoretical studies. (pp. 8–9)

Thus, we did not set out to prove hypotheses. We entered
the field with the inductive premise that our questions and answers would be discovered in the social situation. Like others before us (Spradley, 1980; Black and Metzger, 1964), we believe that
questions imply answers and that statements of any kind imply
questions. Hence, we entered the field with a theoretical framework based on the assumption that organizations are socially constructed, and we were armed with "foreshadowed problems." Our
questions, however, arose in the field.

The five-person team consisted of individuals versed in organizational behavior (the project director), anthropology, statistics,
political science, and communication. The director assembled the
team in the summer of 1984. We selected sites, outlined group and
individual tasks, and prepared for fall visits. We utilized the Higher
Education General Information Survey (HEGIS), a federal data
base on all U.S. regionally accredited institutions of higher education, and the Institutional Performance Survey (IPS), a survey data
base on a stratified random sample of 334 four-year institutions
from the National Center for Higher Education Management Systems, to make site selections. We selected the sample in order to
examine the applicability of our findings to diverse kinds of institutions, to the extent that a small sample permits. The key structural
dimensions on which the selections rested were size and control.
Research sites included four public and three private institutions,
three of them colleges and four of them universities.

We omitted large schools and two-year schools primarily because of other selection criteria. We wanted time-series data on
these institutions to the maximum feasible extent. Therefore, we
limited the sample to the 334 institutions that participated in the
original 1983 IPS survey. The survey included no two-year colleges
and few institutions larger than 10,000 students. Institutions over
10,000 were simply too large and complex for the research team
to gain in-depth knowledge in the time allowed. Located throughout the United States, the institutions ranged from a minimum of
900 students to a maximum of 7,500 students.

The director initiated contact with the college presidents by
letter and a follow-up phone call, described the nature of the
project, and asked if they were willing to participate. Only one

institution declined. When the presidents agreed, they appointed a contact person at their institutions who conversed frequently with the research team prior to the fall visits. The contact person arranged interviews with a diverse sample of the college community—administrators, faculty, staff, students, trustees, executive administrators, and representatives of the community, local and state governments. We stressed that we wanted to interview a diverse sample, such as "actively involved or not involved, women and men, minority and majority races, liberal arts and professional, senior and junior, long and short service, optimists and pessimists, leaders and followers." During the interviews, we also asked individuals if there were other people with whom we should speak.

The contact person sent the team documents such as the campus newspaper, college catalog, institutional histories, or information the institution sends to prospective students, donors, parents, legislators, and alumni. We asked to be put on campus mailing lists and requested minutes from recent administrative meetings, faculty meetings, and board meetings. We requested a copy of any campus master plan. Our contact person also provided local press clippings and accreditation reports. If the institution had a movie or slide show about itself, we viewed it. We asked the contact person to provide materials we may have neglected to ask for but which the institution considered important. Finally, we asked to attend any scheduled meetings or ceremonies such as the faculty senate, administrative council, or honors day celebrations.

We examined the materials and interview lists to ensure that we had received a complete and fair sample. For example, Covenant University had not arranged any faculty interviews because of extreme administrative sensitivity about the faculty union. When we arrived on campus, we asked the contact person if we could speak with the union president. She arranged the interview, and the union president readily agreed to faculty participation. Indeed, the union president turned out to be a primary informant. In this case, permitting the exclusion of data would have jeopardized the integrity of the study.

Procedures for Team Research

Validity, obtaining a correct interpretation of the observed situation, depends on thick description (Geertz, 1973). Four procedures that help a researcher interpret data correctly are (a) longitudinal analysis, (b) quantitative analysis, (c) multiple interviews and interview formats, and (d) data presentation style.

LONGITUDINAL ANALYSIS

The team made every effort to place present events and people into an historical context. The assumption was that for a portrait of an organization to have any meaning, it had to be fleshed out, thick in description and rich in nuance. Cultural research of colleges and universities requires that the researchers observe at least an academic year, in order to see a full season of the unit of analysis. Repeat visits to each campus were an essential element in the research design. Had we made only one visit, we would have missed a number of important, sometimes crucial, insights into the dynamics of organizational culture and processes of organizational change.

In the fall, for example, Rural State College exhibited a strong degree of consensus about decision-making, leadership, and the perception of organizational culture. However, when we returned in the spring the institution was in an uproar over administrative decisions and violations of cultural norms. Although our findings from the fall visit were not inaccurate, the inclusion of a second visit refocused the case study.

What we did not desire was "blitzkrieg ethnography" (Rist, 1980), where one person spends an afternoon at the research site, interviews only top administrators, and never returns. While one short visit to an institution may be helpful for many reasons, that visit defies the research design advocated here. Longitudinal analysis strengthens the validity of team findings in several ways.

First, one key requirement for understanding an organization is to learn the language of the informants. If researchers cannot speak the language, they will not understand the situation. Organizational language can range from jargon or slang to the acronyms and words the individuals use for different meetings and ceremonies. The researcher also wants to identify language patterns individuals use when they interact with one another, such as the use of first names, or the use of pronouns "we" and "they" to identify with whom the speaker's sentiments lie.

Second, a research scientist will build up rapport over time with the persons contacted. During the course of the fieldwork, we reinterviewed some initial informants and communicated with others by letter. People became more open with us on our return visits. Rapport does not occur instantaneously, but gradually over time. Further, rapport provides another means of checking data. The more comfortable people are with an interviewer, the more willing they will be to tell the interviewer "what's really going on around here."

Third, longitudinal analysis allows questions to develop over time. Lincoln and Guba note, "The negotiation of outcomes is a continuous process that goes on, formally and informally, from the very inception of the study" (1985, p. 213). When the researchers use the inductive approach, questions and hypotheses develop from the data. Necessarily, the research demands time-series data from which the team can formulate better questions.

QUANTITATIVE ANALYSIS

Denzin (1978) uses the term triangulation to describe the integration of different methods within a study. He writes, "No single method ever adequately solves the problems of rival causal factors. Because each method reveals different aspects of empirical reality, multiple methods of observation must be employed. This is termed triangulation" (p. 28). Qualitative researchers can employ quantitative techniques as one way to triangulate their observations.

We developed the IPS in order to statistically assess constituents' perceptions of various aspects of institutional performance. The eight sections of the hundred-item questionnaire were environment, enrollments, revenues, functioning, culture, strategy, resource allocation, and effectiveness. We surveyed each institution one year prior to the initial visit and again between the first and second visits.

The IPS provided useful statistical data in five ways. First, because each institution had been surveyed prior to the site visits, we could compare how respondents' perceptions had changed during the two years before the second survey. Second, the data either confirmed or questioned the qualitative findings from the fall visit. Third, the data provided additional questions for the return visit. Fourth, the IPS was a critical component in enabling us to disentangle institutional perceptions across categories of respondents. For example, at Present State College we found that the top administration felt they made budget cuts on a prioritized basis, yet the rest of the institution did not. This evidence confirmed our interviews with staff, faculty, and midmanagement.

Fifth, because we used the same instrument at each site, we had statistical data that could be cross-analyzed. For example, we found that trustees at all institutions were most at variance with others in their understanding of the organization. At one college, however, faculty perception of shared governance was considerably lower than at the other institutions. Thus, the IPS offered a sophisticated means of correlating perceptual and empirical evidence.

MULTIPLE INTERVIEWS AND INTERVIEW FORMATS

We have described above the importance of interviewing diverse individuals. In addition, four forms of interviews by different research members provided a way to cross-check our findings. Two of the interview formats occurred during the fall visits, and two additional formats occurred in the spring. First, one interviewer used a structured interview with predefined questions asked at each site. These questions dealt with general items such as institutional mission, leadership, and decisionmaking. A second individual asked open-ended questions in the ethnographic tradition (Tierney, 1985; Spradley, 1979). Spradley calls these interviews "grand tour questions" (p. 86) because they allow the informant to give the interviewer a grand tour of the research site. The interview is free-flowing and focuses on what the respondent finds important.

The interviewers compared findings and preliminary conclusions at the end of each research visit. The different interview styles provided data to cross-check the validity of one another's interviews. For example, at one institution, respondents in grand tour interviews consistently brought up their view of the organization as a "family." The structured interviews supported this observation by examples of how decision-making and leadership took into account the feelings and ideas of all organizational members. Similar findings from different kinds of interviews added another means of interpretation and analysis.

During the spring visits, new interviewees and a small group of key informants from the first group provided a third interview format. Structured and ethnographic styles of interviewing gave way to specific questions related to the initial findings. The interviewers asked respondents to provide rationales for discrepancies we had found. We had discovered occasional puzzles between IPS results and fall interviews; spring visits allowed respondents to provide their answers to these paradoxes.

The fourth form of confirming perceptual evidence included a third team member uninvolved in earlier visits. Joining the research in progress, the team member's responsibilities included checking assumptions and findings of the original two team members. The new member's interviews provided additional data from a different point in time in order to ascertain if the initial data were highly dependent upon the specific circumstances surrounding the initial interview. The interviewer also checked the validity of the IPS results. He queried respondents to the IPS about why they had answered the survey the way they had in order to ensure the accuracy of our interpretation.

PRESENTATION OF DATA

The way we presented our data involved a method consistent with anthropology but in many respects new to educational research. Instead of presenting data by reporting incidents to the reader, the reports involve the reader more fully in the interpretation of the data. That is, one goal of the work was to enable the reader to step into the place of the writers and know the institution so well that the reader could interpret the data. Rather than tell the reader about the case, we presented quotes and institutional portraits that showed their cultures.

For example, an interpretive statement about one college president would be, "Many people commented on the president's broad intellectual scope, yet also on his attention to detail." Instead of telling the reader that general conclusion, we reported that:

> Words used to characterize the president were "humble," "intellectual," "a renaissance man." On the other hand, one often heard comments similar to the following, "He gets caught up in the minute activities of the campus. You know he lives in one of the dorms so he's always walking around. He gets upset if there are posters on the doors, or dislikes the color of the carpets. Could you kindly tell me why the president gets involved in things like that?"

This style enables the reader to check the researchers' interpretation against the actual data.

We began writing our field notes in coherent form after the

first visit. Then, two additional team members read each of the case studies. They provided suggestions about the direction the research and writing should take. By the end of the fieldwork, we had rewritten the rough drafts and a fifth team member read the cases. After editing the case studies again, the team sent each president the case dealing with his institution. We asked them for their impressions of the study and corrections of any factual errors. Their responses became an additional set of data.

For example, one president wrote an eight-page letter providing his analysis of the study and including additional information about why he had made certain decisions reported in the study. The point is that the data collection did not stop when we concluded our fieldwork. We viewed writing as an ongoing process, so that research did not occur in isolation or solely prior to writing; research and writing occurred concurrently.

Also, we never used one quote to generalize about a topic. For example, at the institution noted above, several speakers mentioned the president's informal and formal roles. Their comments were recorded by both interviewers at different times. Thus, the quotes exemplify what we heard; they were never exceptions to the rule.

Observation

As with all research, the case studies attempted here have pitfalls and logistical problems. The work is expensive, personally demanding, and time-consuming. Spradley notes that this kind of research "always begins with a sense of uncertainty, a feeling of apprehension" (1979, p. 79). We spent eight of eleven weeks in the fall on the road, away from friends and family. Day-long interviews and observation, coupled with evening debriefing and planning sessions, allow little time for relaxation.

The research occurred over a fifteen-month period. A multisite, multi-member case study demands a large travel budget. However, the validation of the research demanded intense periods of work over a long period of time in different geographic areas. Guba and Lincoln observe,

> It is difficult to find an appropriate balance between settling on an appropriate focus for a study while resisting, on the one hand premature closure, and on the other, changes that ought not to be made. It takes time to sort out the salient factors in a situation and zero in on them.

> There is an enormous press to get the "preliminary" job done so that the "real" inquiry can get under way. But tolerance of ambiguity is a rare characteristic and patience an infrequent virtue. (1981, p. 354)

Collegiality among team members was a critical factor. Team research of this sort demands informal interaction with one another. At the same time, informality can slow down the direction of the project. For this study, Chaffee, the project director, was "first among equals" with instrumental authority. With intellectual tasks, however, disagreements flourished so that spirited debate about the nature of the findings constantly occurred.

Different writing styles and the fact that we began writing in the middle of the research also provided a potential problem. Early writing could have biased our conclusions when we returned in the spring. Because we were critically aware of this problem and merciless when one of us became more attached to our prose than subsequent learning could support, it did not become a problem. Indeed, in two settings we found that our initial conclusions were inaccurate and the case studies had to be rewritten almost entirely. Again, since we saw writing as an additional form of inquiry, our work actually benefited from our different writing styles, how we agreed to the convergence of data, and what we ultimately agreed was important.

Finally, the question arises about what makes a good field researcher. Smith and Robbins have provided a succinct analysis. They note such attributes as "good interviewing and observing skills, ability to critically analyze information, interest in the study, time to devote to the work, willingness to take outside direction, ability to observe without judging or intervening, and good interpersonal skills" (1982, p. 52). In addition, the individual must be able to tolerate ambiguity. None of us claims to be a paragon of all these virtues, but among us we believe we had them covered reasonably well.

Traits such as the ability to critically interview and observe are skills that researchers learn and develop. The procedures we used are not mechanistic principles that can be applied to any situation. Rather, researchers need a background in the theoretical assumptions and framework of qualitative research in order to use optimally various validation procedures.

Appendix B

Sample Documents
— About the Study —

July 31, 1984

Dr. Case Study
President
Home Town University
Home Town, USA 01234

Dear Dr. Study:

The Organizational Studies Division conducted a large-scale survey of the management and performance of over 300 colleges and universities during 1982–83 in which Home Town University participated. As part of our continuing research effort, the Organizational Studies Division is conducting case studies during 1984–85 in eight of the institutions that participated in the earlier project. The purposes of these eight case studies are:

1. To draw our previous findings into a single, integrated set of principles for the management of colleges and universities;

2. To examine the extent to which the principles apply to the experiences of a diverse set of institutions; and

3. To improve our capacity to communicate the validated principles to higher education administrators.

Institutions for the case studies have been selected on the basis of several institutional characteristics, such as enrollment size, geographic region, program emphasis, and institutional control. Based on these considerations, Home Town

University has been selected as a candidate for inclusion in the case studies. I hope that you will allow your institution to participate in this study.

We would like to send two researchers to Home Town University for one week this fall and one week next spring. They would interview individuals, including top administrators, faculty, students, trustees, and community representatives. If possible, they would sit in on meetings of such groups as administrative council or a planning committee. If you have any special activities going on this year, such as preparing for an accreditation visit, it would be helpful if we could observe part of that process. We would like to make specific arrangements through a liaison person named by you to help us with logistics.

In exchange for your help, we offer you a new service of the Division that is further described in the back page of the enclosed brochure—the Institutional Performance Survey (IPS). The IPS is based on the large-scale survey study in which your institution participated in 1982–83. A copy of that instrument is enclosed. The service consists of tailoring the IPS assessment to the needs of your institution, administering the IPS survey, tabulating the results, preparing a comprehensive report, and conducting a seminar on your campus to describe the results and their implications. Colleges using the IPS outside of this research project are paying several thousand dollars for this service.

I will call you in a week to see whether you are interested in participating and if you have any questions. Please feel free to call in the meanwhile if you would like more information (303/497-0322). I hope that you will agree to participate.

Sincerely,

Ellen Earle Chaffee
Director
Organizational Studies

EEC/glt
Enclosures

September 19, 1984

Dr. I. P. Survey
Liaison Representative
Home Town University
Home Town, USA 01234

Dear Dr. Survey:

Thank you for agreeing to arrange our visit to Home Town University. Bill Tierney and I will be there November 19 through 21.

As we discussed, I would appreciate your arranging for us to meet with a number of individuals during our visit. We would like to have about an hour with each person, and we need about 15–30 minutes between interviews in order to allow for any extra time with an interviewee and to get from one place to another. Bill and I would be glad to take interviewees to lunch, so feel free to schedule us all day long. We would like to take you out to lunch on the 21st, if that suits your schedule. It might also work well for us to take students to lunch on the other days or to attend any noon meetings of various groups.

The enclosed material provides more detail on our desired interview schedule, on the written materials we would like to collect, and on the kinds of meetings we would like to observe. We will fill any gaps in our interview schedule with last-minute plans to visit meetings or interview individuals other than those you have scheduled for us. We may well be unable to complete our agenda in three days, so we can plan another visit later.

If you plan to make our visit widely known on campus, please consider the following option. At some time, perhaps at the end of the day on November 19, we could be available for 30–45 minutes to talk with anyone who wants to stop by. If this seems like a good idea, please arrange for a location and for notice of the opportunity.

Thank you for recommending Over Night Hotel. You can leave any message for us there, if you wish. We will check in with you on Monday at 9:00 a.m. We are looking forward to getting to know Home Town University. Thank you again for enabling us to do so.

Sincerely,

Ellen Earle Chaffee
Director
Organizational Studies

EEC/glt
Enclosures

RESEARCH PROJECT: MANAGEMENT
AND PERFORMANCE

Project Description

The Organizational Studies Division conducted a large-scale survey of the management and performance of over 300 colleges and universities during 1982–83 in which Home Town University participated. As part of our continuing research effort, we are conducting case studies during 1984–85 in eight of the institutions that participated in the earlier project. The purposes of the eight case studies are:

1. To draw our previous findings into a single integrated set of principles for the management of colleges and universities;

2. To examine the extent to which the principles apply to the experiences of a diverse set of institutions; and

3. To improve our capacity to communicate the validated principles to higher education administrators.

Institutions for the case studies were selected on the basis of several characteristics, such as enrollment size, geographic region, program emphasis, and institutional control. Based on these considerations, Home Town University was selected, and Dr. Study has agreed on behalf of the institution to participate.

Two researchers, Ellen Chaffee and Bill Tierney, will visit the campus once this fall and again next spring. We will interview a number of individuals on the following general topics: the mission of the institution, changes it has made in recent years, the role of leadership, and assessing how well the institution is doing. Dr. I. P. Survey is coordinating our interview schedules. In addition, we will visit various campus functions and meetings. Our primary purpose is to understand how the institution functions as an organization and to determine whether a wide array of research findings seems to correspond to the experience of the institution.

Each person interviewed is guaranteed that what he or she says will remain confidential both on campus and in any publications. The name of the college will not be revealed to anyone off-campus except the research team. All publications will use a pseudonym instead of the college name. After the case studies are written, the institution will be able to review a draft version to ensure accuracy.

We are very grateful for your willingness to participate in the study. Our aim is to interpret what we learn from you so that ultimately the administration of higher education institutions will improve as a result of this and related research.

Organizational Studies Division
National Center for Higher Education Management Systems
P.O. Drawer P
Boulder, CO 80302
303/497-0322

RESEARCH PROJECT: MANAGEMENT AND PERFORMANCE

Assistance Requested from Liaison Representative

INTERVIEWS

The top priority for our visit is to conduct individual interviews. *Two* researchers will conduct separate interviews with different individuals, except that the researchers will interview the president together. Other than that interview, please create an individual schedule for each of the two researchers. Each should see a mixture of different types of people, as listed below. Please provide us with our interview schedules when we arrive.

The list below identifies the individuals who are so central to the study that we ask you to make every effort to schedule an interview with each of them before filling in any remaining time.

president
academic vice president
business vice president
institutional and/or academic planning officer
admissions director
development director
institutional research officer
dean of students
mix of at least four faculty, such as representatives of:
   actively involved in college or not involved
   women and men, minority and majority races
   liberal arts and professional
   senior and junior
   long and short service here
   optimists and pessimists
   supporters and skeptics of administration
   (Note: Be sure to include at least one skeptic, please!)
mix of at least four students, such as representatives of:
   women and men, minority and majority races
   student leaders and others
   undergraduate and graduate

In addition, we would like to meet with individuals such as those listed below, as the schedule permits:

president's secretary/executive assistant
director of public relations
academic deans
director of alumni affairs
trustees
representatives of the community, executive and legislative
      branches of government, parents of students—whether
      actively involved with the institution or not
other key individuals who may not be listed here

WRITTEN MATERIALS

Please arrange for us to receive as many of the following documents as possible. We can pick them up when we arrive, either from you or whoever can most easily give them to us. Please bill us for any copying charges, as needed.

sample campus newspaper
college catalog
materials the institution sends to:
   prospective students
   prospective donors
   parents
   legislators
   alumni
   (may simply put us on your mailing lists)
calendar of events the week we're on campus
minutes from most recent faculty meeting
minutes from most recent trustee meeting
curriculum vitae for each of the individuals interviewed
any "master plan" or similar document since 1970
current issue of any faculty/staff newsletter
clippings about the college from recent local papers
accreditation reports—visiting team's report from the past two
site visits, and one (most recent) institutional self-study

MEETINGS

If our interview schedule permits and the members of the groups are willing, we would like to attend any regularly scheduled meetings such as the following. Our purpose is only to observe.

We would not participate in or disrupt the meeting in any way.
   faculty senate or subcommittee
   board of trustees or subcommittee
   administrative council or subcommittee
   long-range planning committee or subcommittee
   accreditation study group or subcommittee
   alumni group or committee
   In addition, if the institution has a movie or slide show about
itself (however old it may be), we would like to view it.

Organizational Studies Division
National Center for Higher Education Management Systems
P.O. Drawer P
Boulder, CO 80302
303/497-0322

RESEARCH PROJECT: MANAGEMENT AND PERFORMANCE

Biographies of Researchers

Ellen Earle Chaffee is the Director of the Organizational Studies Division at the National Center for Higher Education Management Systems in Boulder, Colorado, where she has been since 1980. She conducts research on strategic management, planning and budgeting, and organizational decision-making in colleges and universities. Her research has led to a number of articles and books, and she has consulted with several colleges. Dr. Chaffee holds a Ph.D. in Administration and Policy Analysis from Stanford University. Her administrative responsibilities during ten years at Stanford and North Dakota State universities included budget development, equal opportunity, and student affairs administration.

William G. Tierney is Senior Associate for the Organizational Studies Division at the National Center for Higher Education Management Systems in Boulder, Colorado. He holds a Ph.D. in Administration and Policy Analysis and an M.A. in Anthropology from Stanford University. He has published several articles that demonstrate the usefulness of anthropological models and methods for the administration and organization of educational institutions. He spent two years as Academic Dean at Fort Berthold Community College in Newtown, North Dakota, and two years as an English teacher in the Peace Corps in Morocco.

Organizational Studies Division
National Center for Higher Education Management Systems
P.O. Drawer P
Boulder, CO 80302
303/497-0322

INTERVIEW PROTOCOL

Case Studies in Management and Performance

Introduction:

Explain general nature of the study and why we chose college X
   synthesis of three years of research
   topics: the mission of the college
      changes in the college
      leadership
      performance—how the college is doing
   narrowed college selection to 334 in 1983 survey
      deleted colleges over 10,000
      looked for diverse kinds of colleges
   purpose: see if our research ideas hold water in the real world
Both the colleges and the respondents are guaranteed
   anonymity

1. What is the mission of this college? How well-focused is it?
   How and to what extent has the college adapted to its
   environment in the past 5 years? What have been the consequences for the institution? for the people associated
   with the institution?
      Explain linear, adaptive, and interpretive strategy—do
   you see evidence of any of these strategies having been
   used here in the past three years? How do you assess the
   results?
      [changes in niche size/shape]: Do you think enroll-
   ments will increase, decrease, or remain the same at this
   institution over the next three years? What factors contribute to this expected trend? (Look for comments on
   changing population demographics, student interests relative to college programs, economic conditions, competition with other schools, federal and state policies and
   regulations.) If decrease, what could the institution do to
   prevent it?
      Do you think institutional revenues will increase,
   decrease, or remain about the same over the next three
   years? What factors contribute to this expected trend?
   (Look for comments on effects of changing enrollments,
   economic conditions, changing federal and state support.)

[Admissions officer only]: Who are the school's primary competitors for enrollments? Does the competition occur in any particular area? (Make a list.)

Explain domain defense, offense, creation—do you see evidence of any of these strategies having been used here in the past three years? How do you assess the results?

2. Some people say that management makes a critically important difference in the welfare of the institution; others say that environmental forces are so strong that management is virtually helpless. Have you seen evidence here that would tend to support either of these positions?

3. What constitutes leadership? What, to you, is leader credibility? How would you rate it here? What affects your judgment of a leader's credibility? What could be done to improve leader credibility here?

What does the president want the college to be in the next 3–5 years? How do you know? To what extent do you agree with that view?

What are the president's strongest personal skills?

What constituencies are most important to the president?

What indicators does the president use to determine how well the college is doing? . . . for how well *he* is doing?

4. What were the two most important decisions for this institution in the past 3 years? Why were they important? How were they made?

Thinking about each of these decisions, how would you describe the way explicit data or information was used in the decisionmaking process?

What two or three pieces of data or information (if any) seemed most salient in making the decision?

If other or additional data or information had been available at the time of the decision, how might the decision have been different?

Once the decision was taken, what key concepts, words, and pieces of information were used to communicate it to others? What reactions were encountered?

5. Finally, I have some questions that relate to your evaluation of how the college is doing, overall.

Why did you come to this college rather than some other? How have your reasons for being here changed since then? What do you personally want from the college?

On what bases do you personally evaluate the effectiveness of the college? That is, if you want to assess how well the college is doing, how do you do it?

How widely accepted are your personal measures among others on campus? That is, how many others share them?

How explicit are they (quantitative vs. qualitative, hard vs. soft)?

How "numbers-oriented" do you feel current decisionmaking is at this institution?

Do people who invest time and money in the college feel that they get ample return? What do they get? On what do you base your answer? What could be done to improve it?

What 3-4 constituent groups are more important for the college? Why is each important? What does each want from the college? To what extent does each get what it wants? Which one matters most to the college? Why?

Now, let me try to paraphrase some themes I think I've heard you express during the interview. Tell me if I've understood you correctly. . . . [Feed back what you've heard, in terms of our theoretical framework.]

Now that you know the kinds of issues I'm interested in, is there anyone else you think I should be sure to talk with about them?

[For best informants:] You've been exceptionally helpful. May I call you from time to time to ask you more about these issues and what is happening here? (Get phone number.)

OVERVIEW OF CASE STUDIES

Case Studies on Management and Performance

Autumn visit:
  Interviews, meetings, events
    strategy
    effectiveness
    competition (admissions)
    information on decision-making
  Set up IPS administration (institutional research)

Interim:
  Possible visit, interviews, meetings, events
  Administer and analyze IPS

Spring visit:
  Interviews, meetings, events
    strategy
    effectiveness
    competition (admissions)
    information in decision-making
  Feedback session for IPS results

Key concepts for the study:
    investor confidence
    leader credibility
    interpretive strategy
    adaptive strategy, adaptation
    linear strategy
    multiple constituencies
    domain defense, offense, creation
    indicators of effectiveness
    leadership
    changes in niche size/shape
    management vs. environment
    rationality
    selective perception
    information as signal and symbol
    information for decision vs. information for implementation

By_____

FACE SHEET FOR INTERVIEW NOTES

Interviewee _____School_____

Position_____Resume attached__yes__no

Address/phone_____

   I. Topics covered:

— virtually all

— especially management vs. environment

— especially decision/information

— especially mission/adaptation/strategy

— especially leadership

— especially evaluation of college

  II. Key points/stories discussed:

  III. Quotable quotes:

  IV. Issues to be investigated further:

  V. Tentative conclusions re:

      mission/adaptation/strategy—

      leadership—

      decision/information—

      evaluation of college—

      management vs. environment—

1983 and 1985 Rankings of the Cases on Selected Institutional Performance Survey ——— Questions ———

INSTITUTIONAL PERFORMANCE SURVEY

Institution Means
[1983 in Column 1 and 1985 in Column 2]

Scale: 1 = disagree; 5 = agree

Section 4: Institutional Characteristics
    Q 6: People associated with this institution share a common
         definition of its mission.

Family State	4.3	Mission	3.6
Triad	4.0	Family State	3.5
Mission	4.0	Rural State	3.5
Rural State	3.4	Triad	3.2
R&D	2.9	Covenant	2.7
Present State	2.8	R&D	2.5
Convenant	2.7	Present State	2.5

223

INSTITUTIONAL PERFORMANCE SURVEY

Institution Means
[1983 in Column 1 and 1985 in Column 2]

Section 4: Institutional Characteristics
  Q 7: Those who make a personal or financial investment in this
       institution believe that they receive an ample return.

Family State	4.2	Mission	3.8
Mission	4.2	Family State	3.7
Triad	4.1	Rural State	3.6
Rural State	4.1	Triad	3.6
R&D	3.1	Covenant	3.2
Covenant	3.0	R&D	2.9
Present State	3.0	Present State	2.9

Section 4: Institutional Characteristics
  Q 9: Major decisions are very centralized.

Covenant	4.3	R&D	4.3
R&D	4.0	Present State	4.2
Mission	3.9	Mission	4.2
Triad	3.9	Rural State	3.9
Present State	3.6	Covenant	3.9
Family State	3.1	Family State	3.5
Rural State	2.9	Triad	3.5

Section 4: Institutional Characteristics
  Q11: Innovative activity is increasing.

Present State	4.0	Mission	3.6
Mission	4.0	Rural State	3.4
Rural State	3.8	Present State	3.4
Family State	3.8	Triad	3.4
Triad	3.7	Family State	3.3
R&D	3.4	Covenant	3.2
Covenant	2.7	R&D	2.6

INSTITUTIONAL PERFORMANCE SURVEY

Institution Means
[1983 in Column 1 and 1985 in Column 2]

Section 4: Institutional Characteristics
  Q15: Morale is increasing among members of this institution.

Present State	3.6	Covenant	3.4
Rural State	3.6	Family State	3.3
Mission	3.5	Mission	3.1
Family State	3.5	Present State	2.8
Triad	3.3	Triad	2.7
R&D	2.7	Rural State	2.6
Covenant	1.7	R&D	2.2

Section 4: Institutional Characteristics
  Q16: We have no place that we could cut expenditures without
       severely damaging the school.

Rural State	3.6	Rural State	3.6
Present State	3.4	R&D	3.0
Family State	2.9	Family State	2.9
R&D	2.9	Covenant	2.7
Triad	2.8	Present State	2.7
Covenant	2.7	Triad	2.7
Mission	2.0	Mission	2.3

Section 4: Institutional Characteristics
  Q18: Top administrators have high credibility.

Rural State	4.2	Rural State	3.7
Family State	4.1	Family State	3.5
Triad	3.8	Mission	3.3
Mission	3.8	Triad	3.1
Present State	3.2	Covenant	2.7
R&D	2.7	Present State	2.7
Covenant	2.3	R&D	2.5

INSTITUTIONAL PERFORMANCE SURVEY

Institution Means
[1983 in Column 1 and 1985 in Column 2]

Section 4: Institutional Characteristics
    Q19: When cutbacks occur, they are done on a prioritized basis.

Present State	4.0	Rural State	3.5
Family State	3.8	Mission	3.4
Rural State	3.7	Family State	3.4
Mission	3.7	Triad	3.1
Covenant	3.7	R&D	3.0
Triad	3.6	Present State	3.0
R&D	3.1	Covenant	2.8

Section 4: Institutional Characteristics
    Q20: Conflict is increasing within this institution.

Covenant	4.3	R&D	3.3
R&D	2.9	Present State	3.3
Mission	2.6	Triad	3.0
Rural State	2.5	Covenant	2.6
Present State	2.2	Rural State	2.5
Triad	2.1	Mission	2.4
Family State	1.8	Family State	2.3

Section 4: Institutional Characteristics
    Q21: Top administrators believe that factors outside the institution
        largely determine its condition.

R&D	4.0	R&D	3.7
Triad	3.1	Triad	3.5
Rural State	3.1	Rural State	3.2
Covenant	3.0	Covenant	3.1
Family State	2.7	Family State	3.0
Present State	2.4	Present State	2.8
Mission	2.3	Mission	2.5

INSTITUTIONAL PERFORMANCE SURVEY

Institution Means
[1983 in Column 1 and 1985 in Column 2]

Section 6: Institutional Strategy
  Q 1: We are making our academic programs more diverse.

Family State	4.1	Rural State	4.1
Present State	4.0	Family State	3.7
Triad	4.0	Mission	3.7
Rural State	4.0	Triad	3.4
Mission	3.7	Covenant	3.2
Covenant	3.0	Present State	3.0
R&D	2.4	R&D	2.9

Section 6: Institutional Strategy
  Q 2: We are changing the composition of our student body,
       making it more diverse.

Rural State	3.9	Rural State	3.7
Family State	3.7	Family State	3.5
Covenant	3.3	Covenant	3.1
Present State	3.2	Present State	3.1
Mission	3.2	Mission	2.7
Triad	3.0	Triad	2.7
R&D	2.9	R&D	2.7

Section 6: Institutional Strategy
  Q 7: Our top administrators educate important outsiders about the
       value of the institution in order to improve its legitimacy in
       their eyes.

Family State	4.5	Family State	4.1
Triad	4.1	Present State	4.1
Rural State	4.1	Rural State	3.9
Mission	4.0	Mission	3.6
R&D	4.0	Covenant	3.5
Present State	3.5	Triad	3.4
Covenant	3.0	R&D	3.3

INSTITUTIONAL PERFORMANCE SURVEY

Institution Means
[1983 in Column 1 and 1985 in Column 2]

Section 6: Institutional Strategy
    Q 8: This institution tends to do more of what it does well, to expand in areas we have expertise.

Present State	4.0	Rural State	3.7
Family State	4.0	Mission	3.7
Mission	4.0	Triad	3.6
Triad	3.9	Family State	3.5
Rural State	3.8	Present State	3.4
R&D	3.7	Covenant	3.1
Covenant	3.3	R&D	3.0

Section 6: Institutional Strategy
    Q 9: This institution establishes new domains of activity.

Present State	4.0	Rural State	3.5
Rural State	3.8	Family State	3.4
Family State	3.8	Present State	3.3
R&D	3.7	Mission	3.2
Mission	3.3	R&D	3.2
Covenant	3.3	Covenant	3.1
Triad	2.9	Triad	2.7

Section 6: Institutional Strategy
    Q10: We are increasing the quality of the individuals in top administrative positions.

Family State	4.2	Rural State	3.4
Present State	4.0	Family State	3.1
Triad	3.8	Mission	3.1
Mission	3.6	Covenant	3.1
Rural State	3.3	Triad	3.1
R&D	3.0	Present State	2.9
Covenant	2.7	R&D	2.4

INSTITUTIONAL PERFORMANCE SURVEY

Institution Means
[1983 in Column 1 and 1985 in Column 2]

Section 7: Institutional Decision Processes
  Q 3: People at this institution make resource allocation decisions
       collegially.

Triad	3.4	Rural State	3.1
Mission	3.3	Family State	2.8
Family State	3.2	Mission	2.8
Rural State	3.0	Triad	2.5
R&D	2.6	Covenant	2.4
Present State	2.5	Present State	2.2
Covenant	1.7	R&D	1.9

Section 7: Institutional Decision Processes
  Q 4: A rational process is used to make resource allocation
       decisions at this institution.

Mission	3.8	Family State	3.3
Present State	3.7	Mission	3.3
Triad	3.7	Rural State	3.2
Family State	3.7	Triad	3.0
Rural State	3.6	Covenant	2.9
R&D	3.1	Present State	2.9
Covenant	3.0	R&D	2.7

Section 7: Institutional Decision Processes
  Q 7: Resource allocation is decided bureaucratically at this
       institution.

Covenant	4.0	Covenant	3.3
Family State	2.9	R&D	3.3
R&D	2.9	Present State	3.1
Triad	2.8	Rural State	3.1
Rural State	2.6	Family State	3.1
Present State	2.5	Triad	3.0
Mission	2.4	Mission	2.8

INSTITUTIONAL PERFORMANCE SURVEY

Institution Means
[1983 in Column 1 and 1985 in Column 2]

Section 7: Institutional Decision Processes
    Q 8: Resource allocation is decided autocratically.

Covenant	3.3	R&D	3.7
Present State	3.2	Present State	3.5
R&D	3.0	Covenant	3.2
Rural State	2.5	Family State	3.1
Family State	2.4	Triad	3.0
Mission	2.3	Rural State	2.9
Triad	1.9	Mission	2.9

Section 7: Institutional Decision Processes
    Q12: Persuasion, negotiation, and coalition-building are examples
         of what determines resource allocation.

Triad	3.6	Present State	3.3
Present State	3.5	Family State	3.1
Family State	3.1	Mission	3.0
R&D	3.0	Covenant	3.0
Mission	2.9	Triad	3.0
Rural State	2.8	Rural State	2.9
Covenant	2.7	R&D	2.5

Section 8: Institutional Effectiveness
    OE1: Student educational satisfaction

Mission	4.6	Rural State	4.0
Family State	4.3	Triad	3.7
Rural State	4.2	Family State	3.9
Triad	4.2	R&D	3.5
R&D	3.9	Mission	3.3
Present State	3.5	Covenant	3.2
Covenant	2.7	Present State	2.8

INSTITUTIONAL PERFORMANCE SURVEY

Institution Means
[1983 in Column 1 and 1985 in Column 2]

Section 8: Institutional Effectiveness
  OE2: Student academic development

Mission	3.2	Mission	2.9
R&D	3.0	R&D	2.6
Covenant	2.9	Covenant	2.4
Family State	2.8	Rural State	2.3
Triad	2.8	Family State	2.3
Rural State	2.6	Triad	2.3
Present State	2.1	Present State	2.0

Section 8: Institutional Effectiveness
  OE3: Student career development

Triad	4.1	Rural State	4.3
Family State	4.0	Family State	4.3
Rural State	3.9	R&D	4.3
R&D	3.8	Triad	4.0
Mission	3.7	Covenant	3.9
Covenant	3.6	Mission	3.8
Present State	3.1	Present State	3.5

Section 8: Institutional Effectiveness
  OE4: Student personal development

Mission	4.1	Mission	3.9
Family State	3.8	Family State	3.5
Present State	3.7	Rural State	3.2
Covenant	3.4	Covenant	3.2
Rural State	3.3	Present State	3.2
Triad	2.7	Triad	2.7
R&D	2.2	R&D	2.2

INSTITUTIONAL PERFORMANCE SURVEY

Institution Means
[1983 in Column 1 and 1985 in Column 2]

Section 8: Institutional Effectiveness
    OE5: Faculty and administrator employment satisfaction

Triad	4.0	Mission	4.4
Rural State	3.9	Rural State	4.1
Family State	3.9	Family State	4.0
Mission	3.9	Triad	3.7
Covenant	3.4	Covenant	3.5
R&D	3.4	R&D	3.1
Present State	3.3	Present State	3.1

Section 8: Institutional Effectiveness
    OE6: Professional development and quality of the faculty

R&D	3.8	R&D	4.1
Mission	3.5	Mission	3.3
Family State	3.0	Triad	2.6
Triad	2.9	Covenant	2.5
Covenant	2.9	Family State	2.4
Rural State	2.6	Present State	2.3
Present State	2.1	Rural State	2.1

Section 8: Institutional Effectiveness
    OE7: System openness and community interaction

Family State	4.0	Family State	3.5
Mission	3.8	Mission	3.4
Rural State	3.6	Rural State	3.3
Present State	3.2	Present State	3.1
R&D	3.1	Covenant	2.9
Covenant	3.0	Triad	2.7
Triad	2.9	R&D	2.6

INSTITUTIONAL PERFORMANCE SURVEY

Institution Means
[1983 in Column 1 and 1985 in Column 2]

Section 8: Institutional Effectiveness
    OE8: Ability to acquire resources

R&D	3.5	Mission	3.2
Mission	3.5	R&D	2.5
Family State	2.9	Family State	2.4
Rural State	2.6	Rural State	2.3
Triad	2.3	Covenant	2.2
Covenant	2.2	Triad	1.9
Present State	2.1	Present State	1.8

Section 8: Institutional Effectiveness
    OE9: Organizational health

Family State	3.9	Rural State	3.7
Rural State	3.9	Mission	3.7
Mission	3.8	Family State	3.5
Triad	3.7	Triad	3.4
Present State	3.5	Covenant	3.0
R&D	3.2	Present State	3.0
Covenant	2.9	R&D	2.7

APPENDIX D

Tables of Financial and Enrollment Data

Rural State College

Rural State College, Reported Revenues for 1974-75 to 1981-82

YEAR	TUITION AND FEES	APPROPRIATIONS	GRANTS AND CONTRACTS	ENDOWMENT INCOME	GIFTS	OTHER REVENUE	TOTAL REVENUE
1975	$1,088,506	$2,938,253	$335,029	$0	$0	$1,176,697	$5,538,485
1976	1,032,599	2,795,983	574,071	0	10,288	1,507,873	5,920,814
1977	1,116,981	3,293,912	639,982	760	15,815	1,700,663	6,768,113
1978	1,206,592	3,634,531	518,911	959	12,970	1,691,699	7,065,662
1979	1,187,349	4,146,728	526,676	1,460	30,214	1,806,934	7,699,361
1980	1,645,388	3,654,894	501,721	0	19,636	1,822,644	7,644,283
1981	1,570,004	5,146,337	1,264,130	0	19,560	2,091,765	10,091,796
1982	1,912,945	5,243,407	1,053,410	0	44,290	2,294,661	10,548,713

Rural State College, Reported Expenditures for 1974–75 to 1981–82

Year	Instruction	Research	Public Service	Academic Support	Student Services	Institutional Support	Operation and Maintenance of Physical Plant	Scholarships and Fellowships	Mandatory Transfers	Total Educational and General Expenditure	Total Expenditure
1975	$2,731,184	$40,745	$146,194	$177,869	$156,843	$371,203	$532,660	$9,638	$0	$4,166,336	$5,122,541
1976	2,714,911	20,824	262,896	493,496	290,291	436,055	642,168	160,057	2,080	5,022,778	6,103,315
1977	3,210,186	13,736	24,739	578,051	344,351	396,568	698,968	177,598	21,229	5,465,426	6,620,505
1978	3,297,878	0	76,805	602,281	357,421	446,265	784,995	176,479	0	5,742,124	6,886,628
1979	3,723,058	0	57,686	598,129	395,905	555,140	895,104	156,347	2,290	6,383,659	7,710,608
1980	3,870,932	0	35,991	828,196	475,475	543,614	1,031,054	142,236	0	6,927,498	8,199,933
1981	4,594,384	0	68,035	703,736	443,196	644,437	1,148,555	835,094	785	8,438,222	9,879,683
1982	4,910,447	0	54,634	810,077	496,916	780,838	1,302,264	833,147	0	9,188,323	10,817,223

Rural State College, Percent Revenues of Total Revenue for 1974–75 to 1981–82

Year	Tuition and Fees	Appropriations	Grants and Contracts	Endowment Income	Gifts	Other Revenue
1975	19.7%	53.1%	6.0%	0.0%	0.0%	21.2%
1976	17.4	47.2	9.7	0.0	0.2	25.5
1977	16.5	48.7	9.5	.0	0.2	25.1
1978	17.1	51.4	7.3	.0	0.2	23.9
1979	15.4	53.9	6.8	.0	0.4	23.5
1980	21.5	47.8	6.6	0.0	0.3	23.8
1981	15.6	51.0	12.5	0.0	0.2	20.7
1982	18.1	49.7	10.0	0.0	0.4	21.8

Rural State College, Percent Expenditures of Total Expenditures for 1974-75 to 1981-82

Year	Instruction	Research	Public Service	Academic Support	Student Services	Institutional Support	Operation and Maintenance of Physical Plant	Scholarships and Fellowships	Mandatory Transfers	Total Educational and General Expenditures
1975	53.3%	0.8%	2.9%	3.5%	3.1%	7.2%	10.4%	0.2%	0.0%	81.3%
1976	44.5	0.3	4.3	8.1	4.8	7.1	10.5	2.6	.0	82.3
1977	48.5	0.2	0.4	8.7	5.2	6.0	10.6	2.7	0.3	82.6
1978	47.9	0.0	1.1	8.7	5.2	6.5	11.4	2.6	0.0	83.4
1979	48.3	0.0	0.7	7.8	5.1	7.2	11.6	2.0	.0	82.8
1980	47.2	0.0	0.4	10.1	5.8	6.6	12.6	1.7	0.0	84.5
1981	46.5	0.0	0.7	7.1	4.5	6.5	11.6	8.5	.0	85.4
1982	45.4	0.0	0.5	7.5	4.6	7.2	12.0	7.7	0.0	84.9

Rural State College, Four Selected Student Full Time Equivalent Ratios for 1974-75 to 1981-82, per Student

Year	Tuition and Fees	Instruction	Scholarships	Student Services	Total
1975	$554	$1,390	$5	$80	1,965
1976	519	1,366	81	146	1,988
1977	532	1,529	85	164	2,100
1978	573	1,567	84	170	2,104
1979	541	1,696	71	180	2,195
1980	795	1,871	69	230	2,069
1981	697	2,041	371	197	2,251
1982	845	2,169	368	219	2,264

Rural State College, Reported Revenues and Full-Time Equivalent (FTE) Students: Value, Index Based on 1975, and % Change Between Years

YEAR	TUITION AND FEES		GIFTS		ENDOWMENT		TOTAL REVENUE		FTE STUDENTS	
1975	$1,088,506		$0		$0		$5,538,485		1,965	
	100.0		NA		NA		100.0		100.0	
1976	$1,032,599		$10,288		$0		$5,920,814		1,988	
	94.9	−5.1%	NA	100.0%	NA	0.0%	106.9	6.9%	101.2	1.2%
1977	$1,116,981		$15,815		$760		$6,768,113		2,100	
	102.6	8.2%	NA	53.7%	NA	100.0%	122.2	14.3%	106.9	5.6%
1978	$1,206,592		$12,970		$959		$7,065,662		2,104	
	110.8	8.0%	NA	−18.0%	NA	26.2%	127.6	4.4%	107.1	0.2%
1979	$1,187,349		$30,214		$1,460		$7,699,361		2,195	
	109.1	−1.6%	NA	133.0%	NA	52.2%	139.0	9.0%	111.7	4.3%
1980	$1,645,388		$19,636		$0		$7,644,283		2,069	
	151.2	38.6%	NA	−35.0%	NA	−100.0%	138.0	−0.7%	105.3	−5.7%
1981	$1,570,004		$19,560		$0		$10,091,796		2,251	
	144.2	−4.6%	NA	−0.4%	NA	0.0%	182.2	32.0%	114.6	8.8%
1982	$1,912,945		$44,290		$0		$10,548,713		2,264	
	175.7	21.8%	NA	126.4%	NA	0.0%	190.5	4.5%	115.2	0.6%

238

Rural State College, Reported Expenditures: Value, Index Based on 1975, and % Change Between Years

Year	Scholarships and Fellowships	Total Educational and General Expenditures	Total Expenditures
1975	$9,638	$4,166,336	$5,122,541
	100.0	100.0	100.0
1976	$160,057	$5,022,778	$6,103,315
	1660.7	120.6	119.1
	1560.7%	20.6%	19.1%
1977	$177,598	$5,465,426	$6,620,505
	1842.7	131.2	129.2
	11.0%	8.8%	8.5%
1978	$176,479	$5,742,124	$6,886,628
	1831.1	137.8	134.4
	−0.6%	5.1%	4.0%
1979	$156,347	$6,383,659	$7,710,608
	1622.2	153.2	150.5
	−11.4%	11.2%	12.0%
1980	$142,236	$6,927,498	$8,199,933
	1475.8	166.3	160.1
	−9.0%	8.5%	6.3%
1981	$835,094	$8,438,222	$9,879,683
	8664.6	202.5	192.9
	487.1%	21.8%	20.5%
1982	$833,147	$9,188,323	$10,817,223
	8644.4	220.5	211.2
	−0.2%	8.9%	9.5%

Rural State College, Reported Endowment: Value, Index Based on 1975, and % Change Between Years

Year	Book Value Beginning of Year	Market Value Beginning of Year	Book Value End of Year	Market Value End of Year	Yield
1975	$9,918	$9,918	$10,235	$10,235	$291
	100.0	100.0	100.0	100.0	100.0
1976	$10,235	$10,235	$10,235	$10,235	$696
	103.2	103.2	100.0	100.0	239.2
	3.2%	3.2%	0.0%	0.0%	139.2%
1977	$10,234	$10,234	$10,234	$10,234	$760
	103.2	103.2	100.0	100.0	261.2
	.0%	.0%	.0%	.0%	9.2%
1978	$10,234	$10,234	$20,039	$20,039	$959
	103.2	103.2	195.8	195.8	329.6
	0.0%	0.0%	95.8%	95.8%	26.2%
1979	$20,039	$20,039	$46,229	$46,229	$1,460
	202.0	202.0	451.7	451.7	501.7
	95.8%	95.8%	130.7%	130.7%	52.2%
1980	$46,229	$46,229	$85,273	$85,273	$5,109
	466.1	466.1	833.2	833.2	1755.7
	130.7%	130.7%	84.5%	84.5%	249.9%
1981	$85,273	$85,273	$249,203	$249,203	$29,904
	859.8	859.8	2434.8	2434.8	10276.3
	84.5%	84.5%	192.2%	192.2%	485.3%
1982	$249,203	$249,203	$286,516	$286,516	$31,429
	2512.6	2512.6	2799.4	2799.4	10800.3
	192.2%	192.2%	15.0%	15.0%	5.1%

Rural State College, Reported Physical Plant Indebtedness: Value, Index Based on 1975, and % Change Between Years

Year	Balance Owed Beginning of Year	Additional Borrowed	Payments Made	Balance Owed End of Year	Interest Payments
1975	$2,174,000	$0	$45,000	$2,129,000	$80,977
	100.0	NA	100.0	100.0	100.0
1976	$2,129,000	$0	$45,000	$2,084,000	$79,156
	97.9	NA	100.0	97.9	97.8
	−2.1%	0.0%	0.0%	−2.1%	−2.2%
1977	$2,084,000	$0	$45,000	$2,039,000	$77,918
	95.9	NA	100.0	95.8	96.2
	−2.1%	0.0%	0.0%	−2.2%	−1.6%
1978	$2,039,000	$0	$47,000	$1,992,000	$75,976
	93.8	NA	104.4	93.6	93.8
	−2.2%	0.0%	4.4%	−2.3%	−2.5%
1979	$1,992,000	$0	$47,000	$1,945,000	$74,395
	91.6	NA	104.4	91.4	91.9
	−2.3%	0.0%	0.0%	−2.4%	−2.1%
1980	$1,945,000	$550,000	$57,000	$2,438,000	$72,706
	89.5	NA	126.7	114.5	89.8
	−2.4%	100.0%	21.3%	25.3%	−2.3%
1981	$2,438,000	$0	$65,000	$2,373,000	$71,947
	112.1	NA	144.4	111.5	88.8
	25.3%	−100.0%	14.0%	−2.7%	−1.0%
1982	$2,373,000	$0	$65,000	$2,308,000	$84,877
	109.2	NA	144.4	108.4	104.8
	−2.7%	0.0%	0.0%	−2.7%	18.0%

241

Family State College

Family State College, Reported Revenues for 1974-75 to 1981-82

Year	Tuition and Fees	Appropriations	Grants and Contracts	Endowment Income	Gifts	Other Revenue	Total Revenue
1975	$930,228	$6,630,106	$1,581,081	$0	$0	$644,592	$9,786,007
1976	1,250,811	5,906,846	791,923	0	0	1,293,619	9,243,199
1977	1,589,446	6,971,000	1,020,683	0	0	1,742,869	11,323,998
1978	1,670,549	7,309,853	2,029,090	0	0	1,800,875	12,810,367
1979	1,783,918	9,507,040	371,186	0	0	2,557,138	14,219,282
1980	2,214,560	11,614,552	359,435	0	0	2,699,512	16,888,059
1981	2,220,126	11,970,392	326,335	0	200,000	2,853,527	17,570,380
1982	2,459,260	12,098,053	252,963	0	134,000	3,014,730	17,959,006

Family State College, Reported Expenditures for 1974-75 to 1981-82

Year	Instruction	Research	Public Service	Academic Support	Student Services	Institutional Support	Operation and Maintenance of Physical Plant	Scholarships and Fellowships	Mandatory Transfers	Total Educational and General Expenditure	Total Expenditure
1975	$3,981,408	$0	$0	$607,678	$347,117	$0	$2,145,651	$65,593	$0	$7,147,447	$7,595,502
1976	3,653,570	0	0	547,470	275,000	0	1,901,327	126,780	0	6,504,147	7,571,947
1977	4,201,605	0	0	629,590	307,500	109,684	2,186,526	579,445	0	8,014,350	9,293,314
1978	4,621,765	0	0	692,549	332,100	118,458	2,049,194	1,609,706	0	9,423,772	10,720,434
1979	4,442,928	371,186	0	745,137	793,817	700,193	1,967,446	1,449,231	0	10,469,938	12,096,878
1980	4,998,748	305,624	0	784,902	1,063,241	683,630	1,776,758	3,012,426	2,502,928	15,128,257	16,888,059
1981	5,725,703	311,385	0	820,441	1,252,276	925,312	2,025,504	2,150,839	2,504,874	15,716,334	17,570,380
1982	5,821,288	246,315	0	987,990	1,397,832	716,949	2,107,168	2,019,701	2,772,063	16,069,306	17,959,006

Family State College, Percent Revenues of Total Revenue for 1974–75 to 1981–82

Year	Tuition and Fees	Appropriations	Grants and Contracts	Endowment Income	Gifts	Other Revenue
1975	9.5%	67.8%	16.2%	0.0%	0.0%	6.6%
1976	13.5	63.9	8.6	0.0	0.0	14.0
1977	14.0	61.6	9.0	0.0	0.0	15.4
1978	13.0	57.1	15.8	0.0	0.0	14.1
1979	12.5	66.9	2.6	0.0	0.0	18.0
1980	13.1	68.8	2.1	0.0	0.0	16.0
1981	12.6	68.1	1.9	0.0	1.1	16.2
1982	13.7	67.4	1.4	0.0	0.7	16.8

Family State College, Percent Expenditures of Total Expenditures for 1974–75 to 1981–82

Year	Instruction	Research	Public Service	Academic Support	Student Services	Institutional Support	Operation and Maintenance of Physical Plant	Scholarships and Fellowships	Mandatory Transfers	Total Educational and General Expenditures
1975	52.4%	0.0%	0.0%	8.0%	4.6%	0.0%	28.2%	0.9%	0.0%	94.1%
1976	48.3	0.0	0.0	7.2	3.6	0.0	25.1	1.7	0.0	85.9
1977	45.2	0.0	0.0	6.8	3.3	1.2	23.5	6.2	0.0	86.2
1978	43.1	0.0	0.0	6.5	3.1	1.1	19.1	15.0	0.0	87.9
1979	36.7	3.1	0.0	6.2	6.6	5.8	16.3	12.0	0.0	86.6
1980	29.6	1.8	0.0	4.6	6.3	4.0	10.5	17.8	14.8	89.6
1981	32.6	1.8	0.0	4.7	7.1	5.3	11.5	12.2	14.3	89.4
1982	32.4	1.4	0.0	5.5	7.8	4.0	11.7	11.2	15.4	89.5

Family State College, Four Selected Full-Time Equivalent Student Ratios for 1974-75 to 1981-82, per Student

Year	Tuition and Fees	Instruction	Scholarships	Student Services	Total
1975	$212	$907	$15	$79	4,392
1976	272	796	28	60	4,591
1977	366	967	133	71	4,345
1978	393	1,088	379	78	4,248
1979	401	998	325	178	4,453
1980	509	1,149	693	244	4,350
1981	459	1,184	445	259	4,836
1982	536	1,268	440	304	4,592

Family State College, Reported Revenues and Full-Time Equivalent (FTE) Students: Value, Index Based on 1975, and % Change Between Years

Year	Tuition and Fees	Gifts	Endowment	Total Revenue	FTE Students
1975	$930,228	$0	$0	$9,786,007	4,392
	100.0	NA	NA	100.0	100.0
1976	$1,250,811	$0	$0	$9,243,199	4,591
	134.5	NA	NA	94.5	104.5
	34.5%			−5.5%	4.5%
1977	$1,589,446	$0	$0	$11,323,998	4,345
	170.9	NA	NA	115.7	98.9
	27.1%	0.0%	0.0%	22.5%	−5.4%
1978	$1,670,549	$0	$0	$12,810,367	4,248
	179.6	NA	NA	130.9	96.7
	5.1%	0.0%	0.0%	13.1%	−2.2%
1979	$1,783,918	$0	$0	$14,219,282	4,453
	191.8	NA	NA	145.3	101.4
	6.8%	0.0%	0.0%	11.0%	4.8%
1980	$2,214,560	$0	$0	$16,888,059	4,350
	238.1	NA	NA	172.6	99.0
	24.1%	0.0%	0.0%	18.8%	−2.3%
1981	$2,220,126	$200,000	$0	$17,570,380	4,836
	238.7	NA	NA	179.5	110.1
	0.3%	100.0%	0.0%	4.0%	11.2%
1982	$2,459,260	$134,000	$0	$17,959,006	4,592
	264.4	NA	NA	183.5	104.6
	10.8%	−33.0%	0.0%	2.2%	−5.0%

Family State College, Reported Expenditures: Value, Index Based on 1975, and % Change Between Years

Year	Scholarships and Fellowships			Total Educational and General Expenditures			Total Expenditures		
1975	$65,593			$7,147,447			$7,595,502		
	100.0			100.0			100.0		
1976	$126,780			$6,504,147			$7,571,947		
	193.3	93.3%		91.0	−9.0%		99.7	−0.3%	
1977	$579,445			$8,014,350			$9,293,314		
	883.4	357.0%		112.1	23.2%		122.4	22.7%	
1978	$1,609,706			$9,423,772			$10,720,434		
	2454.1	177.8%		131.8	17.6%		141.1	15.4%	
1979	$1,449,231			$10,469,938			$12,096,878		
	2209.4	−10.0%		146.5	11.1%		159.3	12.8%	
1980	$3,012,426			$15,128,257			$16,888,059		
	4592.6	107.9%		211.7	44.5%		222.3	39.6%	
1981	$2,150,839			$15,716,334			$17,570,380		
	3279.1	−28.6%		219.9	3.9%		231.3	4.0%	
1982	$2,019,701			$16,069,306			$17,959,006		
	3079.1	−6.1%		224.8	2.2%		236.4	2.2%	

245

Family State College, Reported Endowment: Value, Index Based on 1975, and % Change Between Years

YEAR	BOOK VALUE BEGINNING OF YEAR		MARKET VALUE BEGINNING OF YEAR		BOOK VALUE END OF YEAR		MARKET VALUE END OF YEAR		YIELD
1975	$0		$0		$0		$0		$0
	NA		NA		NA		NA		NA
1976	$0		$0		$0		$0		$0
	NA	0.0%	NA	0.0%	NA	0.0%	NA	0.0%	NA
1977	$0		$0		$0		$0		$0
	NA	0.0%	NA	0.0%	NA	0.0%	NA	0.0%	NA
1978	$0		$0		$0		$0		$0
	NA	0.0%	NA	0.0%	NA	0.0%	NA	0.0%	NA
1979	$0		$0		$0		$0		$0
	NA	0.0%	NA	0.0%	NA	0.0%	NA	0.0%	NA
1980	$0		$0		$0		$0		$0
	NA	0.0%	NA	0.0%	NA	0.0%	NA	0.0%	NA
1981	$0		$0		$0		$0		$0
	NA	0.0%	NA	0.0%	NA	0.0%	NA	0.0%	NA
1982	$0		$0		$0		$0		$0
	NA	0.0%	NA	0.0%	NA	0.0%	NA	0.0%	NA

246

Family State College, Reported Physical Plant Indebtedness: Value, Index Based on 1975, and % Change Between Years

Year	Balance Owed Beginning of Year		Additional Borrowed		Payments Made		Balance Owed End of Year		Interest Payments	
1975	$0		$0		$0		$0		$0	
	NA		NA		NA		NA		NA	
1976	$0		$0		$0		$0		$0	
	NA	0.0%	NA	0.0%	NA	0.0%	NA	0.0%	NA	0.0%
1977	$0		$0		$0		$0		$0	
	NA	0.0%	NA	0.0%	NA	0.0%	NA	0.0%	NA	0.0%
1978	$0		$0		$0		$0		$0	
	NA	0.0%	NA	0.0%	NA	0.0%	NA	0.0%	NA	0.0%
1979	$0		$0		$0		$0		$0	
	NA	0.0%	NA	0.0%	NA	0.0%	NA	0.0%	NA	0.0%
1980	$0		$0		$0		$0		$0	
	NA	0.0%	NA	0.0%	NA	0.0%	NA	0.0%	NA	0.0%
1981	$0		$0		$0		$0		$0	
	NA	0.0%	NA	0.0%	NA	0.0%	NA	0.0%	NA	0.0%
1982	$0		$0		$0		$0		$0	
	NA	0.0%	NA	0.0%	NA	0.0%	NA	0.0%	NA	0.0%

Mission University

Mission University, Reported Revenues for 1974-75 to 1981-82

Year	Tuition and Fees	Appropriations	Grants and Contracts	Endowment Income	Gifts	Other Revenue	Total Revenue
1975	$11,748,123	$0	$734,938	$255,654	$268,914	$6,751,043	$19,758,672
1976	13,229,417	0	941,230	378,257	995,473	4,823,762	20,368,139
1977	13,825,167	0	952,708	366,540	1,150,032	5,784,795	22,079,242
1978	15,531,341	0	3,721,231	340,803	1,163,483	6,486,447	27,243,305
1979	16,589,388	0	1,354,513	459,286	1,226,009	7,184,322	26,813,518
1980	18,528,534	0	1,368,321	771,575	1,446,679	8,142,794	30,257,903
1981	21,141,571	0	1,472,117	1,080,173	1,883,192	9,277,001	34,854,054
1982	24,765,590	0	1,377,429	1,474,744	2,109,129	3,069,125	32,796,017

Mission University, Reported Expenditures for 1974-75 to 1981-82

Year	Instruction	Research	Public Service	Academic Support	Student Services	Institutional Support	Operation and Maintenance of Physical Plant	Scholarships and Fellowships	Mandatory Transfers	Total Educational and General Expenditure	Total Expenditure
1975	$6,370,816	$762,906	$198,735	$826,235	$737,254	$1,575,602	$1,402,332	$1,536,403	$0	$13,410,283	$17,482,684
1976	6,687,063	973,879	188,099	1,179,282	828,692	2,255,696	1,316,829	1,660,502	0	15,090,042	19,722,808
1977	6,963,476	976,820	655,200	1,299,897	889,997	2,361,567	1,533,769	1,971,397	0	16,652,123	21,747,702
1978	7,750,394	1,211,528	827,349	1,211,331	952,639	2,468,444	2,026,574	4,612,914	0	21,061,173	26,385,780
1979	8,659,519	1,445,020	833,175	1,223,400	928,472	3,396,776	2,467,365	2,031,634	0	20,985,361	26,858,328
1980	9,961,164	1,446,824	814,574	1,402,447	1,149,316	3,818,303	3,157,978	2,270,634	0	24,021,240	30,473,056
1981	11,515,937	1,606,865	1,265,475	1,635,965	1,362,682	4,181,565	3,780,803	2,531,985	0	27,081,277	34,239,437
1982	13,272,626	1,532,874	937,094	1,855,383	1,850,615	4,749,938	3,360,124	2,942,847	0	30,501,501	37,603,248

Mission University, Percent Revenues of Total Revenue for 1974–75 to 1981–82

Year	Tuition and Fees	Appropriations	Grants and Contracts	Endowment Income	Gifts	Other Revenue
1975	59.5%	0.0%	3.7%	1.3%	1.4%	34.2%
1976	65.0	0.0	4.6	1.9	4.9	23.7
1977	62.6	0.0	4.3	1.7	5.2	26.2
1978	57.0	0.0	13.7	1.3	4.3	23.8
1979	61.9	0.0	5.1	1.7	4.6	26.8
1980	61.2	0.0	4.5	2.5	4.8	26.9
1981	60.7	0.0	4.2	3.1	5.4	26.6
1982	75.5	0.0	4.2	4.5	6.4	9.4

Mission University, Percent Expenditures of Total Expenditures for 1974–75 to 1981–82

Year	Instruction	Research	Public Service	Academic Support	Student Services	Institutional Support	Operation and Maintenance of Physical Plant	Scholarships and Fellowships	Mandatory Transfers	Total Educational and General Expenditures
1975	36.4%	4.4%	1.1%	4.7%	4.2%	9.0%	8.0%	8.8%	0.0%	76.7%
1976	33.9	4.9	1.0	6.0	4.2	11.4	6.7	8.4	0.0	76.5
1977	32.0	4.5	3.0	6.0	4.1	10.9	7.1	9.1	0.0	76.6
1978	29.4	4.6	3.1	4.6	3.6	9.4	7.7	17.5	0.0	79.8
1979	32.2	5.4	3.1	4.6	3.5	12.6	9.2	7.6	0.0	78.1
1980	32.7	4.7	2.7	4.6	3.8	12.5	10.4	7.5	0.0	78.8
1981	33.6	4.7	3.7	4.8	4.0	12.2	11.0	7.4	0.0	81.4
1982	35.3	4.1	2.5	4.9	4.9	12.6	8.9	7.8	0.0	81.1

Mission University, Four Selected Full-Time Equivalent Student Ratios for 1974–75 to 1981–82, per Student

Year	Tuition and Fees	Instruction	Scholarships	Student Services	Total
1975	$2,115	$1,147	$277	$133	5,555
1976	2,478	1,253	311	155	5,338
1977	2,437	1,228	348	157	5,672
1978	2,620	1,307	778	161	5,928
1979	2,904	1,516	356	163	5,712
1980	3,392	1,824	416	210	5,462
1981	3,731	2,032	447	240	5,667
1982	4,608	2,469	548	344	5,375

Mission University, Reported Revenues and Full-Time Equivalent (FTE) Students: Value, Index Based on 1975, and % Change Between Years

Year	Tuition and Fees	Gifts	Endowment	Total Revenue	FTE Students
1975	$11,748,123	$268,914	$255,654	$19,758,672	5,555
	100.0	100.0	100.0	100.0	100.0
1976	$13,229,417	$995,473	$378,257	$20,368,139	5,338
	112.6	370.2	148.0	103.1	96.1
	12.6%	270.2%	48.0%	3.1%	−3.9%
1977	$13,825,167	$1,150,032	$366,540	$22,079,242	5,672
	117.7	427.7	143.4	111.7	102.1
	4.5%	15.5%	−3.1%	8.4%	6.3%
1978	$15,531,341	$1,163,483	$340,803	$27,243,305	5,928
	132.2	432.7	133.3	137.9	106.7
	12.3%	1.2%	−7.0%	23.4%	4.5%
1979	$16,589,388	$1,226,009	$459,286	$26,813,518	5,712
	141.2	455.9	179.7	135.7	102.8
	6.8%	5.4%	34.8%	−1.6%	−3.6%
1980	$18,528,534	$1,446,679	$771,575	$30,257,903	5,462
	157.7	538.0	301.8	153.1	98.3
	11.7%	18.0%	68.0%	12.8%	−4.4%
1981	$21,141,571	$1,883,192	$1,080,173	$34,854,054	5,667
	180.0	700.3	422.5	176.4	102.0
	14.1%	30.2%	40.0%	15.2%	3.8%
1982	$24,765,590	$2,109,129	$1,474,744	$32,796,017	5,375
	210.8	784.3	576.9	166.0	96.8
	17.1%	12.0%	36.5%	−5.9%	−5.2%

Mission University, Reported Expenditures: Value, Index Based on 1975, and % Change Between Years

Year	Scholarships and Fellowships		Total Educational and General Expenditures		Total Expenditures	
1975	$1,536,403		$13,410,283		$17,482,684	
	100.0		100.0		100.0	
1976	$1,660,502		$15,090,042		$19,722,808	
	108.1	8.1%	112.5	12.5%	112.8	12.8%
1977	$1,971,397		$16,652,123		$21,747,702	
	128.3	18.7%	124.2	10.4%	124.4	10.3%
1978	$4,612,914		$21,061,173		$26,385,780	
	300.2	134.0%	157.1	26.5%	150.9	21.3%
1979	$2,031,634		$20,985,361		$26,858,328	
	132.2	−56.0%	156.5	−0.4%	153.6	1.8%
1980	$2,270,634		$24,021,240		$30,473,056	
	147.8	11.8%	179.1	14.5%	174.3	13.5%
1981	$2,531,985		$27,881,277		$34,239,437	
	164.8	11.5%	207.9	16.1%	195.8	12.4%
1982	$2,942,847		$30,501,501		$37,603,248	
	191.5	16.2%	227.4	9.4%	215.1	9.8%

Mission University, Reported Endowment: Value, Index Based on 1975, and % Change Between Years

Year	Book Value Beginning of Year			Market Value Beginning of Year			Book Value End of Year			Market Value End of Year			Yield		
1975	$8,551,983	100.0		$8,094,356	100.0		$9,531,216	100.0		$9,290,144	100.0		$462,363	100.0	
1976	$9,531,216	111.5	11.5%	$9,290,144	114.8	14.8%	$10,239,615	107.4	7.4%	$10,494,167	113.0	13.0%	$459,133	99.3	−0.7%
1977	$10,239,615	119.7	7.4%	$10,494,167	129.6	13.0%	$10,908,942	114.5	6.5%	$11,482,489	123.6	9.4%	$421,399	91.1	−8.2%
1978	$10,908,942	127.6	6.5%	$11,605,994	143.4	10.6%	$12,286,346	128.9	12.6%	$13,560,494	146.0	18.1%	$568,595	123.0	34.9%
1979	$12,286,346	143.7	12.6%	$13,560,494	167.5	16.8%	$16,178,787	169.7	31.7%	$17,806,097	191.7	31.3%	$840,817	181.9	47.9%
1980	$16,178,787	189.2	31.7%	$17,806,097	220.0	31.3%	$20,132,879	211.2	24.4%	$21,650,377	233.0	21.6%	$1,398,172	302.4	66.3%
1981	$20,132,879	235.4	24.4%	$21,650,377	267.5	21.6%	$25,423,035	266.7	26.3%	$28,396,391	305.7	31.2%	$1,825,931	394.9	30.6%
1982	$21,879,300	255.8	8.7%	$28,402,302	350.9	31.2%	$26,754,847	280.7	5.2%	$32,168,373	346.3	13.3%	$1,512,218	327.1	−17.2%

Mission University, Reported Physical Plant Indebtedness: Value, Index Based on 1975, and % Change Between Years

Year	Balance Owed Beginning of Year			Additional Borrowed			Payments Made			Balance Owed End of Year			Interest Payments		
1975	$6,781,000	100.0		$4,000,000	100.0		$144,000	100.0		$10,637,000	100.0		$230,740	100.0	
1976	$10,637,000	156.9	56.9%	$946,848	23.7	−76.3%	$265,542	184.4	84.4%	$11,318,306	106.4	6.4%	$539,061	233.6	133.6%
1977	$11,318,306	166.9	6.4%	$0	0.0	−100.0%	$294,686	204.6	11.0%	$11,023,620	103.6	−2.6%	$525,270	227.6	−2.6%
1978	$11,023,620	162.6	−2.6%	$0	0.0	0.0%	$141,580	98.3	−52.0%	$10,882,040	102.3	−1.3%	$539,678	233.9	2.7%
1979	$10,882,040	160.5	−1.3%	$0	0.0	0.0%	$455,716	316.5	221.9%	$10,426,324	98.0	−4.2%	$522,230	226.3	−3.2%
1980	$10,426,324	153.8	−4.2%	$0	0.0	0.0%	$364,115	252.9	−20.1%	$10,062,209	94.6	−3.5%	$502,532	217.8	−3.8%
1981	$10,062,209	148.4	−3.5%	$0	0.0	0.0%	$360,515	250.4	−1.0%	$9,701,694	91.2	−3.6%	$482,018	208.9	−4.1%
1982	$9,701,694	143.1	−3.6%	$0	0.0	0.0%	$393,823	273.5	9.2%	$9,307,871	87.5	−4.1%	$523,891	227.0	8.7%

253

Present State College

Present State College, Reported Revenues for 1974-75 to 1981-82

Year	Tuition and Fees	Appropriations	Grants and Contracts	Endowment Income	Gifts	Other Revenue	Total Revenue
1975	$1,400,000	$1,200,000	$587,733	$0	$0	$625,000	$3,812,733
1976	1,201,351	1,007,489	594,935	120	7,214	1,072,564	3,883,673
1977	1,410,253	1,150,540	783,185	11	29,211	1,029,110	4,402,310
1978	1,277,173	1,308,885	890,865	0	0	1,101,720	4,578,643
1979	1,429,069	1,381,891	890,381	0	0	1,285,202	4,986,543
1980	1,624,969	1,685,018	782,629	0	16,555	1,520,504	5,629,675
1981	1,791,132	1,558,880	1,177,461	0	0	1,565,005	6,092,478
1982	1,864,894	1,756,000	1,290,091	0	0	1,688,727	6,599,712

Present State College, Reported Expenditures for 1974-75 to 1981-82

Year	Instruction	Research	Public Service	Academic Support	Student Services	Institutional Support	Operation and Maintenance of Physical Plant	Scholarships and Fellowships	Total Educational and General Expenditure	Mandatory Transfers	Total Expenditure
1975	$1,500,000	$0	$50,000	$250,000	$150,000	$300,000	$202,779	$600,724	$3,203,503	$150,000	$3,818,292
1976	1,402,045	2,995	60,432	155,696	219,895	449,778	425,456	213,242	3,247,806	318,267	4,046,081
1977	1,472,664	0	57,315	166,170	391,918	459,245	461,499	271,313	3,613,375	333,251	4,437,426
1978	1,533,750	0	222,638	202,402	508,520	447,165	320,005	630,147	3,872,729	8,102	4,854,904
1979	1,585,265	0	234,830	287,094	197,694	628,917	287,980	553,698	3,827,278	51,800	4,850,616
1980	1,807,839	3,919	254,265	355,936	654,252	596,321	451,021	126,120	4,249,673	0	5,653,153
1981	2,042,405	0	236,710	353,305	367,226	792,043	489,763	289,846	4,571,298	0	6,063,346
1982	2,114,209	0	369,507	451,183	358,823	929,811	578,091	444,243	5,303,191	57,324	6,696,566

Present State College, Percent Revenues of Total Revenue for 1974-75 to 1981-82

Year	Tuition and Fees	Appropriations	Grants and Contracts	Endowment Income	Gifts	Other Revenue
1975	36.7%	31.5%	15.4%	0.0%	0.0%	16.4%
1976	30.9	25.9	15.3	.0	0.2	27.6
1977	32.0	26.1	17.8	.0	0.7	23.4
1978	27.9	28.6	19.5	0.0	0.0	24.1
1979	28.7	27.7	17.9	0.0	0.0	25.8
1980	28.9	29.9	13.9	0.0	0.3	27.0
1981	29.4	25.6	19.3	0.0	0.0	25.7
1982	28.3	26.6	19.5	0.0	0.0	25.6

Present State College, Percent Expenditures of Total Expenditures for 1974-75 to 1981-82

Year	Instruction	Research	Public Service	Academic Support	Student Services	Institutional Support	Operation and Maintenance of Physical Plant	Scholarships and Fellowships	Mandatory Transfers	Total Educational and General Expenditures
1975	39.3%	0.0%	1.3%	6.5%	3.9%	7.9%	5.3%	15.7%	3.9%	83.9%
1976	34.7	0.1	1.5	3.8	5.4	11.1	10.5	5.3	7.9	80.3
1977	33.2	0.0	1.3	3.7	8.8	10.3	10.4	6.1	7.5	81.4
1978	31.6	0.0	4.6	4.2	10.5	9.2	6.6	13.0	0.2	79.8
1979	32.7	0.0	4.8	5.9	4.1	13.0	5.9	11.4	1.1	78.9
1980	32.0	0.1	4.5	6.3	11.6	10.5	8.0	2.2	0.0	75.2
1981	33.7	0.0	3.9	5.8	6.1	13.1	8.1	4.8	0.0	75.4
1982	31.6	0.0	5.5	6.7	5.4	13.9	8.6	6.6	0.9	79.2

255

Present State College, Four Selected Full Time Equivalent Student Ratios for 1974–75 to 1981–82, per Student

Year	Tuition and Fees	Instruction	Scholarships	Student Services	Total
1975	$1,134	$1,215	$486	$121	1,235
1976	1,039	1,213	184	190	1,156
1977	1,280	1,336	246	356	1,102
1978	1,246	1,496	615	496	1,025
1979	1,496	1,660	580	207	955
1980	1,778	1,978	138	716	914
1981	1,763	2,010	285	361	1,016
1982	1,943	2,202	463	374	960

Present State College, Reported Revenues and Full-Time Equivalent (FTE) Students: Value, Index Based on 1975, and % Change Between Years

Year	Tuition and Fees	Gifts	Endowment	Total Revenue	FTE Students
1975	$1,400,000	$0	$0	$3,812,733	1,235
	100.0	NA	NA	100.0	100.0
1976	$1,201,351	$7,214	$120	$3,883,673	1,156
	85.8	NA	NA	101.9	93.6
	−14.2%	100.0%	100.0%	1.9%	−6.4%
1977	$1,410,253	$29,211	$11	$4,402,310	1,102
	100.7	NA	NA	115.5	89.2
	17.4%	304.9%	−90.8%	13.4%	−4.7%
1978	$1,277,173	$0	$0	$4,578,643	1,025
	91.2	NA	NA	120.1	83.0
	−9.4%	−100.0%	−100.0%	4.0%	−7.0%
1979	$1,429,069	$0	$0	$4,986,543	955
	102.1	NA	NA	130.8	77.3
	11.9%	0.0%	0.0%	4.0%	−7.0%
1980	$1,624,969	$16,555	$0	$5,629,675	914
	116.1	NA	NA	147.7	74.0
	13.7%	100.0%	0.0%	8.9%	−6.8%
1981	$1,791,132	$0	$0	$6,092,478	1,016
	127.9	NA	NA	159.8	82.3
	10.2%	−100.0%	0.0%	12.9%	−4.3%
1982	$1,864,894	$0	$0	$6,599,712	960
	133.2	NA	NA	173.1	77.7
	4.1%	0.0%	0.0%	8.3%	−5.5%

Present State College, Reported Expenditures: Value, Index Based on 1975, and % Change Between Years

Year	Scholarships and Fellowships			Total Educational and General Expenditures			Total Expenditures		
1975	$600,724	100.0		$3,203,503	100.0		$3,818,292	100.0	
1976	$213,242	35.5	−64.5%	$3,247,806	101.4	1.4%	$4,046,081	106.0	6.0%
1977	$271,313	45.2	27.2%	$3,613,375	112.8	11.3%	$4,437,426	116.2	9.7%
1978	$630,147	104.9	132.3%	$3,872,729	120.9	7.2%	$4,854,904	127.1	9.4%
1979	$553,698	92.2	−12.1%	$3,827,278	119.5	−1.2%	$4,850,616	127.0	−0.1%
1980	$126,120	21.0	−77.2%	$4,249,673	132.7	11.0%	$5,653,153	148.1	16.5%
1981	$289,846	48.2	129.8%	$4,571,298	142.7	7.6%	$6,063,346	158.8	7.3%
1982	$444,243	74.0	53.3%	$5,303,191	165.5	16.0%	$6,696,566	175.4	10.4%

Present State College, Reported Endowment: Value, Index Based on 1975, and % Change Between Years

Year	Book Value Beginning of Year	Market Value Beginning of Year	Book Value End of Year	Market Value End of Year	Yield
1975	$0	$0	$0	$0	$0
	NA	NA	NA	NA	NA
1976	$0	$0	$8,476	$8,476	$120
	NA	NA	NA 100.0%	NA 100.0%	NA 100.0%
1977	$8,476 0.0%	$8,476 0.0%	$9,337	$9,337	$0
	NA	NA	NA 10.2%	NA 10.2%	NA −100.0%
1978	$9,337 100.0%	$9,337 100.0%	$12,121	$12,121	$682
	NA	NA	NA 29.8%	NA 29.8%	NA 100.0%
1979	$12,347 10.2%	$12,347 10.2%	$25,693	$25,693	$1,716
	NA	NA	NA 112.0%	NA 112.0%	NA 151.6%
1980	$25,693 32.2%	$25,693 32.2%	$25,693	$25,693	$1,747
	NA	NA	NA 0.0%	NA 0.0%	NA 1.8%
1981	$25,693 108.1%	$25,693 108.1%	$94,760	$94,760	$2,400
	NA	NA	NA 268.8%	NA 268.8%	NA 37.4%
1982	$94,760 0.0%	$94,760 0.0%	$67,281	$67,281	$4,853
	NA 268.8%	NA 268.8%	NA −29.0%	NA −29.0%	NA 102.2%

258

Present State College, Reported Physical Plant Indebtedness: Value, Index Based on 1975, and % Change Between Years

Year	Balance Owed Beginning of Year		Additional Borrowed		Payments Made		Balance Owed End of Year		Interest Payments	
1975	$0		$0		$0		$0		$0	
	NA		NA		NA		NA		NA	
1976	$0		$0		$0		$0		$0	
	NA	0.0%	NA	0.0%	NA	0.0%	NA	0.0%	NA	0.0%
1977	$0		$0		$0		$0		$0	
	NA	0.0%	NA	0.0%	NA	0.0%	NA	0.0%	NA	0.0%
1978	$0		$0		$0		$0		$0	
	NA	0.0%	NA	0.0%	NA	0.0%	NA	0.0%	NA	0.0%
1979	$0		$0		$0		$0		$0	
	NA	0.0%	NA	0.0%	NA	0.0%	NA	0.0%	NA	0.0%
1980	$0		$0		$0		$0		$0	
	NA	0.0%	NA	0.0%	NA	0.0%	NA	0.0%	NA	0.0%
1981	$0		$0		$0		$0		$0	
	NA	0.0%	NA	0.0%	NA	0.0%	NA	0.0%	NA	0.0%
1982	$0		$0		$0		$0		$0	
	NA	0.0%	NA	0.0%	NA	0.0%	NA	0.0%	NA	0.0%

259

Covenant University

Covenant University, Reported Revenues for 1974-75 to 1981-82

Year	Tuition and Fees	Appropriations	Grants and Contracts	Endowment Income	Gifts	Other Revenue	Total Revenue
1975	$11,168,000	$0	$1,011,000	$171,000	$1,008,000	$3,214,000	$16,572,000
1976	14,283,000	0	1,475,000	141,000	1,911,000	3,566,000	21,376,000
1977	16,185,000	0	1,916,000	122,000	1,302,000	3,992,000	23,517,000
1978	20,132,000	0	1,782,000	164,000	1,485,000	4,383,000	27,946,000
1979	22,527,708	0	1,782,000	164,000	1,485,000	4,864,643	30,823,351
1980	24,196,000	0	2,516,000	185,000	1,828,000	5,269,000	33,994,000
1981	26,765,005	0	2,925,018	842,443	2,342,273	5,803,595	38,678,334
1982	29,726,189	0	2,450,175	554,530	1,815,022	6,983,073	41,528,989

Covenant University, Reported Expenditures for 1974-75 to 1981-82

Year	Instruction	Research	Public Service	Academic Support	Student Services	Institutional Support	Operation and Maintenance of Physical Plant	Scholarships and Fellowships	Mandatory Transfers	Total Educational and General Expenditure	Total Expenditure
1975	$6,582,000	$547,000	$284,000	$1,728,000	$1,118,000	$2,132,000	$1,035,000	$883,000	$114,000	$14,423,000	$17,230,000
1976	9,834,000	711,000	347,000	1,380,000	1,374,000	2,148,000	1,156,000	827,000	107,000	17,884,000	20,708,000
1977	10,764,000	593,000	416,000	1,329,000	1,668,000	2,595,000	1,668,000	1,199,000	115,000	20,347,000	23,404,000
1978	12,300,000	592,000	603,000	2,925,000	2,067,000	3,456,000	1,772,000	1,810,000	0	25,525,000	28,940,000
1979	13,763,700	638,176	650,034	3,153,150	2,312,973	3,725,568	1,910,216	1,951,180	0	28,104,997	31,926,382
1980	14,021,000	837,000	470,000	3,699,000	2,564,000	5,146,000	2,848,000	2,342,000	233,000	32,160,000	36,858,000
1981	14,229,874	684,681	620,683	4,211,219	1,673,248	5,868,454	3,009,192	2,794,696	293,667	33,385,714	38,425,777
1982	14,483,249	548,813	551,195	4,125,250	1,593,847	5,974,761	3,622,514	3,443,735	504,094	34,847,458	40,454,334

Covenant University, Percent Revenues of Total Revenue for 1974–75 to 1981–82

Year	Tuition and Fees	Appropriations	Grants and Contracts	Endowment Income	Gifts	Other Revenue
1975	67.4%	0.0%	6.1%	1.0%	6.1%	19.4%
1976	66.8	0.0	6.9	0.7	8.9	16.7
1977	68.8	0.0	8.1	0.5	5.5	17.0
1978	72.0	0.0	6.4	0.6	5.3	15.7
1979	73.1	0.0	5.8	0.5	4.8	15.8
1980	71.2	0.0	7.4	0.5	5.4	15.5
1981	69.2	0.0	7.6	2.2	6.1	15.0
1982	71.6	0.0	5.9	1.3	4.4	16.8

Covenant University, Percent Expenditures of Total Expenditures for 1974–75 to 1981–82

Year	Instruction	Research	Public Service	Academic Support	Student Services	Institutional Support	Operation and Maintenance of Physical Plant	Scholarships and Fellowships	Mandatory Transfers	Total Educational and General Expenditures
1975	38.2%	3.2%	1.6%	10.0%	6.5%	12.4%	6.0%	5.1%	0.7%	83.7%
1976	47.5	3.4	1.7	6.7	6.6	10.4	5.6	4.0	0.5	86.4
1977	46.0	2.5	1.8	5.7	7.1	11.1	7.1	5.1	0.5	86.9
1978	42.5	2.0	2.1	10.1	7.1	11.9	6.1	6.3	0.0	88.2
1979	43.1	2.0	2.0	9.9	7.2	11.7	6.0	6.1	0.0	88.0
1980	38.0	2.3	1.3	10.0	7.0	14.0	7.7	6.4	0.6	87.3
1981	37.0	1.8	1.6	11.0	4.4	15.3	7.8	7.3	0.8	86.9
1982	35.8	1.4	1.4	10.2	3.9	14.8	9.0	8.5	1.2	86.1

Covenant University, Four Selected Full Time Equivalent Student Ratios for 1974-75 to 1981-82, per Student

Year	Tuition and Fees	Instruction	Scholarships	Student Services	Total
1975	$2,198	$1,296	$174	$220	5,080
1976	2,667	1,836	154	257	5,356
1977	3,057	2,033	226	315	5,294
1978	3,941	2,408	354	405	5,108
1979	4,374	2,673	379	449	5,150
1980	4,731	2,742	458	501	5,114
1981	5,446	2,895	569	340	4,915
1982	6,539	3,186	758	351	4,546

Covenant University, Reported Revenues and Full-Time Equivalent Students: (FTE) Value, Index Based on 1975, and % Change Between Years

Year	Tuition and Fees	Gifts	Endowment	Total Revenue	FTE Students
1975	$11,168,000	$1,008,000	$171,000	$16,572,000	5,080
	100.0	100.0	100.0	100.0	100.0
1976	$14,283,000	$1,911,000	$141,000	$21,376,000	5,356
	127.9	189.6	82.5	129.0	105.4
1977	27.9%	89.6%	-17.5%	29.0%	5.4%
	$16,185,000	$1,302,000	$122,000	$23,517,000	5,294
	144.9	129.2	71.3	141.9	104.2
1978	13.3%	-31.9%	-13.5%	10.0%	-1.2%
	$20,132,000	$1,485,000	$164,000	$27,946,000	5,108
	180.3	147.3	95.9	168.6	100.6
1979	24.4%	14.1%	34.4%	18.8%	-3.5%
	$22,527,708	$1,485,000	$164,000	$30,823,351	5,150
	201.7	147.3	95.9	186.0	101.4
1980	11.9%	0.0%	0.0%	10.3%	0.8%
	$24,196,000	$1,828,000	$185,000	$33,994,000	5,114
	216.7	181.3	108.2	205.1	100.7
1981	7.4%	23.1%	12.8%	10.3%	-0.7%
	$26,726,005	$2,342,273	$842,443	$38,678,334	4,915
	239.7	232.4	492.7	233.4	96.8
1982	10.6%	28.1%	355.4%	13.8%	-3.9%
	$29,726,189	$1,815,022	$554,530	$41,528,989	4,546
	266.2	180.1	324.3	250.6	89.5
	11.1%	-22.5%	-34.2%	7.4%	-7.5%

262

Covenant University, Reported Expenditures: Value, Index Based on 1975, and % Change Between Years

Year	Scholarships and Fellowships			Total Educational and General Expenditures			Total Expenditures		
1975	$883,000	100.0		$14,423,000	100.0		$17,230,000	100.0	
1976	$827,000	93.7	−6.3%	$17,884,000	124.0	24.0%	$20,708,000	120.2	20.2%
1977	$1,199,000	135.8	45.0%	$20,347,000	141.1	13.8%	$23,404,000	135.8	13.0%
1978	$1,810,000	205.0	51.0%	$25,525,000	177.0	25.4%	$28,940,000	168.0	23.7%
1979	$1,951,180	221.0	7.8%	$28,104,997	194.9	10.1%	$31,926,382	185.3	10.3%
1980	$2,342,000	265.2	20.0%	$32,160,000	223.0	14.4%	$36,858,000	213.9	15.4%
1981	$2,794,696	316.5	19.3%	$33,385,714	231.5	3.8%	$38,425,777	223.0	4.3%
1982	$3,443,735	390.0	23.2%	$34,847,458	241.6	4.4%	$40,454,334	234.8	5.3%

263

Covenant University, Reported Endowment: Value, Index Based on 1975, and % Change Between Years

Year	Book Value Beginning of Year	Market Value Beginning of Year	Book Value End of Year	Market Value End of Year	Yield
1975	$4,542,000 100.0	$4,073,000 100.0	$5,261,000 100.0	$5,210,000 100.0	$174,000 100.0
1976	$5,261,000 115.8 15.8%	$5,210,000 127.9 27.9%	$4,617,000 87.8 −12.2%	$4,646,000 89.2 −10.8%	$180,000 103.4 3.4%
1977	$4,617,000 101.7 −12.2%	$4,646,000 114.1 −10.8%	$5,003,000 95.1 8.4%	$4,799,000 92.1 3.3%	$196,000 112.6 8.9%
1978	$5,003,000 110.1 8.4%	$4,799,000 117.8 3.3%	$5,024,000 95.5 0.4%	$4,844,000 93.0 0.9%	$164,000 94.3 −16.3%
1979	$5,024,000 110.6 0.4%	$4,844,000 118.9 0.9%	$5,024,000 95.5 0.0%	$4,844,000 93.0 0.0%	$164,000 94.3 0.0%
1980	$5,751,000 126.6 14.5%	$5,843,000 143.5 20.6%	$5,937,000 112.8 18.2%	$6,052,000 116.2 24.9%	$399,000 229.3 143.3%
1981	$6,094,905 134.2 6.0%	$6,189,000 152.0 5.9%	$7,875,437 149.7 32.7%	$7,980,000 153.2 31.9%	$581,246 334.0 45.7%
1982	$7,875,437 173.4 29.2%	$7,980,000 195.9 28.9%	$8,183,775 155.6 3.9%	$8,262,426 158.6 3.5%	$646,577 371.6 11.2%

Covenant University, Reported Physical Plant Indebtedness: Value, Index Based on 1975, and % Change Between Years

Year	Balance Owed Beginning of Year	Additional Borrowed	Payments Made	Balance Owed End of Year	Interest Payments
1975	$7,694,000	$0	$222,000	$7,472,000	$255,000
	100.0	NA	100.0	100.0	100.0
1976	$7,472,000	$0	$692,000	$6,780,000	$235,000
	97.1	NA	311.7	90.7	92.2
	-2.9%	0.0%	211.7%	-9.3%	-7.8%
1977	$7,003,000	$0	$178,000	$6,825,000	$227,000
	91.0	NA	80.2	91.3	89.0
	-6.3%	0.0%	-74.3%	0.7%	-3.4%
1978	$7,003,000	$5,794,000	$1,438,000	$11,359,000	$239,000
	91.0	NA	647.7	152.0	93.7
	0.0%	100.0%	707.9%	66.4%	5.3%
1979	$11,359,000	$0	$1,438,000	$9,921,000	$239,000
	147.6	NA	647.7	132.8	93.7
	62.2%	-100.0%	0.0%	-12.7%	0.0%
1980	$12,245,000	$0	$406,000	$11,839,000	$735,000
	159.1	NA	182.9	158.4	288.2
	7.8%	0.0%	-71.8%	19.3%	207.5%
1981	$11,839,023	$0	$439,801	$11,399,222	$615,629
	153.9	NA	198.1	152.6	241.4
	-3.3%	0.0%	8.3%	-3.7%	-16.2%
1982	$11,399,222	$0	$341,393	$11,057,829	$622,451
	148.2	NA	153.8	148.0	244.1
	-3.7%	0.0%	-22.4%	-3.0%	1.1%

265

Triad University

Triad University, **Reported Revenues** for 1974–75 to 1981–82

Year	Tuition and Fees	Appropriations	Grants and Contracts	Endowment Income	Gifts	Other Revenue	Total Revenue
1975	$7,957,517	$0	$230,123	$339,455	$63,234	$212,302	$8,802,631
1976	8,835,644	0	482,773	347,682	102,589	79,845	9,848,533
1977	10,335,473	0	145,882	438,226	151,041	130,496	11,201,118
1978	11,675,310	0	169,193	510,733	206,986	163,634	12,725,856
1979	12,956,723	0	214,896	483,107	396,616	289,670	14,341,012
1980	14,539,892	0	825,958	531,718	717,176	434,712	17,049,456
1981	16,137,130	0	889,429	718,478	625,953	692,332	19,063,322
1982	18,013,209	0	995,276	608,053	626,753	892,191	21,135,482

Triad University, **Reported Expenditures** for 1974–75 to 1981–82

Year	Instruction	Research	Public Service	Academic Support	Student Services	Institutional Support	Operation and Maintenance of Physical Plant	Scholarships and Fellowships	Mandatory Transfers	Total Educational and General Expenditure	Total Expenditure
1975	$3,168,000	$0	$0	$508,064	$176,617	$2,149,746	$1,093,188	$813,354	$0	$7,908,969	$7,908,969
1976	3,606,599	0	0	466,874	200,418	2,671,051	1,704,027	1,104,864	0	9,753,833	9,753,833
1977	4,410,111	0	122,087	2,184,457	219,429	1,354,923	1,277,202	891,432	553,342	11,012,983	11,012,983
1978	4,775,510	0	257,781	1,773,382	927,164	1,563,246	1,274,635	1,022,924	570,126	12,164,768	12,164,768
1979	4,945,039	0	234,615	2,054,792	1,136,395	1,767,060	1,358,875	1,217,958	1,693,086	14,407,820	14,407,820
1980	5,422,716	0	346,442	2,181,890	1,161,335	2,117,385	1,486,482	1,899,768	1,553,328	16,169,346	16,169,346
1981	6,226,686	0	236,259	2,517,272	1,359,827	2,419,970	1,696,084	2,072,669	2,090,778	18,619,545	18,619,545
1982	7,206,377	0	211,647	2,923,604	1,593,122	2,772,516	2,239,722	2,359,629	1,785,818	21,092,435	21,092,435

Triad University, Percent Revenues of Total Revenue for 1974–75 to 1981-82

YEAR	TUITION AND FEES	APPROPRIATIONS	GRANTS AND CONTRACTS	ENDOWMENT INCOME	GIFTS	OTHER REVENUE
1975	90.4%	0.0%	2.6%	3.9%	0.7%	2.4%
1976	89.7	0.0	4.9	3.5	1.0	0.8
1977	92.3	0.0	1.3	3.9	1.3	1.2
1978	91.7	0.0	1.3	4.0	1.6	1.3
1979	90.3	0.0	1.5	3.4	2.8	2.0
1980	85.3	0.0	4.8	3.1	4.2	2.5
1981	84.7	0.0	4.7	3.8	3.3	3.6
1982	85.2	0.0	4.7	2.9	3.0	4.2

Triad University, Percent Expenditures of Total Expenditures for 1974–75 to 1981-82

YEAR	INSTRUCTION	RESEARCH	PUBLIC SERVICE	ACADEMIC SUPPORT	STUDENT SERVICES	INSTITUTIONAL SUPPORT	OPERATION AND MAINTENANCE OF PHYSICAL PLANT	SCHOLARSHIPS AND FELLOWSHIPS	MANDATORY TRANSFERS	TOTAL EDUCATIONAL AND GENERAL EXPENDITURES
1975	40.1%	0.0%	0.0%	6.4%	2.2%	27.2%	13.8%	10.3%	0.0%	100.0%
1976	37.0	0.0	0.0	4.8	2.1	27.4	17.5	11.3	0.0	100.0
1977	40.0	0.0	1.1	19.8	2.0	12.3	11.6	8.1	5.0	100.0
1978	39.3	0.0	2.1	14.6	7.6	12.9	10.5	8.4	4.7	100.0
1979	34.3	0.0	1.6	14.3	7.9	12.3	9.4	8.5	11.8	100.0
1980	33.5	0.0	2.1	13.5	7.2	13.1	9.2	11.7	9.6	100.0
1981	33.4	0.0	1.3	13.5	7.3	13.0	9.1	11.1	11.2	100.0
1982	34.2	0.0	1.0	13.9	7.6	13.1	10.6	11.2	8.5	100.0

Triad University, Four Selected Full-Time Equivalent Student Ratios for 1974–75 to 1981–82, per Student.

Year	Tuition and Fees	Instruction	Scholarships	Student Services	Total
1975	$1,938	$772	$198	$43	4,106
1976	2,056	839	257	47	4,298
1977	2,346	1,001	202	50	4,405
1978	2,685	1,098	235	213	4,348
1979	2,903	1,108	273	255	4,463
1980	2,783	1,038	364	222	5,225
1981	3,696	1,426	475	311	4,366
1982	4,317	1,727	565	382	4,173

Triad University, Reported Revenues and Full-Time Equivalent (FTE) Students: Value, Index Based on 1975, and % Change Between Years

Year	Tuition and Fees			Gifts			Endowment			Total Revenue			FTE Students		
1975	$7,957,517	100.0		$63,234	100.0		$339,455	100.0		$8,802,631	100.0		4,106	100.0	
1976	$8,835,644	111.0	11.0%	$102,589	162.2	62.2%	$347,682	102.4	2.4%	$9,848,533	111.9	11.9%	4,298	104.7	4.7%
1977	$10,335,473	129.9	17.0%	$151,041	238.9	47.2%	$438,226	129.1	26.0%	$11,201,118	127.2	13.7%	4,405	107.3	2.5%
1978	$11,675,310	146.7	13.0%	$206,986	327.3	37.0%	$510,733	150.5	16.5%	$12,725,856	144.6	13.6%	4,348	105.9	-1.3%
1979	$12,956,723	162.8	11.0%	$396,616	627.2	91.6%	$483,107	142.3	-5.4%	$14,341,012	162.9	12.7%	4,463	108.7	2.6%
1980	$14,539,892	182.7	12.2%	$717,176	1134.2	80.8%	$531,718	156.6	10.1%	$17,049,456	193.7	18.9%	5,225	127.3	17.1%
1981	$16,137,130	202.8	11.0%	$625,953	989.9	-12.7%	$718,478	211.7	35.1%	$19,063,322	216.6	11.8%	4,366	106.3	-i6.4%
1982	$18,013,209	226.4	11.6%	$626,753	991.2	0.1%	$608,053	179.1	-15.4%	$21,135,482	240.1	10.9%	4,173	101.6	-4.4%

Triad University, Reported Expenditures: Value, Index Based on 1975, and % Change Between Years

Year	Scholarships and Fellowships		Total Educational and General Expenditures		Total Expenditures	
1975	$813,354		$7,908,969		$7,908,969	
	100.0		100.0		100.0	
1976	$1,104,864		$9,753,833		$9,753,833	
	135.8	35.8%	123.3	23.3%	123.3	23.3%
1977	$891,432		$11,012,983		$11,012,983	
	109.6	−19.3%	139.2	12.9%	139.2	12.9%
1978	$1,022,924		$12,164,768		$12,164,768	
	125.8	14.8%	153.8	10.5%	153.8	10.5%
1979	$1,217,958		$14,407,820		$14,407,820	
	149.7	19.1%	182.2	18.4%	182.2	18.4%
1980	$1,899,768		$16,169,346		$16,169,346	
	233.6	56.0%	204.4	12.2%	204.4	12.2%
1981	$2,072,669		$18,619,545		$18,619,545	
	254.8	9.1%	235.4	15.2%	235.4	15.2%
1982	$2,359,629		$21,092,435		$21,092,435	
	290.1	13.8%	266.7	13.3%	266.7	13.3%

269

Triad University, Reported Endowment: Value, Index Based on 1975, and % Change Between Years

	Book Value Beginning of Year	Market Value Beginning of Year	Book Value End of Year	Market Value End of Year	Yield
1975	$6,999,214	$5,180,714	$7,282,049	$5,998,745	$339,455
	100.0	100.0	100.0	100.0	100.0
1976	$7,282,049	$6,421,318	$7,322,015	$7,078,494	$347,682
	104.0	123.9	100.5	118.0	102.4
	4.0%	23.9%	0.5%	18.0%	2.4%
1977	$7,322,015	$6,886,137	$7,410,824	$7,489,457	$429,617
	104.6	132.9	101.8	124.9	126.6
	0.5%	7.2%	1.2%	5.8%	23.6%
1978	$7,410,824	$7,489,457	$7,692,243	$7,185,318	$510,733
	105.9	144.6	105.6	119.8	150.5
	1.2%	8.8%	3.8%	-4.1%	18.9%
1979	$7,692,243	$7,185,318	$7,776,749	$7,111,715	$483,107
	109.9	138.7	106.8	118.6	142.3
	3.8%	-4.1%	1.1%	-1.0%	-5.4%
1980	$7,776,749	$7,111,715	$7,766,680	$7,111,389	$531,718
	111.1	137.3	106.7	118.5	156.6
	1.1%	-1.0%	-0.1%	.0%	10.1%
1981	$7,766,680	$7,111,389	$7,997,409	$7,325,399	$718,478
	111.0	137.3	109.8	122.1	211.7
	-0.1%	.0%	3.0%	3.0%	35.1%
1982	$7,997,409	$7,325,399	$8,272,522	$7,478,829	$508,053
	114.3	141.4	113.6	124.7	149.7
	3.0%	3.0%	3.4%	2.1%	-29.3%

Triad University, Reported Physical Plant Indebtedness: Value, Index Based on 1975, and % Change Between Years

Year	Balance Owed Beginning of Year	Additional Borrowed	Payments Made	Balance Owed End of Year	Interest Payments
1975	$0	$0	$0	$0	$0
	NA	NA	NA	NA	NA
1976	$0	$0	$0	$0	$0
	NA	NA	NA	NA	NA
	0.0%	0.0%	0.0%	0.0%	0.0%
1977	$0	$30,000	$2,500	$27,500	$1,400
	NA	NA	NA	NA	NA
	0.0%	100.0%	100.0%	100.0%	100.0%
1978	$27,500	$0	$27,500	$0	$1,100
	NA	NA	NA	NA	NA
	100.0%	-100.0%	1000.0%	-100.0%	-21.4%
1979	$0	$0	$0	$0	$0
	NA	NA	NA	NA	NA
	-100.0%	0.0%	-100.0%	0.0%	-100.0%
1980	$0	$0	$0	$0	$0
	NA	NA	NA	NA	NA
	0.0%	0.0%	0.0%	0.0%	0.0%
1981	$0	$0	$0	$0	$0
	NA	NA	NA	NA	NA
	0.0%	0.0%	0.0%	0.0%	0.0%
1982	$0	$0	$0	$0	$0
	NA	NA	NA	NA	NA
	0.0%	0.0%	0.0%	0.0%	0.0%

271

R&D University

R&D University, Reported Revenues for 1974–75 to 1981–82

Year	Tuition and Fees	Appropriations	Grants and Contracts	Endowment Income	Gifts	Other Revenue	Total Revenue
1975	$188,785	$6,025,759	$4,176,482	$73,921	$456,907	$225,113	$11,146,967
1976	1,063,510	11,695,753	6,558,927	41,093	870,528	2,634,297	22,864,108
1977	1,733,775	14,473,237	6,426,775	59,348	1,019,018	2,346,843	26,058,996
1978	1,961,766	14,242,273	5,923,018	63,098	1,127,501	2,862,886	26,180,542
1979	2,144,860	14,462,797	5,466,307	76,336	1,205,191	2,920,425	26,275,916
1980	2,599,096	16,894,677	5,155,106	117,512	1,322,831	3,773,171	29,862,393
1981	2,834,633	18,473,022	4,962,084	170,980	1,287,875	5,842,468	33,571,062
1982	3,357,616	23,351,909	5,279,150	164,922	1,505,235	6,219,769	39,878,601

R&D University, Reported Expenditures for 1974–75 to 1981–82

Year	Instruction	Research	Public Service	Academic Support	Student Services	Institutional Support	Operation and Maintenance of Physical Plant	Scholarships and Fellowships	Mandatory Transfers	Total Educational and General Expenditure	Total Expenditure
1975	$1,522,637	$3,841,586	$176,157	$1,199,512	$262,559	$2,056,715	$1,599,013	$62,740	$121,852	$10,842,771	$11,024,836
1976	7,761,006	5,707,829	270,620	1,181,612	328,108	1,661,446	2,849,258	101,281	505,408	20,366,568	21,478,489
1977	8,548,556	5,795,571	394,858	1,299,188	431,401	2,025,124	3,075,465	177,449	635,359	22,382,971	23,857,354
1978	8,930,796	5,423,408	348,551	1,557,615	480,379	2,555,394	3,494,672	157,322	798,393	23,746,530	25,363,823
1979	9,596,164	5,061,229	452,976	1,609,602	521,431	2,691,447	3,454,877	180,193	1,393,753	24,961,672	26,858,099
1980	11,590,732	4,274,492	534,548	1,812,731	470,577	2,136,320	4,000,295	316,215	1,125,051	26,260,961	28,180,209
1981	13,462,657	4,121,028	405,191	1,806,478	537,820	2,651,098	5,256,168	519,305	1,457,412	30,217,157	32,685,885
1982	15,821,292	4,633,774	352,874	2,589,326	555,224	3,188,603	5,669,184	579,993	1,613,693	35,003,963	37,812,835

R&D University, Percent Revenues of Total Revenue for 1974–75 to 1981–82

Year	Tuition and Fees	Appropriations	Grants and Contracts	Endowment Income	Gifts	Other Revenue
1975	1.7%	54.1%	37.5%	0.7%	4.1%	2.0%
1976	4.7	51.2	28.7	0.2	3.8	11.5
1977	6.7	55.5	24.7	0.2	3.9	9.0
1978	7.5	54.4	22.6	0.2	4.3	10.9
1979	8.2	55.0	20.8	0.3	4.6	11.1
1980	8.7	56.6	17.3	0.4	4.4	12.6
1981	8.4	55.0	14.8	0.5	3.8	17.4
1982	8.4	58.6	13.2	0.4	3.8	15.6

R&D University, Percent Expenditures of Total Expenditures for 1974–75 to 1981–82

Year	Instruction	Research	Public Service	Academic Support	Student Services	Institutional Support	Operation and Maintenance of Physical Plant	Scholarships and Fellowships	Mandatory Transfers	Total Educational and General Expenditures
1975	13.8%	34.8%	1.6%	10.9%	2.4%	18.7%	14.5%	0.6%	1.1%	98.3%
1976	36.1	26.6	1.3	5.5	1.5	7.7	13.3	0.5	2.4	94.8
1977	35.8	24.3	1.7	5.4	1.8	8.5	12.9	0.7	2.7	93.8
1978	35.2	21.4	1.4	6.1	1.9	10.1	13.8	0.6	3.1	93.6
1979	35.7	18.8	1.7	6.0	1.9	10.0	12.9	0.7	5.2	92.9
1980	41.1	15.2	1.9	6.4	1.7	7.6	14.2	1.1	4.0	93.2
1981	41.2	12.6	1.2	5.5	1.6	8.1	16.1	1.6	4.5	92.4
1982	41.8	12.3	0.9	6.8	1.5	8.4	15.0	1.5	4.3	92.6

R&D University, Four Selected Full-Time Equivalent Student Ratios for 1974-75 to 1981-82, per Student.

Year	Tuition and Fees	Instruction	Scholarships	Student Services	Total
1975	$387	$3,120	$129	$538	488
1976	521	3,801	50	161	2,042
1977	562	2,770	58	140	3,086
1978	550	2,506	44	135	3,564
1979	727	3,253	61	177	2,950
1980	773	3,447	94	140	3,363
1981	818	3,883	150	155	3,467
1982	748	3,527	129	124	4,486

R&D University, Reported Revenues and Full-Time Equivalent (FTE) Students: Value, Index Based on 1975, and % Change Between Years

Year	Tuition and Fees	Gifts	Endowment	Total Revenue	FTE Students
1975	$188,785	$456,907	$73,921	$11,146,967	488
	100.0	100.0	100.0	100.0	100.0
1976	$1,063,510	$870,528	$41,093	$22,864,108	2,042
	563.3	190.5	55.6	205.1	418.4
	463.3%	90.5%	−44.4%	105.1%	318.4%
1977	$1,733,775	$1,019,018	$59,348	$26,058,996	3,086
	918.4	223.0	80.3	233.8	632.4
	63.0%	17.1%	44.4%	14.0%	51.1%
1978	$1,961,766	$1,127,501	$63,098	$26,180,542	3,564
	1039.2	246.8	85.4	234.9	730.3
	13.1%	10.6%	6.3%	0.5%	15.5%
1979	$2,144,860	$1,205,191	$76,336	$26,275,916	2,950
	1136.1	263.8	103.3	235.7	604.5
	9.3%	6.9%	21.0%	0.4%	−17.2%
1980	$2,599,096	$1,322,831	$117,512	$29,862,393	3,363
	1376.7	289.5	159.0	267.9	689.1
	21.2%	9.8%	53.9%	13.6%	14.0%
1981	$2,834,633	$1,287,875	$170,980	$33,571,062	3,467
	1501.5	281.9	231.3	301.2	710.5
	9.1%	−2.6%	45.5%	12.4%	3.1%
1982	$3,357,616	$1,505,235	$164,922	$39,878,601	4,486
	1778.5	329.4	223.1	357.8	919.3
	18.4%	16.9%	−3.5%	18.8%	29.4%

R&D University, Reported Expenditures: Value, Index Based on 1975, and % Change Between Years

YEAR	SCHOLARSHIPS AND FELLOWSHIPS			TOTAL EDUCATIONAL AND GENERAL EXPENDITURES			TOTAL EXPENDITURES		
1975	$62,740	100.0		$10,842,771	100.0		$11,024,836	100.0	
1976	$101,281	161.4	61.4%	$20,366,568	187.8	87.8%	$21,478,489	194.8	94.8%
1977	$177,449	282.8	75.2%	$22,382,971	206.4	9.9%	$23,857,354	216.4	11.1%
1978	$157,322	250.8	−11.3%	$23,746,530	219.0	6.1%	$25,363,823	230.1	6.3%
1979	$180,193	287.2	14.5%	$24,961,672	230.2	5.1%	$26,858,099	243.6	5.9%
1980	$316,215	504.0	75.5%	$26,260,961	242.2	5.2%	$28,180,209	255.6	4.9%
1981	$519,305	827.7	64.2%	$30,217,157	278.7	15.1%	$32,685,885	296.5	16.0%
1982	$579,993	924.4	11.7%	$35,003,963	322.8	15.8%	$37,812,835	343.0	15.7%

R&D University, Reported Endowment: Value, Index Based on 1975, and % Change Between Years

Year	Book Value Beginning of Year	Market Value Beginning of Year	Book Value End of Year	Market Value End of Year	Yield
1975	$1,216,853	$895,073	$1,360,761	$1,000,160	$64,229
	100.0	100.0	100.0	100.0	100.0
1976	$1,360,761	$1,000,160	$7,713,600	$7,352,999	$75,300
	111.8	111.7	566.9	735.2	117.2
	11.8%	11.7%	466.9%	635.2%	17.2%
1977	$7,713,600	$7,713,600	$7,842,717	$7,842,717	$79,834
	633.9	861.8	576.3	784.1	124.3
	466.9%	671.2%	1.7%	6.7%	6.0%
1978	$7,842,717	$7,842,717	$7,720,735	$7,720,735	$83,077
	644.5	876.2	567.4	771.9	129.3
	1.7%	1.7%	-1.6%	-1.6%	4.1%
1979	$7,720,735	$7,720,735	$8,426,277	$8,426,277	$111,064
	634.5	862.6	619.2	842.5	172.9
	-1.6%	-1.6%	9.1%	9.1%	33.7%
1980	$8,426,277	$8,426,277	$8,528,470	$8,528,470	$181,850
	692.5	941.4	626.7	852.7	283.1
	9.1%	9.1%	1.2%	1.2%	63.7%
1981	$8,528,470	$8,528,470	$14,932,671	$14,932,671	$187,740
	700.9	952.8	1097.4	1493.0	292.3
	1.2%	1.2%	75.1%	75.1%	3.2%
1982	$14,932,671	$14,932,671	$19,629,910	$19,629,910	$1,364,407
	1227.2	1668.3	1442.6	1962.7	2124.3
	75.1%	75.1%	31.5%	31.5%	626.8%

R&D University, Reported Physical Plant Indebtedness: Value, Index Based on 1975, and % Change Between Years

Year	Balance Owed Beginning of Year	Additional Borrowed	Payments Made	Balance Owed End of Year	Interest Payments
1975	$0	$0	$0	$0	$0
1976	NA	NA	NA	NA	NA
1977	$0	$0	$0	$0	$0
	NA 0.0%	NA 0.0%	NA 0.0%	NA 0.0%	NA 0.0%
1978	$0	$0	$0	$0	$0
	NA 0.0%	NA 0.0%	NA 0.0%	NA 0.0%	NA 0.0%
1979	$0	$9,000,000	$0	$9,000,000	$275,094
	NA 0.0%	NA 100.0%	NA 0.0%	NA 0.0%	NA 0.0%
1980	$9,000,000	$10,125,000	$140,000	$18,985,000	$545,463
	NA 100.0%	NA 12.5%	NA 100.0%	NA 100.0%	NA 100.0%
1981	$18,985,000	$0	$385,000	$18,600,000	$1,323,793
	NA 110.9%	NA -100.0%	NA 175.0%	NA 110.9%	NA 98.3%
1982	$18,600,000	$0	$410,000	$18,190,000	$1,293,943
	NA -2.0%	NA 0.0%	NA 6.5%	NA -2.0%	NA 142.7%
				NA -2.2%	NA -2.3%

Index